Networking

A Beginner's Guide
Sixth Edition

About the Author

Bruce Hallberg has 30 years' experience in information technology, including executive management, system implementations, and global network consulting for Fortune 1000 companies. He is the author of more than 30 books on a wide variety of computing topics, including operating systems, networking, and both server and desktop applications. He holds an MBA from Heriot Watt University, and resides in the Silicon Valley area of California with his two daughters.

About the Technical Editor

Steve Langford has over 17 years of network administration experience in several industries, such as biotechnology, chemical manufacturing, and venture capital. Currently at a private school, he has been the IT project manager for software upgrades and new building construction.

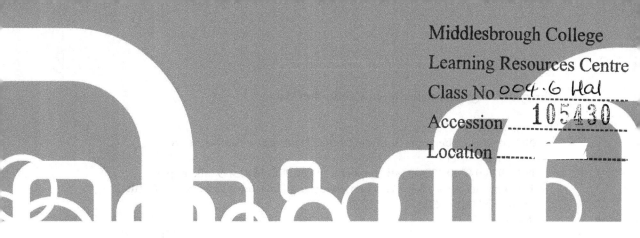

Networking

A Beginner's Guide
Sixth Edition

BRUCE **HALLBERG**

Mc
Graw
Hill
Education

New York   Chicago   San Francisco   Athens
London   Madrid   Mexico City   Milan
New Delhi   Singapore   Sydney   Toronto

Library of Congress Cataloging-in-Publication Data

Hallberg, Bruce A., 1964–
    Networking : a beginner's guide / Bruce Hallberg. — Sixth edition.
        pages   cm
    ISBN 978-0-07-181224-5 (alk. paper) — ISBN 0-07-181224-5 (alk. paper)
    1. Computer networks.   2. Internetworking (Telecommunication)   I. Title.
    TK5105.5.H318   2014
    004.6—dc23

                                                                    2013034579

McGraw-Hill Education books are available at special quantity discounts to use as premiums and sales promotions, or for use in corporate training programs. To contact a representative, please visit the Contact Us pages at www.mhprofessional.com.

Networking: A Beginner's Guide, Sixth Edition

4 5 6 7 8 9 QVS/QVS 20 19 18 17

ISBN   978-0-07-181224-5
MHID   0-07-181224-5

Sponsoring Editor
  Amy Jollymore
	Technical Editor
	  Steve Langford
		Composition
		  Cenveo Publisher Services

Editorial Supervisor
  Patty Mon
	Copy Editor
	  Lisa McCoy
		Illustration
		  Cenveo Publisher Services

Project Manager
  Sandhya Gola,
  Cenveo® Publisher Services
	Proofreader
	  Carol Shields
		Art Director, Cover
		  Jeff Weeks

Acquisitions Coordinator
  Amanda Russell
	Indexer
	  James Minkin
		Cover Designer
		  Jeff Weeks

	Production Supervisor Jean Bodeaux	

With all my love, for Bonnie Gordon,
and my two daughters, Vivian and Maxine.

At a Glance

Part II	Hands-On Knowledge

Contents

Part I

Networking Ins and Outs

Part II

Hands-On Knowledge

Acknowledgments

'd like to thank Amy Jollymore for putting this project together. An acquisition editor's job is rarely an easy one (think "herding cats"), but Amy was unfailingly pleasant to work with.

Amanda Russell was the editorial coordinator for this book, which means she had the daunting job of ensuring that all of the myriad tasks were tracked and accomplished. Amanda brought to this job an amazing combination of poise and ability.

Sandhya Gola was our project manager, and once the manuscript was written, took charge of managing the overall copyedit process and the production of the book. I'd like to thank Sandhya for her competent work on the project; I enjoyed working with her!

I'd like to also thank Lisa McCoy, who copyedited the entire book. I really appreciate Lisa's deft improvements to the text of the book.

Finally, Steve Langford was the technical editor of the edition of this book. I've known Steve for many years, originally when we were colleagues and Steve was the network administrator for a fairly complex network. I'm grateful to Steve that he was willing to take on this job.

Introduction

've run into many people over the years who have gained good—even
impressive—working knowledge of PCs, operating systems, applications,
and common problems and solutions. Many of these people are wizards
with desktop computers. Quite a few of them have been unable to make the
transition into working with networks, however, and they have had trouble
gaining the requisite knowledge to conceptualize, understand, install, administer,
and troubleshoot networks. In many cases, this inability limits their career
growth because most companies believe networking experience is fundamental
to holding higher-level information technology (IT) positions. And, in fact,
networking experience *is* very important.

Certainly, networks can be complicated beasts to learn about. To add to the
difficulty, most companies aren't willing to let people unskilled with networks
experiment and learn about them using the company's production network! This
leaves the networking beginner in the difficult position of having to learn about
networks by

- Reading an endless number of books and articles
- Attending classes
- Building small experimental networks at home, using cobbled-together
  and/or borrowed parts and software

This book is designed for people who understand computers and the rudiments of computer science, but who want to begin an education about networks and networking. I assume you understand and are comfortable with the following topics:

- How bits and bytes work
- The notion of binary, octal, decimal, and hexadecimal notation
- How basic PC hardware works, and how to install and replace PC peripheral components
- Two or three desktop operating systems in detail, such as Windows, Mac OS, Linux, or Unix
- Detailed knowledge of a wide variety of application software

The purpose of this book is both to educate and familiarize. The first part of the book discusses basic networking technology and hardware. Its purpose is to help you understand the basic components of networking so you can build a conceptual framework into which you can fit knowledge that is more detailed in your chosen area of expertise. The second part of the book is concerned with familiarizing you with two important network operating systems: Windows Server 2012 and Oracle Linux. In the second part, you learn the basics of setting up and administering these network operating systems, as well as about virtualization.

This book is meant to be a springboard from which you can start pursuing more detailed knowledge in the areas that interest you. Following are some areas that you may wish to continue exploring, depending on your career goals:

- **Small-to-medium network administrator**   If you plan on building and administering networks with 200 or fewer users, you should extend your knowledge by studying the network operating systems you intend to use, server hardware, client PC administration, and network management. You may find more detailed knowledge of network hardware, like routers, bridges, gateways, switches, and the like, to be useful, but these may not be an important focus for you.

- **Large network administrator**   If you plan on working with networks with more than 200 users, then you need to pursue detailed knowledge about TCP/IP addressing and routing and network hardware, including routers, bridges, gateways, switches, and firewalls. Also, in large networks, administrators tend to specialize in certain areas, so you should consider several areas of particular specialization, such as e-mail servers like Microsoft Exchange, or database servers like Oracle or SQL Server.

- **Internet administrator**   Many people these days are pursuing specialization in Internet-based technologies. Depending on what area you want to work in, you should learn more about web and FTP servers, HTTP and other application-level Internet protocols, CGI and other web scripting technologies, HTML design, and SMTP mail connections. You may also want to become an expert in TCP/IP and all its related protocols, addressing rules, and routing techniques.

- **End-user support**   If your primary job is supporting end users, perhaps with application or client computer support, you may still benefit from a deeper understanding of networking. Client computer applications usually interact with the network, and understanding networks will undoubtedly help you be more effective.

TIP   If you're working toward getting a job in the field of networking, find job postings on the Internet and carefully study the job requirements. This can be a useful technique to direct your studies appropriately. When you do this, you will notice that for their most important jobs, most employers ask for people who are certified by Microsoft, Cisco, or other companies. You should seriously consider pursuing an appropriate certification. While certifications can never replace experience, they are one way that a person can demonstrate a needed level of knowledge and expertise in a particular area. This difference may be key in getting the best possible job offers and in being able to gain more experience. Often, an appropriate certification can be worth several years' experience in terms of compensation and job responsibilities, so it's an investment in yourself that will usually pay for itself over a fairly short period of time.

PART I | Networking Ins and Outs

CHAPTER 1 | The Business of Networking

This book is a soup-to-nuts beginner's guide to networking. Before delving into the bits and bytes of networking, which are covered in the rest of the book, you should start by understanding the whys and wherefores of networking.

This chapter discusses networking from a business perspective. You'll learn about the benefits that networking brings a company and the different types of networking jobs available. You'll also discover how networks are supported from the business perspective, and how you can begin a career in networking. Finally, you'll learn about the Sarbanes-Oxley Act of 2002 and how its requirements affect networking professionals.

Understanding Networking: The Corporate Perspective

To be truly effective in the field of networking, you need to start by understanding networking from the corporate perspective. Why are networks important to companies? What do they accomplish for the company? How can networking professionals more clearly meet the needs of the company with the networks that they build and maintain? It's important to realize that there are no single correct answers to these questions. Every company will have different needs and expectations with regard to their network. What is important is that you learn the relevant questions to ask about networking for your company and arrive at the best possible answers to those questions for your particular company. Doing so will ensure that the company's network best meets its needs.

What Does the Company Need?

There are many possible reasons that a company might need or benefit from a network. In order to understand your particular company, you should start by exploring the following questions. You may need to ask a variety of different people in the company their perspective on these questions. Some of the managers that you may need to interview include the chief executive officer or owner, the chief financial officer, and the heads of the various key departments within the company, such as manufacturing, sales and marketing, accounting, purchasing and materials, retail operations, and so forth. The range of managers that you interview will depend on the type of business in which the company is engaged.

It's important that you first start by understanding the business itself and the business-oriented perspectives of these different individuals and the people in their departments. Consider the following questions for each of these key areas of the organization:

- What is their function for the company?
- How do their objectives tie into the company objectives?
- What are the key goals for their function in the coming year? How about in the coming five years?
- What do they see as the chief challenges to overcome in achieving their objectives?

- How might information technology (IT) play a role in supporting their objectives?
- What sorts of automation do they think might help them accomplish their objectives?
- How is the work in their area accomplished? For instance, do most of the employees do mechanical work, like on a production line, or are most of them so-called "knowledge workers" who generate documents, analyze information, and so forth?
- What are the key inputs for the functional area in terms of information or materials, and what are the key outputs for the functional area? What processes convert the inputs into the outputs?
- Does the current performance of the network meet their needs? If not, how does it affect them? What level of improved performance is needed, and what benefits will accrue to the company as a whole by addressing them?
- Do the capabilities of the existing network meet their needs? If not, what capabilities are needed, and how will adding those capabilities benefit their functional area and the company?

Your objective in asking these questions, and others that may occur to you, is to get a good understanding of each functional area: what it does and how it does it, as well as what it wants to be able to do in the future. With this knowledge, you can then start to analyze the impact that the network—or improvements to the existing network—might have in those various areas.

Beginning from a business perspective is absolutely essential. Networks are not built and improved "just because." Instead, any particular network or network upgrade needs to be driven by the needs of the business. Justifications for networks or improvements to existing networks should clearly show how they are necessary to the proper functioning of the business or how they will play an important role in the company achieving its objectives, consistent with the cost and effort involved.

How Will the Network Benefit the Company?

After getting a good understanding of the company, its objectives, and how it accomplishes its work, you can then analyze different ideas that you may have for the network and how those ideas will benefit some or all parts of the business. In doing so, you need to consider at least the following areas:

- Are there any areas in which the lack of a network, or some failing of the existing network, is inhibiting the company from realizing its goals or accomplishing its work? For example, if an existing network is undersized and this causes people to waste too much time on routine tasks (such as saving or sending files, transacting in the system, or getting information from the system), what improvements might address those shortcomings? Or maybe the network and its servers are unreliable, and so people are frequently losing their work or are unproductive while problems are addressed.

- Are there capabilities that you could add to the network that would provide benefits to the business? For example, if many people in the company are constantly sending faxes (for instance, salespeople sending price quotations to customers), would adding a network-based fax system produce significant productivity benefits? What about other network-based applications? (Chapter 2 lists some common network features that you may want to review to help in answering this question.)

- What other automation plans exist that will require the support of the network? For example, say you're the network administrator in a company. What new applications or features will be added to the network that you need to support? Is the company planning on installing some kind of videoconferencing system, for instance? If so, do you know what changes you will need to make to the network to support the system?

- What needs to be done to the network simply to maintain it? In most companies, file space requirements grow rapidly, even if the business itself isn't expanding. How much additional storage space does the network need to keep going forward? How many additional servers and other components will be needed to keep the network working smoothly?

Obviously, a list such as the preceding one can't be exhaustive. The important point is that you need to approach the job of networking first from the perspective of the company and its needs. Within that framework, use your creativity, knowledge, experience, and business and technical acumen to propose and execute a plan for the network. The remainder of this book discusses the information you need to start learning about this important part of any company's infrastructure.

Understanding Networking Jobs

If you're planning on entering the field of networking (and this book is designed as a good start for that), it's important to have some understanding of the various networking jobs that you're likely to encounter and what they typically require. Of course, actual job requirements will vary widely between companies and for different established networks. Also, companies may have different entry-level opportunities through which you can enter a networking career. That said, the following descriptions are broad overviews of some key jobs.

Network Administrator

Network administrators are responsible for the operations of a network or, in larger companies, for the operations of key parts of the network. In a smaller company that has only one network administrator, duties include the following:

- Creating, maintaining, and removing user accounts
- Ensuring that necessary backups are made on a regular basis

- Managing the "keys" to the network, such as the administrative accounts and their passwords
- Managing network security policies
- Adding new networking equipment, such as servers, routers, hubs, and switches, and managing that equipment
- Monitoring the network, its hardware, and its software for potential problems and for utilization levels for planning network upgrades
- Troubleshooting network problems

In larger firms, individual jobs may cover just one or two of the aforementioned bullets. In these cases, the level of expertise in that more narrow set of responsibilities would be expected to be much higher.

Network administrators may also be called system administrators, local area network (LAN) administrators, and other variations on that theme.

Typically, you should have several years' experience performing network-related duties with a similar network for this job. Certifications such as the Microsoft Certified Solutions Associate/Expert/Master (MCSA/MCSE/MCSM), one of the appropriate Cisco certifications, or one of the appropriate CompTIA certifications can reduce the amount of experience that an employer will require. Employers usually consider these certifications important because they clearly establish that a candidate meets minimum requirements for the networking system in question.

TIP   The Computing Technology Industry Association (CompTIA) offers a number of different vendor-neutral certifications that can help you enter the field of networking. You can learn more about them at http://certification.comptia.org/.

Network Engineer

Network engineers are more deeply involved in the bits and bytes of a network. They are expected to be expert in the network operating systems with which they work, especially in the network's key hardware, such as its hubs, routers, switches, and so forth. Network engineers are also usually the troubleshooters of last resort, who are brought in to diagnose and fix the most vexing problems that surpass the ability of the network administrator to resolve.

Aside from often holding a degree in electrical engineering or computer science, network engineers typically have at least five years' experience running and troubleshooting complex networks. Also, network engineers typically carry certifications from networking equipment companies, such as Cisco's well-regarded certification program.

TIP   Learn more about Cisco's certification programs at http://www.cisco.com.

Network Architect/Designer

Network architects (sometimes also called network designers) usually work for companies that sell and support networks or for organizations with large networks that are constantly changing and expanding. Essentially, network architects design networks. They need to combine important qualities to be successful. They must know the business requirements that the network needs to meet and have a thorough *current* understanding of all of the networking products available, as well as how those products interact. Network architects are also important when growing a sophisticated network and helping to ensure that new additions to the network don't cause problems elsewhere in the network.

Other Network-Related Jobs

There are a wide variety of other network-related jobs, including some that do not involve working directly with the network, such as the job of database administrator. Organizations employ e-mail administrators, webmasters, web designers, network support technicians, and so on. In fact, a dizzying number of different jobs are available in the networking field.

If you've chosen to enter the field of networking, it would make sense to spend time browsing job ads for the various networking jobs and to get a sense of what these different types of jobs require. Once you find one that reflects your interests, you can then analyze what additional skills, classes, or certifications you may need to enter one of those jobs. Many opportunities are available. The important thing is to get started and pursue your objectives.

Sarbanes-Oxley Act of 2002

You may be wondering what a law that was passed by the U.S. Congress has to do with the field of networking and why it's discussed in this book. The reason is that this law has an important impact on the networks of all public companies, and so it's important for you to understand what all the fuss is about.

The Sarbanes-Oxley Act of 2002 (usually referred to as SOX, pronounced "socks") was an act sponsored by Senator Sarbanes and Representative Oxley in response to the many cases of corporate wrongdoing that preceded it, such as Enron, Global Crossing, Arthur Andersen, Tyco, and others. The act makes sweeping changes to a number of areas of corporate governance and accounting. One change in particular is likely to impact most networking professionals, especially those involved in day-to-day network operations, such as network administrators.

Section 404 of the act places new requirements on public companies to annually assess their system of internal controls, and on their outside auditors to examine the company's internal controls and to attest to the effectiveness of the company's internal controls over the company's use and reporting of financial information. This may sound like a requirement that pertains only to accounting departments, and in fact, it mostly does. However, accounting internal controls rely heavily on network system controls—in particular, those system controls that impact important systems the company uses for managing and reporting financial information.

Generally, outside auditors classify company systems as being either within the scope of their audit ("in scope") or outside the scope of their audit. Systems that are in scope include the company's accounting system, payroll system, stock administration system, materials management system, shipping system, billing system, banking system, and so forth. The computers and all related hardware and software that perform those functions or host or run the software that performs those functions are also in scope. In addition, other network operations that support those systems may be in scope, such as the network-wide password settings, backup and restore procedures, new and terminated user account management, and so forth.

Accordingly, network administrators for publicly traded companies will need to work closely with their accounting departments to comply with the SOX 404 requirements on an ongoing basis. Doing so will include activities such as the following:

- Documentation of all user account creation, maintenance, and deactivation activities, including appropriate sign-offs for new, changed, and terminated users of in-scope systems

- Creation of a change-control system for any systems that the company modifies from time to time, such as an accounting system for which the company uses custom-developed reports or processing programs

- Documentation of the security settings of the network

- Documentation of the security settings and user account and password management of the in-scope systems

- Documentation of routine maintenance activities for in-scope systems

- Collaboration with the accounting staff and the auditors to prove that all of the controls that are in place are being followed, without exceptions

- Creation and maintenance of systems (even manual procedural systems) to detect unauthorized changes to any in-scope systems

Obviously, a book about networking cannot fully address all of the factors involved in Sarbanes-Oxley compliance. You should, however, have a general idea of what it is and what is involved. The accounting professionals charged with this important requirement will have more detailed information about the exact steps required for your company.

Chapter Summary

Many people I've met who work in some area of information technology, such as networking, don't consider the business reasons for the network when they go about their day-to-day jobs or when they propose improvements to the network. This certainly isn't limited to the field of networking; many people who work in any area of a company sometimes forget that the reason their function exists is to support the objectives of the company in which they work. The most successful employees of any company keep firmly in mind why they do what they do before they consider how best to do it. Some of the suggestions in this chapter should help you to approach managing and improving a network successfully by keeping in mind the benefits the network brings to the company. Once you know what the company needs, you can then propose the best solutions to solve problems that arise or make appropriate improvements to the network.

This chapter also discussed several broad areas you might consider pursuing in the field of networking. Demand for trained, capable networking people is extremely high, salaries are top-notch, and people working in the networking field have jobs that are—more than most—fun, stimulating, and rewarding in many ways.

Finally, you learned a little about the Sarbanes-Oxley Act of 2002 and how it impacts networking professionals.

The next chapter starts exploring the technical details of networking by briefly discussing some basic computer science concepts that you need to understand. If you already know about different numbering systems and about how data rates are measured, you can probably skip the next chapter and move on to the networking topics that follow, although be warned that you need a strong grasp of how binary numbers work to understand some of the discussion surrounding network protocols in Chapter 6.

CHAPTER 2 | Understanding Networking

There are *a lot* of aspects to networking, and this tends to make the subject seem more complex than it really is. This chapter discusses some basic and key networking concepts. If you're new to networking, getting a good understanding of the subjects in this chapter will enable you to build a mental framework into which you can fit more detailed knowledge as it is presented in the remainder of this book. In addition, the rest of this book assumes you're comfortable with all the concepts presented in this chapter.

Laying the Foundation

Many people who read this book do not come from a technical background. In order to ensure that everyone starts with some important background information, this chapter first will cover some basic computer terminology and knowledge.

Bits, Nibbles, and Bytes

Most people know that computers, at their most fundamental level, work entirely using only 1's and 0's for numbers. Each of these numbers (whether it is a 0 or 1) is called a *bit*, which is short for *binary digit*. String eight bits together, and you have a byte; string about 1,000 bits together, and you have a *kilobit*; or you can string about 1,000 bytes together for a *kilobyte*. A rarely used unit is composed of four bits strung together, called a *nibble*. Remember this for when you play *Jeopardy*!

Understanding Binary Numbers

Before you learn about binary numbers, it's useful to recall a few things about the numbering system that people use on a daily basis. This is called the *decimal numbering system* or, alternatively, the *base-10 numbering system*. The decimal numbering system is built using ten different symbols, each of which represents a quantity from zero to nine. Therefore, ten possible digits can be used: 0 through 9. (The base-10 numbering system gets its name from the fact that only ten digits are possible in the system.)

An important part of any numbering system is the use of *positions* in which the numerical symbols can be placed. Each position confers a different quantity to the number being represented in that position. Therefore, the number 10 in the decimal system represents the quantity ten. There is a 1 in the *tens position* and a 0 in the *ones position*. This can also be represented as $(1 \times 10) + (0 \times 1)$. Now consider the number 541. This number uses the *hundreds position* as well as the tens and ones positions. It can be represented as $(5 \times 100) + (4 \times 10) + (1 \times 1)$. In English, you could state this number as five hundred plus forty plus one.

Every written number has a *least-significant digit* and a *most-significant digit*. The least-significant digit is the one farthest to the right, and the most-significant digit is the one farthest to the left. For binary numbers, people also talk about the least- and most-significant bits, but it's the same idea.

So far, this section has simply reviewed basic number knowledge that you learned in grade school. What grade school probably didn't cover is the fact that basing a numbering system on ten is completely arbitrary; there is no mathematical reason to favor a base-10 system over any other. You can create numbering systems for any base you like. You can have a base-3 numbering system, a base-11 numbering system, and so on. Humans have come to favor the base-10 system, probably because we have ten fingers and thus tend to think in tens. Computers, on the other hand, have only two digits with which they can work—1 and 0—on and off—so they need to use a different numbering system. The natural numbering system for a computer to use would, therefore, be the base-2 numbering system, and, in fact, that's what they do use. This system is called the *binary numbering system*. Computers use only 1's and 0's at their most basic level because they understand only two states: on and off. In the binary numbering system, a 1 represents on and a 0 represents off.

Recall that in the decimal numbering system, the position of each number is important. It is the same in the binary numbering system, except that each position doesn't correspond to powers of 10, but instead to powers of 2. Here are the values of the lowest eight positions used in the binary numbering system:

128   64   32   16   8   4   2   1

So, suppose that you encounter the following binary number:

1   0   1   0   1   1   0   1

You would follow the same steps that you use to understand a decimal numbering system number. In this example, the binary number represents 128 + 32 + 8 + 4 + 1, or 173 in the decimal system. You can also write (or calculate) this number as follows:

$(128 \times 1) + (64 \times 0) + (32 \times 1) + (16 \times 0) + (8 \times 1) + (4 \times 1) + (2 \times 0) + (1 \times 1)$

So two main things separate the decimal numbering system from the binary numbering system:

- The binary system uses only 1's and 0's to represent every value.
- The value of digits in the different positions varies.

You might be wondering how you can tell whether you're reading a binary number or a decimal number. For instance, if you're reading a book about computers and you see the number 10101, how do you know whether it's supposed to represent ten thousand one hundred and one or twenty-one? There are several ways that you can tell:

- Usually, binary numbers are shown with at least eight positions (a full byte), even if the leading digits are 0s.
- If you're looking at a bunch of numbers and see only 1's and 0's, it's a pretty good bet that they are binary numbers.
- Binary numbers don't use the decimal point to represent fractional values, so 10100.01 should be assumed to be a decimal system number.

■   Decimal numbers should use commas as you were taught in school. So, the number 10,100 should be read as ten thousand one hundred.

■   Sometimes people put the letter *b* at the end of a binary number, although this convention isn't widely followed.

Put all these things together, plus a little common sense, and you'll usually have no doubt whether you're reading a binary or decimal value.

Other Important Numbering Systems

Two other important numbering systems that you encounter in the world of networking are octal and hexadecimal. Hexadecimal is far more prevalent than octal, but you should understand both.

The octal numbering system is also called the base-8 numbering system. In this scheme, each position in a number can hold only the numerals 0 to 7. The number 010 in the octal numbering system corresponds to 8 in the decimal numbering system. Octal numbers can be indicated with a leading zero, a leading percent symbol (%), or a trailing capital letter *O*.

The hexadecimal numbering system is fairly common in networking, and is often used to represent network addresses, memory addresses, and the like. The hexadecimal system (also called the base-16 numbering system) can use 16 different symbols in each

How to Quickly Convert Hexadecimal, Decimal, Octal, and Binary Numbers

The Calculator application that comes with all versions of Windows allows you to convert values quickly between hexadecimal, decimal, octal, and binary. With the calculator open, place it into Programmer mode (older versions of Windows Calculator use the Scientific mode for this purpose). This mode reveals a lot of advanced features in the calculator. In the upper-left area of the calculator, you can now see four option buttons labeled Hex, Dec, Oct, and Bin. These correspond to the hexadecimal, decimal, octal, and binary numbering systems. Just choose which system you want to use to enter a number, and then click any of the other options to convert the number instantly.

For instance, suppose that you click the Bin option button and enter the number 110100100110111010. If you then click the Dec button, the calculator reveals that the number you just entered is 215,482 in the decimal system. If you click the Hex button, you find that the binary number that you entered is 349BA in the hexadecimal numbering system. And if you click the Oct button, you discover that the number is 644672 in the octal numbering system. You can also go in the other direction: Click the Dec button, enter some number, and then click the other option buttons to see how the number looks in those other numbering systems.

of its positions. Since we have written numerals for only 0 to 9, the hexadecimal system uses the letters *A* through *F* to represent the extra symbols.

Hexadecimal numbers are usually preceded with a leading zero followed by the letter *x* and then the hexadecimal number. The letter *x* can be either lowercase or uppercase, so both 0x11AB and 0X11AB are correct. Hexadecimal numbers may also be shown with a trailing letter *h*, which can be lowercase or uppercase. Rarely, they may be preceded with the dollar sign ($), as in $11AB. Often, you can easily recognize hexadecimal numbers simply by the fact that they include some letters (*A* to *F*). For hexadecimal numbers, *A* equals 10 in the decimal system, *B* equals 11, *C* equals 12, *D* equals 13, *E* equals 14, and *F* equals 15.

> **NOTE**   Each digit of a hexadecimal number requires 4 bits—a nibble—for storage.

You can determine the decimal value for a hexadecimal value manually using the same method as shown earlier in this chapter for decimal and binary numbers. The hexadecimal position values for the first four digits are as follows:

| 4096 | 256 | 16 | 1 |

So, the number 0x11AB can be converted to decimal with the formula $(1 \times 4096) + (1 \times 256) + (10 \times 16) + (11 \times 1)$, or 4,523 in decimal.

Basic Terminology to Describe Networking Speeds

The business of networking is almost entirely about moving data from one point to another. Accordingly, one of the most important things that you need to understand about any network connection is how much data it can carry. Broadly, this capacity is called *bandwidth*, which is measured by the amount of data that a connection can carry in a given period of time.

The most basic measurement of bandwidth is *bits per second*, abbreviated as *bps*. Bandwidth is how many bits the connection can carry within a second. More commonly used are various multiples of this measurement, including thousands of bits per second (Kbps), millions of bits per second (Mbps), or billions of bits per second (Gbps).

> **TIP**   Remember that bits per second is not bytes per second. To arrive at the bytes per second when you know the bits per second (approximately), divide the bps number by 8. In this book, bits per second units are written with a lowercase letter *b* and bytes per second units with an uppercase *B*. For example, 56 Kbps is 56 thousand bits per second, and 56 KBps is 56 thousand bytes per second.

A closely related measurement that you will also see bandied about is *hertz*, which is the number of cycles being carried per second. Hertz is abbreviated as *Hz*. Just as with *bps*, it is the multiples of hertz that are talked about the most, including thousands of hertz (KHz, or kilohertz), millions of hertz (MHz, or megahertz), and billions of hertz (GHz, or gigahertz). For example, a microprocessor running at 2.2 GHz is running at 2.2 billion cycles per second. The electricity in the United States runs at 60 Hz; in Europe, the frequency is 50 Hz.

Hertz and bits per second are essentially the same and are sometimes intermixed. For example, Thin Ethernet cable is said to run at 10 MHz and also to carry 10 Mbps of bandwidth.

Knowing Network Relationship Types

The term *network relationship* refers to how one computer makes use of another computer's resources over the network. Two fundamental types of network relationships exist: peer-to-peer and client/server. These two types of network relationships define the logical structure of a network. To understand them better, you might compare them to different business management philosophies. A *peer-to-peer network* is much like a company with a decentralized management philosophy, where decisions are made locally and resources are managed according to the most immediate needs. A *client/server network* is more like a company that uses centralized management, where decisions are made in a central location by a relatively small group of people. Circumstances exist where both peer-to-peer and client/server relationships are appropriate, and many networks incorporate aspects of both types.

Both peer-to-peer and client/server networks require certain network *layers*. Both types require a physical network connection between the computers, use of the same network protocols, and so forth. In these respects, the two types of network relationships are the same. The difference comes in whether you spread the shared network resources around to all the computers on the network or use centralized network servers.

 NOTE   The mechanics of how a network actually functions are broken down into layers. The concept of layers and what goes into each layer are described later in this chapter, in the "Understanding the OSI Networking Model" section.

Peer-to-Peer Network Relationships

In a peer-to-peer network relationship, the computers on the network communicate with each other as equals. Each computer is responsible for making its own resources available to other computers on the network. These resources might be files, directories, application programs, devices (such as printers, modems, or fax cards), or any combination of these items. Each computer is also responsible for setting up and maintaining its own security for those resources. In addition, each computer is responsible for accessing the network resources it needs from other peer-to-peer computers, knowing where those resources are located in the network, and handling the security required to access them. Figure 2-1 illustrates how this works.

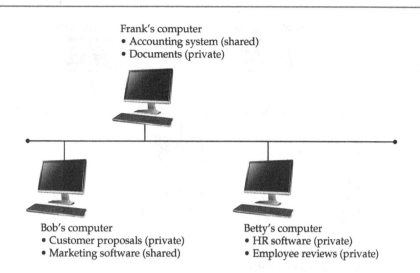

Frank's computer
- Accounting system (shared)
- Documents (private)

Bob's computer
- Customer proposals (private)
- Marketing software (shared)

Betty's computer
- HR software (private)
- Employee reviews (private)

Figure 2-1.   A peer-to-peer network with resources spread across computers

NOTE   Even in a pure peer-to-peer network, using a dedicated computer for certain frequently accessed resources is possible. For example, you might host the application and data files for an accounting system on a single workstation and not use that computer for typical workstation tasks, such as word processing, so that all of the computer's performance is available for the accounting system. The computer is still working in a peer-to-peer fashion; it's just used for a single purpose.

Client/Server Network Relationships

In a client/server network relationship, a distinction exists between the computers that make network resources available (the *servers*) and the computers that use the resources (the *clients*, or *workstations*). A pure client/server network is one in which *all* available network resources—such as files, directories, applications, and shared devices—are centrally managed and hosted, and then are accessed by the client computers. None of the client computers share their resources with other client computers or with the servers. Instead, the client computers are pure consumers of these shared network resources.

NOTE   Don't confuse client/server networks with client/server database systems. While the two mean essentially the same thing (conceptually), a client/server database is one where the processing of the database application is divided between the database server and the database clients. The server is responsible for responding to data requests from the clients and supplying them with the appropriate data, while the clients are responsible for formatting, displaying, and printing that data for the user. For instance, Windows Server 2012 is a client/server network operating system, while an Oracle or Microsoft SQL Server database is a client/server database system.

Server
 • Accounting software (all)
 • Documents (Frank only)
 • HR software (Betty only)
 • Employee reviews (Betty only)
 • Customer proposals (Bob only)
 • Marketing software (all)

Figure 2-2.   A client/server network keeps resources centralized

The server computers in a client/server network are responsible for making available and managing appropriate shared resources, and for administering the security of those resources. Figure 2-2 shows how resources would be located in such a network.

Comparing Peer-to-Peer and Client/Server Networks

As mentioned earlier, most networks have aspects of both peer-to-peer and client/server relationships. Before deciding on setting up a network using one or both types of relationships, you should examine their pros and cons and determine how each meets the needs of your company. Consider the following advantages and disadvantages of using each type.

Pros for Peer-to-Peer Networks

Peer-to-peer networks offer a number of advantages, particularly for smaller firms, as follows:

■ **Use less expensive computer hardware**   Peer-to-peer networks are the least hardware-intensive. In a pure peer-to-peer network, the resources are distributed over many computers, so there is no need for a high-end server computer. The impact on each workstation is usually (but not always) relatively minor.

- **Easy to administer**   Peer-to-peer networks are, overall, easiest to set up and administer, provided that there aren't too many computers within the peer-to-peer network. Because each machine performs its own administration—usually for certain limited resources—the effort of administering the network is widely distributed among many different people.

- **No network operating system required**   Peer-to-peer networks do not require a dedicated network operating system (NOS). You can build a peer-to-peer network using Windows 7 or 8 on all the workstations, or on all Macintosh computers for that matter. These client operating systems include all the features necessary for peer-to-peer networking. Similarly, you can do this with all UNIX- or Linux-based computers (although this is more complicated to set up and maintain).

- **More built-in redundancy**   If you have a small network, with 10 to 20 workstations each storing some important data, and one fails, you still have most of your shared resources available. A peer-to-peer network design can offer more redundancy than a client/server network because fewer single points of failure can affect the entire network and everyone who uses it.

Cons for Peer-to-Peer Networks

There are also various drawbacks to peer-to-peer networks, particularly for larger networks or for networks that have more complex or sophisticated requirements. The disadvantages include the following:

- **Might impact user's performance**   If some workstations have frequently used resources on them, the use of these resources across the network might adversely affect the person using the hosting workstation.

- **Not very secure**   Peer-to-peer networks are not nearly as secure as client/server networks because you cannot guarantee that all of the users will appropriately administer their machines. In fact, in a network of any size (say, more than ten people), you can expect that at least a few people will not follow good administration practices on their own machines. Moreover, the most common desktop operating systems used for peer-to-peer networking, like Windows XP or the Macintosh, are not designed to be secure network operating systems.

- **Difficult to back up**   Reliably backing up all the data scattered over many workstations is difficult, and it is not wise to delegate this job to the user of each machine. Experience shows that leaving this vital task up to users means it will not get done.

- **Hard to maintain version control**   In a peer-to-peer network, with files potentially stored on a number of different machines, it can become extremely difficult to manage different document versions.

Pros for Client/Server Networks

Client/server networks offer the opportunity for centralized administration, using equipment suited to managing and offering each resource. Client/server networks are the type commonly used for networks larger than about ten users, and there are quite a few good reasons for this, as follows:

- **Very secure**   A client/server network's security comes from several things. First, because the shared resources are located in a centralized area, they can be administered at that point. Managing a number of resources is much easier if those resources are all located on centralized server computers, as opposed to needing to administer resources across tens or hundreds of computers. Second, usually the servers are physically in a secure location, such as a lockable server room. Physical security is an important aspect of network security, and it cannot be achieved with a peer-to-peer network. Third, the operating systems on which client/server networks run are designed to be secure. Provided that good security and administration practices are in place, the servers cannot be easily "hacked."

- **Better performance**   While dedicated server computers are more expensive than standard computer workstations, they also offer considerably better performance, and they are optimized to handle the needs of many users simultaneously.

- **Centralized backup**   Backing up a company's critical data is much easier when it is located on a centralized server. Often, such backup jobs can be run overnight when the server is not being used and the data is static. Aside from being easier, centralized backups are also much faster than decentralized backups.

- **Very reliable**   While it is true that more built-in redundancy exists with a peer-to-peer network, a good client/server network can be more reliable overall. Dedicated servers often have much more built-in redundancy than standard workstations. They can handle the failure of a disk drive, power supply, or processor and continue to operate until the failed component can be replaced. Also, because a dedicated server has only one relatively simple job to do, its complexity is reduced and its reliability increased. Contrast this with a peer-to-peer network, where actions on the part of the users can drastically reduce each workstation's reliability. For example, needing to restart a PC or a Macintosh every so often is not uncommon, whereas dedicated servers often run for months without requiring a restart or crashing.

Cons for Client/Server Networks

Client/server networks have some drawbacks, particularly for companies that don't have their own in-house network administration or that want to minimize the expense of the network as much as possible. The following are the disadvantages of client/server networks:

- **Require professional administration** Client/server networks usually need some level of professional administration, even if they are small. Knowing the ins and outs of a network operating system is important and requires experience and training. You can hire a network administrator, or you can use a company that provides professional network administration services.

- **More hardware-intensive** In addition to the client computers, you need a server computer, usually a pretty "beefy" computer with a lot of memory and disk space. Plus, you need a network operating system and an appropriate number of client licenses, which can add at least several thousand dollars to the cost of the server. For large networks, these requirements add tens of thousands of dollars.

In a nutshell, choose a peer-to-peer network for smaller networks with fewer than 10 to 15 users, and choose a client/server network for anything larger. Because most networks are built on a client/server concept, this book generally assumes such a network.

Learning Network Features

Now that you know the two basic ways computers on a network can interact with each other, let's look at the types of tasks you can do with a network. The following sections discuss common network features and capabilities.

File Sharing

Originally, file sharing was the primary reason to have a network. In fact, small and midsize companies in the mid-1980s usually installed networks just so they could perform this function. Often, this was driven by the need to network their accounting systems. Of course, once the networks were in place, sharing other types of files became easier as well.

File sharing typically involves word-processing files, spreadsheets, and other files to which many people need regular access. It requires a shared directory or disk drive that many users can access over the network, along with the underlying programming logic needed to make sure that more than one person doesn't make changes to a file at the same time (called *file locking*). The reason you don't want multiple people making changes to a file at the same time is that they might both be making *conflicting* changes simultaneously without realizing it. Most software programs don't have the ability to allow multiple changes to a single file at the same time and to resolve problems that might arise.

 NOTE Most database programs do allow multiple users to access a database simultaneously. Often, this is done using a technique called *row locking*, which restricts changes to any given record to only one user at a time.

Network operating systems that perform file sharing also administer the security for the shared files. This security can control, with a fine level of detail, who has access to which files and what kinds of access they have. For example, some users might have permission to view only certain shared files, while others have permission to edit or even delete those shared files.

Printer Sharing

A close runner-up in importance to file sharing is printer sharing. While it is true that printers are now so inexpensive that you can afford to put one in every office if you wish, sharing printers among the users on the network is still more economical overall.

Printer sharing enables you to reduce the number of printers you need and also to offer much higher-quality printers. Newer digital copiers—also called multifunction printers (MFPs)—that can handle large print jobs at more than 80 pages per minute and provide special printing features can cost more than $20,000. Sharing such printers among many users makes sense.

Printer sharing can be done in several ways. The most common way is to use *print queues* on a server. A print queue holds print jobs until any currently running print jobs are finished and then automatically sends the waiting jobs to the printer. Using a print queue is efficient for the workstations because they can quickly print to the print queue and don't need to wait for the printer itself to process any waiting print jobs.

Another way to share printers on a network is to let each workstation access the printer directly (most printers can be configured so they are connected to the network just like a network workstation). In this case, usually each workstation must wait its turn if many workstations are vying for the printer.

Networked printers that use printer queues have a *print server* that handles the job of sending each print job to the printer in turn. The print server function can be filled in a number of ways:

- By a file and print server that is connected either directly or across the network to the printer.

- By a computer connected to the network, with the printer connected to that computer. The computer runs special print server software to perform this job.

- Through the use of a built-in print server on a printer's network interface card (NIC), which contains the hardware necessary to act as a print server. For example, many laser printers offer an option to include a NIC, with a built-in print server, in the printer. This is far less expensive than dedicating a stand-alone computer to the job.

- Through the use of a dedicated network print server, which is a box about the size of a deck of cards that connects to the printer's parallel or Universal Serial Bus (USB) port (or even a wireless 802.11 protocol connection), on one end and the network on the other end. Dedicated print servers also contain the hardware necessary to act as print servers. This can be a good option when you need to share a printer that does not contain the necessary networking connections.

Application Services

Just as you can share files on a network, you can often also share applications. For example, if you have the proper type of software license, you can have a shared copy of some applications stored on the network server. When a workstation wants to run the program, it loads the files from the network into its own memory, just as it would from a local disk drive, and runs the program normally. Keeping applications centralized reduces the amount of disk space needed on each workstation and makes it easier to administer the application. (For instance, with some applications, you need to upgrade only the network copy; with others, you also must perform a brief installation for each client.)

Another application service you can host on the network is a shared installation point for applications. Instead of needing to load a CD-ROM onto each workstation to install an application, you can usually copy the contents of the CD-ROM to a folder on a server and then have the installation program run from that folder for each workstation. This makes installing the applications much faster and more convenient.

 CAUTION   Make sure any applications you host on a network server are licensed appropriately. Most software licenses do *not* let you run an application on multiple computers. Even if you need only one actual copy of the application to set up the files on the server, you still must have a license for every user. Different applications have different fine print regarding licensing—some require one license per user, some require one license per computer, some allow your network users to use a copy at home freely, and so forth. Make sure to carefully read the license agreements for your business software and adhere to their terms and conditions.

E-mail

An extremely valuable and important network resource these days is e-mail. Not only can it be helpful for communications within a company, but it is also a preferred vehicle to communicate with people outside a company.

E-mail systems are roughly divided into two different types: file-based and client/server. A file-based e-mail system is one that consists of a set of files kept in a shared location on a server. The server doesn't actually do anything beyond providing access to the files. Connections required from a file-based e-mail system and the outside (say, to the Internet) are usually accomplished with a stand-alone computer—called a *gateway server*—that handles the e-mail interface between the two systems by using gateway software that is part of the file-based e-mail system.

In a client/server e-mail system, an e-mail server contains the messages and handles all the e-mail interconnections, both within and outside the company. Client/server e-mail systems, such as Microsoft Exchange and Lotus Notes, are more secure and far more powerful than their file-based counterparts. They often offer additional features that enable you to use the e-mail system to automate different internal business processes, such as invoicing and purchasing.

For smaller companies (with fewer than 25 employees), e-mail is just as important, but an e-mail server or dedicated e-mail system is usually overkill and too costly to purchase and maintain. Instead, these companies can use a hosted e-mail solution, such as Google for Domains, Microsoft's Office 365 for businesses, or Microsoft's hosted Exchange Server product. There are also many other hosted e-mail services available.

 NOTE   Hosted e-mail solutions let you use your own domain name.

Remote Access

Another important service for most networks is remote access to the network's resources. Users use this feature to access their files and e-mail when they're traveling or working from a remote location, such as a hotel or their home. Remote access systems come in many different flavors. The following are some of the methods used to provide remote access:

- Set up a Virtual Private Network (VPN) server on a Windows server, which is then accessed through the company's Internet connection.
- Employ a workstation on the network and have users connect using a remote control program like Symantec's pcAnywhere or Citrix's GoToMyPC.
- Set up a dedicated VPN server, connected to the Internet, through which users can access resources on the company network in a secure fashion.
- Install Windows Terminal Services (on a Windows server) or Citrix XenDesktop, which allows a single server to host multiple client sessions, each appearing to the end user as a stand-alone computer.

To choose the most suitable remote access solution, you'll need to consider what the users need to do remotely, the number of users (both in total and at any given time), and how much you want to spend. See Chapter 8 for more information about remote access.

Wide Area Networks

You should think of a wide area network (WAN) as a sort of "metanetwork." A WAN is simply multiple local area networks (LANs) connected together. This can be accomplished in many different ways, depending on how often the LANs need to be connected to one another, how much data capacity (bandwidth) is required, and how great the distance is between the LANs. Solutions include full-time leased telephone lines that can carry 56 Kbps of data, dedicated DS1 (T-1) lines carrying 1.544 Mbps, DS3 lines carrying 44.736 Mbps, Ethernet connections carrying 100 Mpbs or 1 Gbps, and other forms (like private satellites) carrying even higher bandwidths. You can also create a WAN using VPNs over the Internet. Although this method usually offers inconsistent bandwidth, it's often the least expensive.

WANs are created when the users of one LAN need frequent access to the resources on another LAN. For instance, a company's Enterprise Resource Planning (ERP) system might be running at the company's headquarters, but the remote warehouse location needs access to it to use its inventory and shipping functions.

As a general rule, if you can design and build a system that doesn't require a WAN, you're usually better off, because WAN links are often expensive to maintain. However, the geographic and management structure of a particular company can dictate the use of a WAN.

Internet and Intranet

The Internet has become vital to the productivity of most businesses, and handling Internet connectivity on a network is often an important network service. Many different types of services are available over the Internet, including e-mail, the Web, and Usenet newsgroups.

An Internet connection for a network consists of a telecommunications network connection to an Internet Service Provider (ISP) using a physical connection. Physical connections can range from a leased Digital Subscriber Line (DSL) line up to 1 Gbps Ethernet connection. This line comes into the building and connects to the internal LAN, usually through a dedicated router. The router then routes data packets between the local network and the Internet. Internet security is provided either by filtering the packets going through the router or, more commonly, by adding a firewall system in between the router and the LAN. A firewall system runs on a computer (or has a computer built into it, if it's an appliance device) and helps you secure your network against various threats.

An *intranet*, as its name suggests, is an internally focused network that mimics the Internet itself. For example, a company might deploy an intranet that hosts a web server, which stores documents such as employee handbooks, purchasing forms, and other information that the company publishes for internal use. Intranets can also host other Internet-type services, such as File Transfer Protocol (FTP) servers or Usenet servers, or these services can be provided by other tools that offer the same functionality. Intranets usually are not accessible from outside the LAN (although they can be) and are just a much smaller version of the Internet that a company maintains for its own use.

Understanding the technologies, services, and features of the Internet is complex. You can learn much more about some of the hardware that makes the Internet work in Chapter 4.

DEFINE-IT! xAN

A myriad of terms refer to what are essentially wide area networks, all with variations on the *x*AN acronym scheme. Some examples include metropolitan area network (MAN), distance area network (DAN), campus area network (CAN), and even—I'm not making this up—personal area network (PAN), which was an IBM demonstration technology where two people shaking hands could exchange data through electrical signals carried on the surface of their skin. All of these different names, and others that I haven't listed here, are a bit silly. I suggest you just stick with the two core terms: LAN and WAN.

Network Security

Any time you share important and confidential information on a network, you need to carefully consider the security of those resources. Users and management must help set the level of security required for the network and the different information it stores, and they need to participate in deciding who has access to which resources.

Network security is provided by a combination of factors, including features of the network operating system, the physical cabling plant, the network connection to other networks, the features of the client workstations, the actions of the users, the security policies of management, and how well the security features are implemented and administered. All these factors form a chain, and any single weak link in the chain can cause it to fail. Security failures can have severe consequences, so network security is usually an extremely important part of any network. For a more detailed discussion of network security, see Chapter 9.

Understanding the OSI Networking Model

The Open Systems Interconnection (OSI) model defines all the methods and protocols needed to connect one computer to any other over a network. It is a conceptual model, used most often in network design and in engineering network solutions. Generally, real-world networks conform to the OSI model, although differences exist between the theory and actual practice in most networks. Still, the OSI model offers an excellent way to understand and visualize how computers network to each other, and it is required knowledge for anyone active in the field of networking. Just about all employers expect networking professionals to be knowledgeable about the OSI model, and it comes up on most networking certification tests. This might be a very dry topic, but it's important to learn!

The OSI model defines a basic framework for how modern networks operate. It separates the methods and protocols needed for a network connection into seven different layers. Each higher layer relies on services provided by a lower layer. If you were to think about a desktop computer in this way, its hardware would be the lowest layer, and the operating system drivers—the next-higher layer—would rely on the lowest layer to do their job. The operating system itself, the next-higher layer, would rely on both of the lower layers working properly. This continues all the way up to the point at which an application presents data to you on the computer screen. Figure 2-3 shows the seven layers of the OSI model.

NOTE   The OSI model is sometimes called the *seven-layer model.* It was developed by the International Standards Organization (ISO) in 1983 and is documented as Standard 7498.

For a complete network connection, data flows from the top layer on one computer, down through all the lower layers, across the wire, and back up the seven layers on the other computer. The following sections discuss each layer, making comparisons to real networking systems as appropriate.

Figure 2-3. The seven layers of the OSI model

Physical Layer

The bottom layer, Layer 1, is called the *physical layer*. It defines the properties of the physical medium used to make a network connection. The physical layer specifications control the lowest level at which data is actually moved between nodes on the physical network. It can be a tangible physical medium, such as a network cable, or it can also be radio waves if that is how the data is carried. The physical layer also includes any devices that make up the physical connection between two networked computers, and so things like routers, switches, satellite antennas, and so forth are part of the physical layer.

The physical connection can be either point to point (between two points) or multipoint (between many points, such as from one point to many others), and it can consist of either *half-duplex* (one direction at a time) or *full-duplex* (both directions simultaneously) transmissions. Moreover, the bits can be transmitted either in series or in parallel. (Most networks use a serial stream of bits, but the OSI model allows for both serial and parallel transmission.) The specification for the physical layer also defines the cable used, the voltages carried on the cable, the timing of the electrical signals, the distance that can be run, and so on.

Data-Link Layer

The *data-link layer*, Layer 2, defines standards that assign meaning to the bits carried by the physical layer. It establishes a reliable protocol through the physical layer so the network layer (Layer 3) can transmit its data. The data-link layer typically includes error detection and correction to ensure a reliable data stream. The data elements carried by the data-link layer are called *frames*. Examples of frame types include X.25 and 802.*x* (802.*x* includes both Ethernet and Token Ring networks).

The data-link layer is usually subdivided into two sublayers, called the *logical link control* (LLC) and *media access control* (MAC) sublayers. If used, the LLC sublayer performs tasks such as call setup and termination (the OSI model can be applied to telecommunications networks as well as LANs) and data transfer. The MAC sublayer handles frame assembly and disassembly, error detection and correction, and addressing. The two most common MAC protocols are 802.3 Ethernet and 802.5 Token Ring. Other MAC protocols include 802.12 100Base-VBG, 802.11 Wireless, and 802.7 Broadband.

 NOTE All network interface cards have unique MAC addresses burned into them. Every company who makes NICs must register with the Institute of Electrical and Electronics Engineers (IEEE), who assigns blocks of unique MAC addresses to each manufacturer.

On most systems, the software drivers for the NIC perform the work done at the data-link layer, and usually NICs are considered part of the data-link layer.

Network Layer

The *network layer*, Layer 3, is where a lot of action goes on for most networks. The network layer defines how data *packets* get from one point to another on a network and what goes into each packet. The network layer uses different packet protocols, such as Internet Protocol (IP) and Internet Protocol Exchange (IPX). These packet protocols include source and destination routing information. The routing information in each packet informs the network where to send the packet to reach its destination and tells the receiving computer from where the packet originated.

The network layer is most important when the network connection passes through one or more *routers*, which are hardware devices that examine each packet and, from their source and destination addresses, send the packets to their proper destination. Over a complex network such as the Internet, a packet might go through ten or more routers before it reaches its destination. On a LAN, a packet might not go through any routers to get to its destination, or it might go through one or more.

Note that breaking the network layer (also known as the *packet layer*) into a separate layer from the physical and data-link layers means the protocols defined in this layer can be carried over any variations of the lower layers. So, to put this into real-world terms, an IP packet can be sent over an Ethernet network, a Token Ring network, or even a serial cable that connects two computers. The same holds true for an IPX packet:

If both computers can handle IPX and they share the lower-level layers (whatever they might be) in common, then the network connection can be made.

Transport Layer

The *transport layer*, Layer 4, manages the flow of information from one network node to another. It ensures that the packets are decoded in the proper sequence and that all packets are received. It also identifies each computer or node on a network uniquely.

The various networking systems (such as Microsoft's or Novell's) implement the transport layer differently. In fact, the transport layer is the first layer where differences between network operating systems occur.

Examples of transport layer protocols include Transmission Control Protocol (TCP) and Sequenced Packet Exchange (SPX), which are used in concert with IP and IPX, respectively.

Session Layer

The *session layer*, Layer 5, defines the connection from a user computer to a network server, or from a peer computer on a network to another peer computer. These virtual connections are referred to as *sessions*. They include negotiation between the client and host (or peer and peer) on matters of flow control, transaction processing, transfer of user information, and authentication to the network. They are called *sessions* because they set up connections that persist for some period of time.

On most computers—whether servers or clients—there are multiple services in parallel. For example, a server might be capable of responding to requests for files, for security authentication, for e-mail transmissions, or for web pages. And a client computer is often making these requests at the same time. The session layer helps ensure that each service is matched up appropriately with each request and that they stay connected (virtually) for the duration of the request.

Presentation Layer

The *presentation layer*, Layer 6, takes the data supplied by the lower-level layers and transforms it so it can be presented to the system (as opposed to presenting the data to the user, which is handled outside the OSI model). The functions that take place at the presentation layer can include data compression and decompression, as well as data encryption and decryption.

Application Layer

The *application layer*, Layer 7, controls how the operating system and its applications interact with the network. The applications you use, such as Microsoft Word or an Oracle database system, are not a part of the application layer, but they certainly benefit from the work that goes on there. The application layer defines how applications can work with the network—in other words, be *network-aware*.

Understanding How Data Travels Through the OSI Layers

As mentioned earlier in this section, data flows from an application program or the operating system and then goes down through the protocols and devices that make up the seven layers of the OSI model, one by one, until the data arrives at the physical layer and is transmitted over the network connection. The computer at the receiving end reverses this process: The data comes in at the physical layer, travels up through all the layers until it emerges from the application layer, and is made use of by the operating system and any application programs.

At each stage of the OSI model, the data is "wrapped" with new control information related to the work done at that particular layer, leaving the previous layers' information intact and wrapped within the new control information. This control information is different for each layer, but it includes *headers, trailers, preambles,* and *postambles.*

For example, when data goes into the networking software and components making up the OSI model, it starts at the application layer and includes an application header and application data (the actual data being sent). Next, at the presentation layer, a presentation header is wrapped around the data, and it is passed to the component at the session layer, where a session header is wrapped around all of the data, and so on, until it reaches the physical layer. At the receiving computer, this process is reversed, with each layer unwrapping its appropriate control information, performing whatever work is indicated by that control information, and passing the data on to the next higher layer. It all sounds rather complex, but it works very well in practice.

Learning About Network Hardware Components

This chapter is really about understanding networks, with a "view from 30,000 feet." An overview of the hardware that enables networks to operate completes this discussion. Understanding the general types of devices you typically encounter in a network is important, not only for planning a network but also for troubleshooting and maintenance.

Servers

A *server* is any computer that performs network functions for other computers. These functions fall into several categories, including the following:

- File and print servers, which provide file sharing and services to share network-based printers.

- Application servers, which provide application-specific services. An example is a server that runs a database that a distributed application uses.

- E-mail servers, which provide e-mail storage and interconnection services to client computers.

- Networking servers, which can provide a host of different network services. Examples of these services include the automatic assignment of TCP/IP addresses

(DHCP servers), routing of packets from one network to another (routing servers), encryption/decryption and other security services, and VPN access.

■ Internet servers, which provide web, Usenet News (NNTP), and Internet e-mail services.

■ Remote access servers, which provide access to a local network for remote users.

As noted earlier, servers typically run some sort of network operating system, such as Windows Server 2012, Linux, or UNIX. Depending on the operating system chosen, the functions previously listed might all be performed on one server or distributed to many servers. Also, not all networks need all the services previously listed.

NOTE   Server computers can be nearly any type of computer, but today they are usually high-end Intel-based PCs. You might also see certain types of servers that use a different platform. For instance, many dedicated web servers run on UNIX-based computers, such as those from Sun Microsystems, IBM, Hewlett-Packard, and other vendors.

A number of features distinguish a true server-class computer from a more pedestrian client computer, including the following:

■ Built-in redundancy with multiple power supplies and fans (for instance) to keep the server running if something breaks.

■ Special high-performance designs for disk subsystems, memory, and network subsystems to optimize the movement of data to and from the server, the network, and the client computers.

■ Special monitoring software and hardware that keeps a close watch on the health of the server, warning of failures before they occur. For example, most servers have temperature monitors; if the temperature starts getting too high, a warning is issued so the problem can be resolved before it causes failure of any of the hardware components in the server.

You can learn more about servers in Chapter 11.

Hubs, Routers, and Switches

Hubs, routers, and switches are the most commonly seen "pure" networking hardware. (They're pure in the sense that they exist only for networking and for no other purpose.) Many people refer to this class of equipment as *internetworking devices*. These are the devices to which all the cables of the network are connected. They pass the data along at the physical, data-link, or network layer of the OSI model.

A *hub*, sometimes called a *concentrator*, is a device that connects a number of network cables coming from connected computers to a network. Hubs come in many different sizes, supporting from as few as 2 computers up to 60 or more computers. (The most common hub size supports 24 network connections.) All the network connections on a hub share a single *collision domain*, which is a fancy way of saying all the connections to a hub "talk" over a single logical wire and are subject to interference from other computers connected to the same hub.

A *switch* is wired very similarly to a hub and actually looks just like a hub. However, on a switch, all of the network connections are on their own collision domain. The switch makes each network connection a private one. Often, switches are connected to one or more backbone switches, which usually run at a much higher speed than the individual switches. If hubs are used (and they're exceedingly rare these days), often the hubs will be connected to a single switch that will serve as a backbone. Figure 2-4 shows a typical switch and hub wiring arrangement.

A *router* routes data packets from one network to another. The two networks connect to the router using their own wiring type and connection type. For example, a router that connects a 100Base-T network to an Integrated Services Digital Network (ISDN) telephone line has two connections: one leading to the 100Base-T network and one leading to the ISDN line provided by the phone company. Routers also usually

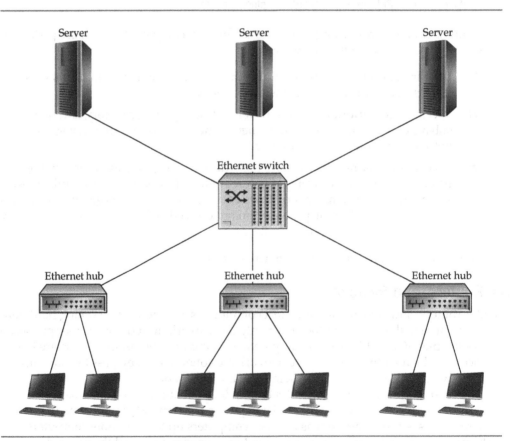

Figure 2-4.   Using switches and hubs in concert

have an additional connection that a terminal can be connected to; this connection is just used to program and maintain the router.

Hubs, routers, and switches are discussed in more detail—along with other networking hardware—in Chapter 4.

Cabling and Cable Plants

Many types of network cable exist, but you need to be concerned with only a few of the more common ones. The most common network cable for LANs is Category 5 (called *Cat-5* for short) twisted-pair cable. This cable carries the network signal to each point through eight wires (four twisted pairs). Cat-5 cable is used to support 100Base-T and 1000Base-T Ethernet networks.

NOTE   The twisting of each pair in the cable jacket reduces the chances of the cable picking up electrical interference.

You will also occasionally see a lower-grade cable used called Category 3 (*Cat-3*) cable. This is similar to Cat-5 cable, but has half as many wires running through it and uses smaller connectors (although they're still the modular phone-style connectors). Cat-3 cable is used for older 10Base-T networks.

NOTE   It is possible to run a Cat-3 network connection over Cat-5 cable. Because of this, many companies installed the higher-grade cable, even if they didn't immediately need it, because the cost of rewiring an entire building is very high.

Cat-5 cable has been improved and is now called *Cat-5E cable*. Also, an even newer standard called *Cat-6* has been approved. Both Cat-5E and Cat-6 are essentially the same as Cat-5, but they meet higher-quality specifications to handle faster network speeds. They are both also backward-compatible with the prior network types. In other words, you can run a 100Base-T network over Cat-6 cable, even though only Cat-5 is required.

Coaxial cable (called *coax*) is not currently used for new cable installations, but you might still come across it in older buildings. Coax cable has a center core of copper (called the *conductor*) surrounded by a plastic wrapper, which is wrapped with braided metal, called the *shield,* and then finally an outer plastic coating. For instance, the cable that you use to connect a television to a cable TV network is a type of coax cable (the same coax is used for cable modems, by the way). Most coax cable used for networks is a type called RG-58, which is used for 10Base-2 (Thin Ethernet) networks. Another is RG-56, used for ARCnet networks. The different types of coax cable refer to the specifications of the cable, which determine whether a particular network type can make use of the cable. You cannot mix different types of coax cable in a single network, and you must use the correct type for the network you are building.

The term *cable plant* refers to the entire installation of all your network cable. It includes not only the cable run throughout a building, but also the connectors, wall plates, patch panels, and so forth. It's extremely important that a new installation of a cable plant be performed by a qualified contractor trained to install that type of cable. Cable may appear simple, but it is actually quite complicated, and its installation is also complex. Moreover, if problems develop in a cable plant, they can be expensive to resolve. It's best to get it right the first time!

Chapter 3 provides more information about network cabling.

Workstation Hardware

Any computer on a network that is used by people is usually referred to as a *network workstation*. Sometimes such workstations are also called *network clients.* Usually, a network client is an Intel-based PC running some version of Windows, which has a NIC and network client software installed, allowing the workstation to participate on the network. Network workstations can also be any other type of computer that includes the necessary network hardware and software, such as an Apple Macintosh or some form of UNIX-based computer.

TIP Don't confuse *network workstations* (a generic term) with workstation-class computers. Workstation-class computers are higher-end desktop computers used for computer-aided design, engineering, and graphics work.

Chapter Summary

This chapter introduced a number of important networking concepts. You first learned about some basic computer knowledge, including numbering systems and bandwidth measures. You then learned about how computers on a network relate to one another, how the different parts of a network connection are logically broken down in the OSI network model, and how this model is useful in understanding networks. You also learned about a number of basic network features and resources.

The following chapters cover these subjects in more detail, starting with the next chapter, which discusses the often-misunderstood world of network wiring.

CHAPTER 3 | Understanding Network Cabling

I f you were to compare a computer network to the human body, the network cabling system would be the nerves that make up the physical manifestation of the nervous system. The network cabling system is what actually carries all the data from one point to another and determines how the network works. How a network is cabled is of supreme importance to how the network functions, how fast it functions, how reliable the network will be as a whole, and how easy it will be to expand and change the network.

With any new network, your first task after assessing the needs for the network is to determine how the network should be wired; all the other components of the network are then built on that foundation. This is much like the OSI seven-layer model you learned about in Chapter 2, in that the network cabling makes up Layer 1 (the physical layer), and all the upper networking layers rely on it.

Many people think that network cabling is relatively simple. After all, what could be simpler than running a wire between two points? However, as you will see, the topic of network cabling encompasses more than meets the eye, and it's an extremely important area to get right. If you make mistakes selecting or installing network cable, your network will likely be unreliable and may perform poorly. Because of the labor costs involved in wiring a network, the best time to address any potential problems in this area is well *before* they occur.

Understanding Cable Topologies

The word *topology* basically means *shape*, and the term *network topology* refers to the shape of a network—how all of the nodes (points) of a network are wired together. Networks may be wired in several different topologies, and the choice of a topology is often your most important decision when you plan a network. The topologies have different costs (both to install and maintain), levels of performance, and levels of reliability.

DEFINE-IT! Network Segment

The term *network segment* can mean somewhat different things depending on the topology of the network, but the concept is simplest to understand when thinking about a bus network, and is essentially the same for any topology. A *segment* is a single length of cable to which all the nodes in that segment are connected. In truth, a segment is not a single continuous length of cable, because it is broken at each computer connection point with a connector that lets the node connect to the network cable, but the cable is *electrically* one single cable.

In any given segment, all the network traffic is "seen" by all the nodes on that segment. You need to take this into account when planning how many nodes you will connect to any given segment. If you have 20 computers, all fully using that segment at the same time, each computer will achieve only approximately one-twentieth of the available maximum bandwidth. This is simplified; you will learn more about how this works later in this chapter and in following chapters.

The main topologies in use today are bus, star, and ring. These topologies are described in this section.

Bus Topology

A *bus topology*, more completely called a *common bus multipoint topology*, is a network where, basically, a single network cable is used from one end of the network to the other, with different network devices (called *nodes*) connected to the cable at different locations. Figure 3-1 illustrates a simple bus topology network.

Different types of bus networks have different specifications, which include the following factors:

- How many nodes can be in a single segment
- How many segments can be used through the use of repeaters
- How close nodes can be to each other
- The total length of a segment
- Which cable type is required
- How the ends of the bus must be terminated

Bus topology networks usually use coaxial cable, described later in this chapter. Each end of each segment of the network has a special cable terminator on it, without which the network will not function. Some bus topology networks, such as Thin Ethernet (10Base-2), use BNC connectors to tie all the individual pieces of cable together. Each computer is connected to the network through the use of a BNC *T-connector* (called that because it's shaped like the letter *T*), which allows the network to continue its bus and lets the computer connect to it. Figure 3-2 shows several different BNC connectors.

Figure 3-1.   A simple bus topology network

BNC T-connector

BNC barrel connector

RG-58 cable with male BNC connector

Figure 3-2.   BNC connectors used in a coax-based bus topology network

Bus network topologies are by far the least expensive to install because they use much less cable than the other two topologies and, accordingly, use less material and need less installation labor.

But bus networks have some big drawbacks. Because all the subcables that make up the segment and run from node to node must be connected at all times, and because a failure in any part of the segment will cause the entire segment to fail, bus networks are prone to trouble. And even more important, that trouble can take a long time to track down because you must work your way through all the cable connections until you find the one causing the problem. Often, the source of the problem isn't visually apparent, so you need to use various techniques and equipment to find it (as discussed in the "Troubleshooting Coaxial Networks" section later in this chapter).

DEFINE-IT! BNC Connectors

Depending on whom you ask, BNC stands for Bayonet Nut Connector, British Naval Connector, or Bayonet Neill-Concelman (with the latter two words standing for its inventors, Mr. Paul Neill of Bell Labs and Carl Concelman of Amphenol Corporation). BNC is a bayonet-style connector that quickly attaches and detaches with a quarter turn. A variety of different parts—T-connectors, barrel connectors, elbow connectors, cable ends that splice onto appropriate cable, and so forth—use BNC connectors, so you can achieve nearly any type of connection needed. The BNC connector is extremely easy to use and makes a secure connection.

Because of the tendency of bus networks to be unreliable, new network wiring installations do not use pure bus topologies.

By far, the most prevalent bus network used in the past (and in very limited existence today) is one called 10Base-2 Ethernet, or more commonly, Thin Ethernet. This network type has the following characteristics:

- Has a rated maximum speed of 10 Mbps
- Uses RG-58/AU or RG-58/CU coaxial cable, with BNC connectors
- Requires a 50-ohm terminating connector at each end of each segment to function
- Can handle a maximum of 30 nodes per segment
- Can be run up to a maximum segment length of 185 meters (607 feet)
- Can use extended segments through the use of repeaters
- Requires each node to be at least 0.5 meter (1.5 feet) of cable distance from any other node

If repeaters are used, you can connect a maximum of three segments together, and each segment may have up to 30 nodes (with the repeater counting as a node). You can also have two additional segments (a total of five) if those extra two segments are used for distance only and do not have any nodes on them. An entire repeated segment must never exceed a total of 925 meters (3,035 feet). Remember the 5-4-3 rule: five segments, four repeaters, three populated segments.

 NOTE   Repeaters are hardware devices that electrically boost the signal on a cable so it can be extended further; they do not route any of the data. In fact, a repeater is "ignorant" of any of the data it carries. Repeaters are inexpensive and reliable. However, remember that extending a cable with a repeater means that all the network traffic on one side of the repeater is echoed to the cable on the other side of the repeater, regardless of whether that traffic needs to go on that other cable. Repeaters are discussed in more detail in Chapter 4.

Star Topology

A *star topology* is one in which a central unit, called a *hub* or *concentrator,* hosts a set of network cables that radiate out to each node on the network. Technically, the hub is referred to as a multistation access unit (MAU), but that particular terminology tends to be used with only Token Ring networks, which use a logical ring topology (see the following section). Each hub usually hosts 24 nodes, although hubs range in size from 2 nodes up to 96 nodes. Regardless of the hub size, you can connect multiple hubs together to grow the network in any way that makes sense. See Chapter 4 for more on connecting hubs together in different configurations. Figure 3-3 shows a simple star topology network.

Figure 3-3. A star topology network

All the network traffic used on any of the network connections to the hub is echoed to all the other connected nodes on that particular hub. Because of this, all the bandwidth of any single node's connection is shared with all other nodes' connections. For example, if one of the nodes connected to the hub is using half the available bandwidth, all the other nodes must contend with that use. In other words, if you're using a network type with a capacity of 100 Mbps, that's the total amount of bandwidth available to all of the nodes connected to the hub.

> **NOTE**   Networks that are physically wired in a star topology are logically either a bus or a ring. This means that, despite what the network looks like, it still "behaves" as either a bus or a ring. Ethernet networks wired in a star fashion are logically a bus. Token Ring networks wired in a star fashion are logically a ring.

Star topology networks can use one of several forms of Ethernet. The most common is 100Base-T Ethernet, which provides 100 Mbps of bandwidth. Older networks use 10Base-T Ethernet, which provides 10 Mbps of bandwidth. Currently, the standard is Gigabit Ethernet (1000Base-T), which offers 1 Gbps of bandwidth. More recently, a standard called 10 Gigabit Ethernet (or alternatively 10GBase-X), which can run at 10 Gbps over various types of cable, has been approved, and various products are available for this standard.

10Base-T requires a type of twisted-pair cable called Category 3 (Cat-3) cable. 100Base-T requires Category 5 (Cat-5) cable. 10Base-T can also use Cat-5, but 100Base-T cannot use Cat-3. These days, you should always use the most recent Cat-5 cable—called Cat-5E—even if it's intended for only a 10Base-T network. (Cat-5 cable provides eight wires—four twisted pairs—and so can carry two connections in each cable if desired.) If cost is not an issue, consider even moving up to Cat-6.

10Base-What?

The various Ethernet standards referred to as, for instance, 10Base-2, 10Base-T, 100Base-T, and so on contain in their name all you need to know about what they do. The first portion—the number—can be 10, 100, or 1000, and this number indicates the data rate (in Mbps) that the standard carries. The word *Base* means the network is *baseband* rather than *broadband*. (A baseband connection carries only one signal at a given instant; a broadband connection carries multiple signals at any time.) The terminating letter or number indicates what sort of cable is used: *T* for twisted pair, 2 for thin coaxial, 5 for thick coaxial, and *F* or *X* usually indicating fiber-optic cable. Here's a quick reference guide to the different standards commonly seen:

10Base-2	10 Mbps, coaxial (RG-58) cable
10Base-5	10 Mbps, coaxial (RG-8) cable
10Base-T	10 Mbps, twisted-pair (two pairs, Cat-3 or higher) cable
100Base-T	100 Mbps, twisted-pair (two pairs, Cat-5) cable; a variant called 100 Base-T4 designates four pairs
100Base-TX	100 Mbps, twisted-pair (two pairs, Cat-5) cable
100Base-FX	100 Mbps, fiber-optic cable
1000Base-T	1 Gbps, twisted-pair (four pairs, Cat-5) cable
10GBase-X	10 Gbps, fiber-optic cable

10Base-T networks share the following wiring characteristics:

- Require four actual wires (two twisted pairs in a single sheath); can be either unshielded twisted-pair or shielded twisted-pair
- Can be run on either Cat-3 or Cat-5 cable
- Are limited to a length of 100 meters (328 feet) for each node connection
- Are not limited in the number of nodes in a single logical segment
- Use RJ-45 connectors for all connections (this type of connector is similar to a modular telephone connector, but the RJ-45 is larger)

100Base-T networks are similar to 10Base-T networks and have these characteristics:

- Require four actual wires (two twisted pairs in a single sheath)
- Must use Cat-5 cable or better
- Are limited to a length of 100 meters (328 feet) for each node connection
- Are not limited in the number of nodes in a single logical segment
- Use RJ-45 connectors for all connections

1000Base-T networks are notable in that they can run over existing Cat-5 cable at ten times the speed of 100Base-T networks. Running over Cat-5 cable is a significant advantage for 1000Base-T, because over 75 percent of installed network cabling today is Cat-5, and rewiring an entire building for a new networking standard is an extremely expensive proposition. 1000Base-T over Cat-5 networks have these characteristics:

- Require eight actual wires (four twisted pairs in a single sheath)
- Must use Cat-5 cable or better
- Are limited to a length of 100 meters (328 feet) for each node connection
- Are not limited in the number of nodes in a single logical segment
- Use RJ-45 connectors for all connections

Compared to bus networks, star topology networks are more expensive. Much more actual wire is required, the labor to install that wire is much greater, and an additional cost exists for the needed hubs. To offset these costs, however, star topologies are far more reliable than bus topologies. With a star topology, if any single network connection goes bad (is cut or damaged in some way), only that one connection is affected. While it is true that hubs echo all the network signals for the connected nodes to all other nodes on the hub, they also have the capability to *partition*, or cut off, any misbehaving node connections automatically—one bad apple won't spoil the whole bunch. In addition, because each cable is run directly from the hub to the node, it is extremely easy to troubleshoot; you don't need to go traipsing over an entire building trying to find the problem.

Ring Topology

A ring topology is actually not a physical arrangement of a network cable, as you might guess. Instead, rings are a logical arrangement; the actual cables are wired in a star, with each node connected on its own cable to the MAU. However, electrically, the network behaves like a ring, where the network signals travel around the ring to each node in turn. Figure 3-4 shows a sample ring topology network.

Ring topology LANs are based on Token Ring instead of Ethernet. Some may also run Fiber Distributed Data Interface (FDDI)—a 100 Mbps fiber-optic network— instead of copper-based cable. Rings are also used for some larger telecommunications networks like Synchronous Optical Network (SONET), as well as in storage area networks and some other applications.

Comparing Rings to Stars and Buses

To compare rings to stars and buses, you first need to understand the basic concept of how Ethernet networks work. Ethernet networks manage all the needed signals on the network using a technique called CSMA/CD, which stands for Carrier Sense Multiple Access with Collision Detection. CSMA/CD allows each node on a segment to transmit data whenever it likes. If two nodes try to transmit at the same time, they each detect this occurrence with their collision detection, and then both nodes wait a random amount of time (counted in milliseconds) to retry their transmissions.

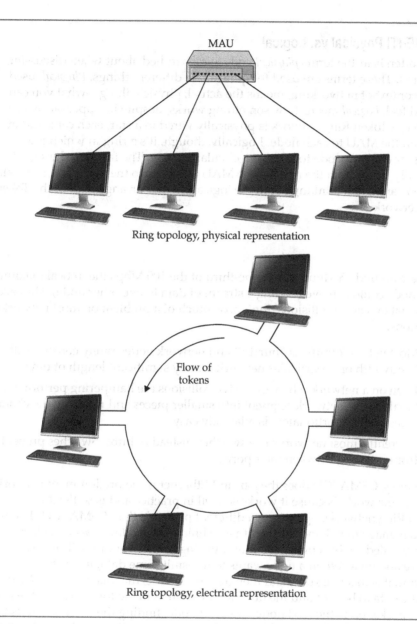

Ring topology, physical representation

Flow of
tokens

Ring topology, electrical representation

Figure 3-4.   A sample ring topology network

Considering how data packets flow on a network using CSMA/CD, you might think that it could quickly become a confusing mess, with data and collision retries causing more collisions. And you would probably think the potential exists for the network to reach a saturation point where virtually nothing gets transmitted because of excessive collisions. You would be right. For 100Base-T networks, this point occurs

DEFINE-IT! Physical vs. Logical

You'll often hear the terms *physical* and *logical* bandied about when discussing networks. These terms are used for quite a few different things. *Physical*, used in the context of networking, means the actual, physical thing—what you can see and feel. *Logical* means how something works, despite its appearance. For example, a Token Ring network is physically wired in a star; each cable radiates out from the MAU to each node. Logically, though, it's a ring in which the signals travel from node to node in a circular fashion. The fact that the signals physically travel from the node to the MAU and back to the next node is usually unimportant when thinking about the logical circular arrangement of the Token Ring network.

somewhere around 35 Mbps (about one-third of the 100 Mbps theoretical maximum that one node could achieve sending a stream of data to one other node). However, the reality is that excessive collisions don't pose much of a problem on most networks, for three reasons:

- Most network traffic is "bursty," and network nodes rarely consume all the bandwidth on a particular network for any significant length of time.

- Even on a network where excessive collisions are hampering performance, breaking the network segment into smaller pieces and reducing the chances of collisions proportionately is relatively easy.

- Currently, most networks use switches instead of hubs. Switches prevent data from colliding between their ports.

Ultimately, CSMA/CD does the job, and Ethernet is the predominant network standard in the world because it works so well in practice and is so flexible.

Token Ring networks operate on a different principle than CSMA/CD. Token Ring networks manage their bandwidth with a technique called *token passing*. Electrically, a data entity called a *token* circulates around the logical network ring. The token has two states: free and busy. When a node wants to transmit some data, it waits until the token coming into it is in a free state, and then the node marks the token as busy. Next, after adding the data to be sent and the destination address to the token packet, the node sends the packet on to the next node. The next node, finding the token set to its busy state, examines the destination address and passes the token on unchanged toward the destination. Once the destination node receives the token, it gets its data, marks the token as free, and sends it along to the next workstation. If the token somehow becomes "lost," then a workstation generates a new, free token automatically after a set period of time passes.

The beauty of Token Ring networks is that they behave predictably as the bandwidth needs of the nodes increase. Also, Token Ring networks are never bogged down by collisions, which are impossible in such a network. However, these benefits of Token Ring networks are offset somewhat by the greater overhead and processing needs to handle the tokens. Overall, Token Ring networks perform about as fast as Ethernet networks with similar bandwidth.

IBM invented the Token Ring network technology in the late 1960s, and the first Token Ring networks started appearing in 1986. While quite a few Token Ring LANs are installed (running at either 4 Mbps or 16 Mbps), you tend to see them predominantly in companies that have a strong IBM relationship and, perhaps, also use an IBM mainframe or minicomputer.

If you're designing a new LAN, generally your best bet is to use Ethernet in a star topology. You'll find network equipment for this choice is readily available and inexpensive. Many qualified installers are available for 100Base-T or 1000Base-T. (There is little sense in installing 10Base-T these days; in fact, the equipment is no longer available.) As noted earlier, for new networks, you should install Cat-5E cable at a minimum, even if you're initially going to use 100Base-T, so that you have a ready upgrade path to the faster standards.

Use Token Ring if some external need is driving this choice, such as connectivity to an old IBM mainframe that doesn't support Ethernet.

Demystifying Network Cabling

Network cabling can be incredibly confusing. Not only are there many different types of network cables—all with their own names and properties—but often you can select different types of cables for a single type of network. For example, Ethernet networks can use an astonishing number of cables, ranging from coaxial cable, to unshielded or shielded twisted-pair cable, to fiber-optic cable. To design or support any given network, you need to know your cable choices and how to maintain the particular type of cable you select.

The focus in this section is on demystifying cabling systems for you. It covers the most common types of network cable—the kinds that you'll find in 99 percent of the networks in existence and that you'll use for 99 percent of any new networks. When appropriate, I will make passing reference to other cable types so that you know what they are, but you should focus your attention on only a few ubiquitous cable types—primarily the ones discussed here.

Overview of Basic Cable Types

The most common network cable types are unshielded twisted-pair (UTP) and coaxial, followed by shielded twisted-pair (STP) and fiber optic. UTP is by far the most common type in use today.

Figure 3-5. UTP cable

UTP cable consists of two or more pairs of plastic-insulated conductors inside a cable sheath (made from either vinyl or Teflon). For each pair, the two conductors are twisted within the cable, helping the cable resist outside electrical interference. Rigid standards exist for how this cable is made, including the proper distance between each twist of the pair. Figure 3-5 shows an example of UTP cable.

STP is similar to UTP, but STP has a braided metal shield surrounding the twisted pairs to further reduce the chance of interference from electrical sources outside the cable.

Coaxial cable consists of a central copper conductor wrapped in a plastic insulation material, which is surrounded by a braided wire shield and, finally, wrapped in a plastic cable sheath. (The coaxial cable used for televisions is similar in design.) Two main types are used for networks: Thin Ethernet (10Base-2), which uses RG-58/AU or RG-58/CU cable, and Thick Ethernet (10Base-5), which uses—you guessed it—a much thicker coaxial cable called RG-8. Figure 3-6 shows an example of coaxial cable.

Fiber-optic cable uses a glass strand and carries the data signals as light instead of electricity. It used to be that fiber-optic cable was required for higher-speed networks, but this is changing, and often UTP or STP can be used instead. This is good news, as fiber-optic cable is extremely expensive to purchase, install, and maintain. However, fiber-optic cable can do one thing that copper cables cannot: span extremely long distances. Fiber-optic cable can easily reach two miles at 100 Mbps. For this reason, fiber-optic cable is often used to connect together buildings in a campus-like setting. But other than when you need to span very long distances, you should avoid fiber-optic cable.

Figure 3-6. Coaxial cable

Twisted-Pair Cabling: The King of Network Cables

For a number of years, virtually all new networks have been built using some form of twisted-pair cabling. Usually, Cat-5–grade twisted-pair cable is used, although you may see some old networks in which Cat-3–grade cable is installed. UTP is used instead of STP in almost all cases because it's less expensive, easier to install and maintain, and not much affected by electrical interference (even without the shield). Both Ethernet and Token Ring networks use twisted-pair cabling. Note that different Ethernet types require different cables, and some higher-speed standards require STP.

When a new twisted-pair network is installed, a number of wiring components form the complete run from the workstation to the hub. As shown in Figure 3-7, the cabling starts at the hub, where a patch cable (usually 6 to 10 feet long, or 2 to 3 meters) connects a port on the hub to a patch panel, using RJ-45 connectors on each end. On the other side of the patch panel, the twisted-pair cable is hard-wired to the patch panel connection and then runs continuously to a wall jack (in an office, for instance) to which it is also hard-wired. The wall jack contains an RJ-45 connector on its other side,

Figure 3-7.   A typical twisted-pair network wiring arrangement

Pin Number	Wire Base Color	Wire Stripe Color	10/100Base-T Use
1	White	Orange	Transmit negative
2	Orange	White	Transmit positive
3	White	Green	Receive negative
4	Blue	White	Not used
5	White	Blue	Not used
6	Green	White	Receive positive
7	White	Brown	Not used
8	Brown	White	Not used

Table 3-1. 10/100Base-T Wire Assignments for RJ-45 Connectors

to which another patch cable connects, and then connects to the computer's network interface card (NIC). The distance from the connector on the hub to the connector on the computer's NIC cannot exceed 100 meters (328 feet) of cable length.

Anywhere twisted-pair cabling isn't hard-wired, it uses RJ-45 modular connectors. These are just like the modular connectors you see on telephones, but they are larger and can accommodate up to eight wires. 10Base-T and 100Base-T use four of those wires (two pairs: one for transmit and one for receive). 1000Base-T uses eight of those wires.

The eight wires in the RJ-45 connector are numbered from one to eight. If you were to hold the connector in your left hand, with the pins in the connector facing up and pointed forward, pin 1 of the connector is the one farthest away from you (see Figure 3-8). Table 3-1 shows both the colors of standard Cat-5 cable that should be wired to each pin and the 10/100Base-T assignments.

Pin 1
Pin 8

Figure 3-8.   An RJ-45 connector

DCE and DTE Wiring

Most communications and network devices, including those designed to use RJ-45 connectors, are either *data communications equipment* (DCE) or *data terminal equipment* (DTE). If you have DTE on one end, you need DCE on the other end. In a way, they're just like screws and nuts. Two screws don't go directly together, and neither do two nuts. The same principle applies here: DCE devices can't talk directly to other DCE devices, nor can DTE devices talk directly to other DTE devices.

The RJ-45 jack on a hub or switch is DCE, while the RJ-45 jack on a computer's NIC is DTE. Note that you cannot communicate between DCE and DCE devices or between DTE and DTE devices using a standard twisted-pair/RJ-45 cable that has been wired as described in Table 3-1. For instance, you cannot use a standard twisted-pair patch cable to connect directly from a network server to a workstation, or between two workstations, because those are all DTE devices. Instead, you must purchase or prepare a *crossover cable* for this connection. For 10/100Base-T networks, Table 3-2 shows the wiring needed for a crossover cable.

NOTE Some network interfaces, such as on network switches, can sense whether their ports are connected to external DTE or DCE devices and can automatically adjust which one the port behaves as, eliminating the need for a crossover cable. You'll have to check the documentation for the switches you have to see if this is the case, and sometimes it's not the case for all of the ports on a particular switch.

TIP You can easily purchase all the tools and parts needed to make twisted-pair/RJ-45 cables, and you should do so if you manage a network of any appreciable size (more than 50 workstations). Knowing how to use these tools and parts to make patch cables or to replace a failed cable is invaluable. This way, you can quickly make cables of any length you need. However, even though you should be able to do this, and it can get you out of a jam quickly, you're better off purchasing premade twisted-pair/RJ-45 cables to use with your network. Professionally made cables are more reliable and should give you fewer problems than the ones that you make yourself. Make your own cables when you're in a pinch.

Cable End 1			Cable End 2		
Pin	Wire Base Color	Wire Stripe Color	Pin	Wire Base Color	Wire Stripe Color
1	White	Orange	1	White	Green
2	Orange	White	2	Green	White
3	White	Green	3	White	Orange
6	Green	White	6	Orange	White

Table 3-2. Twisted-Pair/RJ-45 Crossover Cable Wiring

Level or Category	Rated Performance
Level 1	Not performance rated
Level 2	1 Mbps
Category 3	10 Mbps
Category 4	16 Mbps
Category 5	100 Mbps to 1 Gbps
Category 6	>1 Gbps

Table 3-3. Twisted-Pair Performance Designations

What's All This About Cable Categories?

Twisted-pair network cables are rated in terms of their capability to carry network traffic. These ratings are defined by the Electronic Industries Alliance (EIA) and the Telecommunications Industry Association (TIA) and are referred to as Levels 1 and 2 and Categories 3, 4, 5, and 6. The different category levels are simply called Cat-3 through Cat-6. Table 3-3 shows the rated performance for each of these levels.

To achieve a particular performance rating in practice, you not only need cable certified to that performance level, but you must observe other requirements, including using connectors and patch cables that also meet that level of performance. For example, for a Cat-5 installation, you must have Cat-5 cable, connectors, patch panels, and patch cables. The entire circuit, from where the client computer connects to the hub connection at the other end, needs to be tested and certified to the performance level you need to achieve.

Coaxial Cable

Some older networks (those built prior to circa 1992) still have coaxial cable installed. Most of this coaxial cable is the thin variety, which is RG-58, and is used with Thin Ethernet. A few may also use the thicker RG-8 cable for Thick Ethernet, but this is rare.

Thin Ethernet cabling is wired in a bus arrangement, where each network segment starts with a terminator that connects to the end of the cable, runs to each node in turn, and ends with another terminator on the other end. The terminators contain special 50-ohm resistors, and the network cable will not work unless both are installed.

All the connectors in a Thin Ethernet system are BNC connectors, a quick-release bayonet-style connector, both reliable and easy to use. BNC connectors come in a variety of different styles to enable you to make just about any network connection you need along the bus. T-connectors have two female BNC connectors on each side of the crossbar of the *T* and a male BNC connector at the end of the shaft of the *T*. The two female connectors are used for the RG-58 cable coming into and out of a node, while the male connector attaches to a female BNC connector on the node's Ethernet card. Barrel connectors have two female connectors that are used to connect two Thin Ethernet wires together. Barrel connectors are also available in different shapes, including an elbow bend and a U-shaped bend, but usually the simple straight barrel connector is used. Figure 3-2, earlier in the chapter, shows the various parts of a Thin Ethernet BNC cable system.

Coaxial cable has a central *conductor,* which can be either a solid, single copper wire or a stranded set of wires. A white plastic material surrounds the central conductor, which is surrounded by a metal foil and then a braided wire *shield.* The shield is finally wrapped in a plastic cable sheath.

Plenum vs. Nonplenum Cable

In a building, the area between the ceiling of the rooms and the roof of the building is called the *plenum space.* Most buildings use ducts (big, flexible hoses) to provide conditioned air to the rooms in the building, and they use the open plenum space for air returned from the rooms. Typically, the air returned from the rooms is partially reused by the air conditioning units to save energy because it's already cooled or heated, as appropriate. Occasionally, a building uses ducts for the return air, but the standard for office space is simply to use the open plenum space.

Why is this discussion of office building air handling important in a chapter about cables? Because to run network cable through the ceiling of a building that uses the plenum for return air, you must either install the cable inside special piping, called *conduit piping* (which is extremely expensive), or use plenum-grade cable. The difference between nonplenum cable and plenum cable is that the plastics used in plenum cable do not give off toxic fumes in case of a fire. Because most office buildings reuse the air in the plenum space, the last thing you would want to happen is to have the cables causing toxic fumes if a fire broke out somewhere in the building's roof or plenum space that are then spread throughout the building through the air handling system. A fire in a very small area could cause the fumes from the burning cable to be distributed to a very large area of the building because of how these ventilation systems work—most definitely a bad thing.

Make sure to check with your cabling contractor for details about the municipality in which you are installing network cable, but virtually all local codes in the United States require either conduit or plenum-grade cable for buildings with plenum air returns. It's important for the cable installer to be able to handle any required wall penetrations that cross one-hour, fire-rated corridors or building fire zones. Those wall penetrations must be properly sealed to maintain the building's fire ratings.

CAUTION Cable types must not be mixed in any coaxial network. If the network uses, say, RG-58A/U, then that is what you must always use—not any other coaxial cable. Not mixing RG-58A/U and RG-58/U is also a good idea because they have ever-so-slightly different signaling characteristics. (A/U cable uses a stranded center conductor, while /U—sometimes called C/U—uses a solid center conductor.)

With two special tools, making coaxial cables with BNC connectors is a snap. First, you need a wire stripper that will cut the various parts of the cable to the right length. Many good strippers can do this for you automatically; check with your cable supplier to order one. You also need a crimper that can crimp both the central BNC pin onto the central conductor of the cable and the metal sleeve that holds the entire connector onto the wire. Again, you can buy special crimpers that can easily do both jobs. The best crimpers use a ratcheting mechanism to make it easier to exert the proper amount of force for a solid, reliable connection.

Installing and Maintaining Network Cabling

Not only is the selection of a type of network cabling important, but the cabling must be installed correctly. A cable plant installation should include all of the following:

- Proper cable and connectors for the type of network, including documentation of the components selected and used. (This is so that people adding to the network in the future can make sure to match these selections.)

- Complete labeling of all parts of the network, which should include the wall plates, cables, patch panel ports, patch cables, and hub port assignments. This is important for troubleshooting.

- An as-built drawing of the building showing all the cabling routes and locations.

- A certification report showing that all the installed cables operate properly using a special network cable test device.

CAUTION For bus-type networks, users should be made aware that they should not touch the coaxial cable for any reason whatsoever. The coaxial cable will cause all other nodes in the segment to fail if the cable is separated. Make sure that facilities personnel also know this.

Making sure that a new cable plant is properly installed and well documented will save you time over the long run. The network will be more reliable and much easier to maintain and repair.

Choosing a Cabling Contractor

When building a new network, choosing a cabling contractor is extremely important. A contractor who does high-quality, well-documented work is desirable and, unfortunately, hard to find. Make sure that the contractor you choose has a lot of experience installing networks like the one you're installing. In addition, assess the following issues as part of your selection:

- How will the contractor document the cable plant? What are the contractor's standards, and do you think those documentation standards meet your needs? (Remember that no such thing exists as too much documentation for cable plants.)

- Will the contractor provide a set of as-built drawings showing how the cables were installed in the building?

- How does the contractor install the cable to avoid electrical interference sources in the ceiling and walls?

- Does the contractor recommend a wiring solution that combines telecommunication wiring with data wiring? Generally, keeping these two cable plants separate is best. They have different requirements and respond differently to various building conditions. What works fine for telephones may not work for network cable, and vice versa.

- Has the contractor done any local installations that you can visit and view?

- Does the contractor also provide speedy post-installation support for new wiring drops? This is important, as many wiring contractors who specialize in new construction wiring are not good about returning to do the occasional single drop for new node locations. Ask for references regarding this important information.

- What equipment does the contractor use to certify the cable plant? What certification documentation will the contractor provide upon completion?

- Does the contractor also provide post-installation troubleshooting services?

Make sure to spend time finding the best local cable contractors available to you and compare them carefully. You may want to contact other companies like yours or computer user group members in your area to seek recommendations and learn about their experiences with contractors. Try not to rely on only the references provided by the contractor; even firms that do sloppy work can usually put together a few good references.

TIP   For a large cabling job, make sure to negotiate an appropriate payment schedule. You should aim for something along the lines of 30 percent on inception; 50 percent on completion; and 20 percent on delivery of as-built drawings, certification reports, and any other final deliverables. Make sure to keep no less than 15 percent for these final deliverables to ensure that the cable contractor provides them expediently. Contractors are notorious for dragging their feet on things like this after the wiring itself is done, so you need to make sure you have a way to motivate them to get everything done.

Solving Cable Problems

Cable problems can be extremely hard to diagnose and repair. Many cable problems are intermittent or result in reduced network bandwidth for the affected nodes. Tracking down the source of the problem can be difficult. At times, you may not even be aware that there *is* a problem with the cables!

Problems with network cabling typically exhibit themselves in the following ways:

- Abnormally slow network performance, particularly if one node is much slower than other, similar nodes (for star networks) or if all nodes on one segment have slower network performance than nodes on other segments (for bus networks)

- Sporadic disconnections from the network

- Complete loss of network connectivity, which can also be an intermittent problem

Troubleshooting Star Networks

Star networks are the easiest to troubleshoot. Because each node is on its own network cable leading to the hub, you can often quickly isolate the problem to several lengths of cable.

If you're having trouble with a node on a star topology network, first determine if something is wrong with the computer or the cabling. Move the computer to a different location in the building and see if the same problems occur. If they do, it's a sure bet the problem is in the computer, such as a failing NIC.

If the computer has normal network performance in a different location, try replacing the patch cable leading from the node to the wall. These cables can often become slightly damaged as furniture or computers are moved around.

Next, in the wiring closet, you can try connecting the patch panel from the node's location to a different port on the hub using a different patch cable. While wiring closet patch panels are less likely to fail because they aren't moved around much, they can still have poor connections or wiring that can become problematic over time.

Finally, if you have eliminated all other factors, consider replacing the cable leading from the wiring closet to the node's location. At this point, having a qualified network cabling contractor to assist you can be extremely helpful. The contractor has equipment to test the cable in the wall and to determine if it's bad before pulling a replacement cable through the building. For troubleshooting help, you should expect to pay around $150 for a contractor to come out and test a length of cable. If the contractor must pull a new cable all the way to the location, you'll also need to pay for labor and materials for that work.

Troubleshooting Coaxial Networks

Coaxial networks can be difficult to troubleshoot because many nodes share a single segment of the network. Usually, a problem in one part of the segment affects all nodes on the segment similarly.

By far, the most common problem on coaxial networks is loss of network connectivity for all the nodes in a segment. Someone disconnecting the network cable so it is not a continuous run invariably causes this loss. Find out who is moving to another office, rearranging an office, painting an office, or performing other work of this type in the building. The chances are excellent the problem is there. If this fails, the troubleshooting job becomes more difficult.

To track down cable breaks that aren't obvious, you can try using a coaxial cable scanner. These are handheld instruments that can be attached to a coaxial network cable to detect how far along the cable shorts or breaks are occurring. Keep attaching the cable scanner to the network cable in different locations until you can track down the problem.

Another approach is to test with an extra terminator for the network. Disconnect the cable in a particular location and attach the terminator. See if the computers on the new, smaller segment can log in to a server. (A server must be available in the same segment; otherwise, you can use the PING command, if you're using the TCP/IP protocol on your computers, and try to ping another workstation in the complete segment.) If they can log in, then you know the problem is further on along the cable. Move to a new location, attach the extra terminator, and try again. Eventually, you will find two nearby locations where the terminator will allow the network to work in one spot but not in the next spot. You should find the cable problem somewhere between those two node locations. This approach requires patience, but it works fine in a pinch.

More troublesome still on coaxial networks is a problem that is causing poor network performance but not causing any nodes to actually disconnect from the network. Such problems are often intermittent and not easy to find with a cable scanner. When you have this type of problem, your best approach is to come up with a test that can quickly tell you how fast the nodes are communicating with the network. For example, you can time how long it takes to copy a particular file from the server. Next, use a terminator to close off a large part of the segment and perform the test again. Keep moving the terminator and retrying the test until you discover which part of the cable slows down network performance on the segment. Then either replace all those portions or narrow your search further. This type of problem is usually caused by a poor connection in one of the male cable-end BNC connectors, although a flaky T-connector or barrel connector can also be the culprit. It's usually fastest—providing you narrow the problem to a small enough area—to simply replace all the cable and connectors in that location.

Having a second person help you troubleshoot coaxial cable problems makes the job much easier. One person remains in a fixed location at one end of the segment with a test computer, and the other person moves from location to location with a terminator. While the mobile troubleshooter maps out parts of the segment with the terminator, the stationary person can quickly test to see if any individual parts of the segment prove to be a source of the problem (communicating via a cell phone or portable radio).

TIP   Before going to the trouble of pulling a new section of cable through the wall or replacing various cables and connectors, try simply running an extra cable from one location to another, such as out the door of one room, down the hallway, and into the room of another. Then test to see if this "mapping out" of the suspect portion of the segment fixes the problem. If it does, go ahead and have a new cable run in the walls. If the problem is still there, you need to look further before replacing cable and connectors.

As a general rule, troubleshooting cable problems requires a careful, step-by-step approach and patience. For coaxial cable systems, troubleshooting is made more difficult because a lot of network users are breathing down your neck while you're trying to concentrate and find the problem. You're lucky if you can find a coaxial network problem and solve it within an hour. Some problems may take several hours (or more) to resolve.

Chapter Summary

In this chapter, you learned about network cable systems. It covered the major topologies in which networks are wired, how CSMA/CD and token passing work, what types of cables are commonly used, and how they should be installed. You also learned some tips about selecting cabling contractors and troubleshooting network cable problems.

CHAPTER 4 | Understanding Network Hardware

If network wiring constitutes the nervous system of a network, then the devices discussed in this chapter represent the various organs. These network devices—repeaters, routers, hubs, and such—are responsible for moving data from one network cable to another. Each device has different properties and uses. A good network design uses the correct device for each of the various jobs the network must fulfill.

In this chapter, you learn about essential networking hardware, including the following:

- Repeaters
- Hubs and concentrators
- Switches
- Bridges
- Routers
- Gateways
- Firewalls
- Short-haul modems for short intrabuilding connections

It is essential that you understand these basic components that go into building a network, as well as the job each performs.

Directing Network Traffic

The critical test of any network design is its capability to direct network traffic from one node to another node. You must connect the network's various devices in a configuration that enables the network to pass signals among the devices as efficiently as possible, taking into account the type of network and the different connectivity requirements for the network. The following are the basic network connection devices:

- **Repeaters** extend the distance that network signals can travel over a particular type of network media.
- **Hubs (concentrators)** are used to connect nodes to one another when you use a physical star topology, such as 100Base-T.
- **Bridges** are basically intelligent repeaters that direct traffic from one network segment to another only when the traffic is destined for the other segment.
- **Routers** can intelligently route network traffic in a variety of important ways.
- **Switches** form fast point-to-point connections for all the devices connected to them. Connections from one port on a switch to another port are made on an as-needed basis and are not broadcast to ports that aren't involved in the traffic. By limiting the connections made, switches help eliminate network traffic collisions.

Putting together all the necessary pieces in the proper way is the art of network design. Chapter 13 discusses important aspects of assembling these devices so they work together optimally, but first you need to know what they are and what they can do. The following sections discuss these essential network devices.

Repeaters

A *repeater* is a device that extends the distance of a particular network cable run. It takes a weak network signal in on one side, boosts the signal, and then sends it out its other side. You most often see repeaters on Thin Ethernet networks, but they are available for virtually any network connection. For instance, if you need to run a 100Base-T Cat-5E cable longer than 100 meters (328 feet), a repeater enables you to double that distance.

Repeaters operate at the physical layer of the OSI networking model. They do not have the intelligence to understand the signals they are transmitting. Repeaters merely amplify the signal coming in on either side and repeat it through their other side. (Remember that they also amplify any noise on the cable!) Repeaters are used to connect only the same type of media, such as 10Base-2 Thin Ethernet to 10Base-2 Thin Ethernet, or Token Ring twisted-pair to Token Ring twisted-pair.

Repeaters do have a small amount of intelligence that can be useful. They can separate one of their connections from the other when there is a problem. For example, consider two segments of an Ethernet network that are connected using a repeater. If one of those segments is broken, the repeater allows the good segment to continue working within itself. Users on the good segment will be unable to connect to resources on the broken segment, but they can still use the good segment without trouble. (But remember that this capability does you little good if your servers are on the broken segment and your workstations are on the good segment!) Figure 4-1 shows a network extension using repeaters.

Figure 4-1.   Using repeaters to extend network length (10Base-2 Thin Ethernet shown)

Hubs and Concentrators

Intelligent LAN concentrators—usually just called *concentrators* or, even more simply, *hubs*—are used to connect network nodes to network backbones. Nodes are connected to hubs in a physical star fashion (cables fan out from the hub to each node), whether they are used for a star topology or a ring topology network (these topologies are discussed in Chapter 3). A simple network might consist of just a hub or two; smaller networks usually don't require a network backbone.

Hubs are available for virtually any network media type, with the higher-end units using replaceable modules to support multiple media types. For example, you can purchase a high-end hub chassis that can house both Ethernet and Token Ring modules.

You can purchase hubs in a variety of sizes, ranging from those that support only 2 workstations to those that support more than 100 workstations. Many network designers use stackable hubs, which usually support 24 node connections each. These hubs were once used in concert with switches, but these days, usually only switches are used. Switches are discussed in the next section.

Hubs have two important properties:

- Hubs echo all data from each port to all the other ports on the hub. Although hubs are wired in a star fashion, they actually perform electrically (logically) more like a bus topology segment in this respect. Because of this echoing, no filtering or logic occurs to prevent collisions between packets being transmitted by any of the connected nodes.

- Hubs can automatically partition (in this context, *cut off*) a problematic node from the other nodes—in effect, shutting down that node. Such partitioning occurs if a cable short is detected, if the hub port is receiving excessive packets that are flooding the network, or if some other serious problem is detected for a given port on the hub. Automatic partitioning keeps one malfunctioning connection from causing problems for all of the other connections.

Hubs can have a number of advanced built-in features, including the following:

- Built-in management, where the hub can be centrally managed over the network, using Simple Network Management Protocol (SNMP) or other network management protocols and software.

- Autosensing of different connection speeds. For example, Ethernet hubs that can automatically detect and run each node at either 10 Mbps (10Base-T) or 100 Mbps (100Base-T) are common.

- High-speed uplinks that connect the hub to a backbone. These usually operate at ten times the basic speed of the hub. (For example, for a 100 Mbps hub, the uplink ports might run at 1 Gbps.)

- Built-in bridging and routing functions, which make it unnecessary to use separate devices to perform bridging and routing.

- Built-in switching, where nodes on the hub can be switched instead of shared.

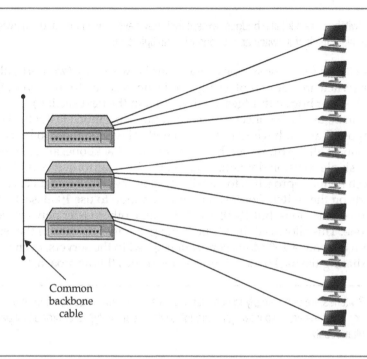

Common
backbone
cable

Figure 4-2.   A typical hub arrangement

When ordering a hub, it's important to know how many nodes you want to connect, how much bandwidth each requires, and what type of network backbone is being used. Your choice of a backbone technology depends on the total amount of bandwidth that you need and the various other network design criteria that you must meet.

Each hub is a separate *collision domain,* or an area of the network in which collisions can occur. Connecting all hubs together in some fashion generally results in a larger collision domain encompassing all the hubs. The exception to this rule is a configuration where all the separate hubs are connected to a switch (see the next section), which keeps each hub in its own collision domain. Figure 4-2 shows an example of a network using hubs.

Switches

Switches, as their name implies, can switch connections from one port to another, and they can do so rapidly. They are connection-oriented and dynamically switch among their various ports to create these connections. Think of a train yard, with many trains coming in on some tracks and leaving on other tracks. The yard manager orders the track "switches" to take place so the trains can get to their destination. A network switch is much like the yard manager, except that the switch directs packets rather than trains and uses Ethernet cabling rather than train tracks to transport its cargo.

NOTE Switches are a lot like bridges, except that they have many ports and otherwise look like hubs. You might think of a switch as a bridge with multiple ports.

Because switches form one-to-one connections between any two ports, all the ports coming into a switch are not part of a single collision domain. In this sense, the switch acts as a sort of super bridge (bridges are discussed in the next section).

Switches can be used to connect a number of hubs to a much faster backbone. For example, suppose that you have 10 hubs, each with 24 workstation nodes connected. If you simply connect all the hubs together on a common backbone, all 240 workstations would share a single collision domain, which could hurt performance quite a bit. Instead, a much better approach is to install a 12-port switch and connect each hub to one of the ports on the switch. For instance, it is common to use 100Base-T Ethernet for workstation connections, but 1000Base-T (or some other faster network connection) for the backbone. This allows all the traffic being generated by each of the ten hubs to continue to run at about a 100 Mbps connection speed to the servers, even though all the hubs are sharing the backbone. Figure 4-3 illustrates this approach.

NOTE Switches are used simply to connect two given ports (such as traffic from port 5 to port 21, for instance), but they are also intelligent enough to echo certain types of broadcast packets to all ports simultaneously.

Figure 4-3. A network built using hubs and switches

Switches have become inexpensive and are blazingly fast. For local area network (LAN) connections, switches make more sense than hubs, partly because of their cost and their relative simplicity.

In addition, most new networks eschew hubs in favor of a 100 percent switched approach. In fact, it's virtually impossible to purchase hubs any longer because manufacturers typically offer only switches. (You may still be able to purchase very small hubs, with four to eight ports, but even in these small applications, switches are preferable and not much more expensive.)

It's important that you understand the difference between hubs and switches because you may still encounter hubs installed in existing networks. For new networks, you will probably use switches exclusively. Doing so dramatically reduces the opportunity for network packet collisions, which are more likely in a hub arrangement.

Bridges

Bridges are, in a nutshell, more intelligent versions of repeaters. Bridges can connect two network segments together, but they have the intelligence to pass traffic from one segment to another *only when that traffic is destined for the other segment.* Bridges are used to segment networks into smaller pieces. Some bridges can span different networking systems and media, such as from coaxial Thin Ethernet to twisted-pair Token Ring.

As you might recall, repeaters operate at the physical layer (Layer 1) of the OSI networking model. Bridges operate one layer higher, at the data-link layer (Layer 2). Bridges examine the media access control (MAC) address of each packet they encounter to determine whether they should forward the packet to the other network. Bridges contain address information about all the parts of your network through either a static routing table that you program or a dynamic, learning-tree system that discovers all the devices and addresses on the network automatically.

Is It Better to Use Fewer Large Switches or More Small Switches?

Larger switches that can host hundreds of connections within a single chassis are generally more powerful than their smaller 24-port siblings, and they tend to have more built-in redundancy, such as redundant power supplies in the unit and so forth. However, sometimes it's easier and less expensive to build a network using smaller 24-port or 48-port switches. You can simply purchase an extra 24-port or 48-port unit as a hot-swap backup (a backup unit that can be quickly swapped in to take the place of a failed unit) that you can manually implement at a moment's notice. The only real disadvantage to this approach is that the redundancy is not automatic. If one switch fails, you'll need to move its connections to the backup switch. In contrast, a larger unit can switch to redundant features automatically. As always, consider such trade-offs carefully for your particular company and its needs.

NOTE   Because they operate below the network layer at which protocols such as TCP/IP and IPX/SPX are defined, bridges don't care about the network protocols they're carrying. They care only about the information required to operate at the data-link layer. This means that whether or not data is carried over the bridge depends on its MAC address.

You should use bridges only on smaller networks, or in cases where you would otherwise use a repeater but would benefit from keeping traffic on one segment from being transmitted on the other segment unnecessarily. Often, routers or switches offer solutions that perform better and create fewer problems, so examine these other options before choosing a bridge.

Routers

Just as bridges are basically more intelligent repeaters, routers are more intelligent bridges. *Routers* operate at the network layer (Layer 3) of the OSI model, and they are far more intelligent than bridges in sending incoming packets off to their destination. Because routers operate at the network layer, a connection across a router requires only that the higher layers use the same protocols. The router can translate from any of the protocols at Layers 1 through 3 to any other protocols at Layers 1 through 3 (provided the router has been configured and designed to do so). Routers can connect both similar and dissimilar networks. They are often used for wide area network (WAN) links.

Routers actually become a node on a network, and they have their own network address. Other nodes send packets to the router, which then examines the contents of the packets and forwards them appropriately. For this reason, routers often have fast microprocessors—usually of the reduced instruction set computer (RISC) type—and memory built into them to perform this job. Routers can also determine the shortest route to a destination and use it. They can perform other tricks to maximize network bandwidth and dynamically adjust to changing problems or traffic patterns on a network.

NOTE   To learn about the networks to which they're connected and what they should do to route various types of packets properly, routers use a process called *discovery*. During the discovery process, the router carefully "listens" to traffic on its ports and also sends out advertisement packets letting other devices know of the router's presence.

Routers form the backbone of the Internet. When you use the TRACERT command to trace the route from a node to a destination, most of the addresses that appear for the hops are actually different routers, each one forwarding the packet to the next until it reaches its destination.

NOTE   Routers can route only protocols that are routable. AppleTalk, NetBIOS, and NetBEUI are examples of protocols that are not routable, while TCP/IP and IPX/SPX are routable.

Routers must be programmed to function correctly. They need to have the addresses assigned to each of their ports, and various network protocol settings must be configured. Routers are usually programmed in one of several ways:

- Most routers include an RS-232C port. You can connect a terminal or PC with terminal emulation software to this port and program the router in text mode.

- Most routers have network-based software that enables you to program the router, often using graphical tools.

- Routers usually have a small web server built in, through which the router can be programmed using a web interface from a connected computer. Home wireless routers, for example, have this feature built in.

The method you use depends on the router and your security needs. (You might want to disable network-based router programming so that unauthorized users cannot change the router's configuration.) Figure 4-4 shows an example of a network that uses routers.

Gateways

Gateways are application-specific interfaces that link all seven layers of the OSI model when they are dissimilar at any or all levels. For instance, if you need to connect a network that uses one of the OSI networking models to one using IBM's Systems Network Architecture (SNA) model, use a gateway. Gateways can also translate from Ethernet to Token Ring, although simpler solutions than gateways exist if you need such a translation. Because gateways must translate so much, they tend to be slower than other solutions, particularly under heavy loads.

Figure 4-4.   A network using routers

The primary use for gateways today is for handling e-mail. Post Office Protocol 3 (POP3) and Simple Mail Transfer Protocol (SMTP) are two examples of protocols that are handled by gateways. Most e-mail systems that can connect to disparate systems either use a computer set up as a gateway for that chore or let the e-mail server handle the gateway chores itself.

Protecting a Network with Firewalls

Firewalls are hardware devices that enforce your network security policies. They often are installed with routers. For instance, firewalls are sometimes installed with routers to create internetwork connections. In most routers designed for small office/home office use, a firewall is part of the router itself. Equipment for larger networks still keeps these duties in separate pieces of equipment, however.

A firewall is a hardware device (which can be a computer set up for the task that runs firewall software or a dedicated firewall device that contains a computer within it) that sits between two networks and enforces network security policies. Generally, firewalls sit between a company LAN and the Internet, but they can also be used between LANs or WANs.

There are basically two different types of firewalls:

- A *network-based firewall* operates at the network level (Layer 3) and usually implements a technique called packet filtering, where packets between networks are compared against a set of rules programmed into the firewall before the packets are allowed to cross the boundary between the two networks. Packet-filtering rules can allow or deny packets based on source or destination address, time of day, or TCP/IP port.

- An *application-based firewall* usually acts in a proxy role between the two networks, such that no network traffic passes directly between the two networks. Instead, the firewall (usually called a *proxy firewall*) acts as a proxy for the users of one network to interact with services on the other network. This proxy interaction is usually done using a technique called network address translation (NAT), where the network addresses on the internal network are not directly exposed to the external network. In the application-based model, the proxy firewall takes care of translating the addresses so that the connections can take place.

 NOTE Firewalls do not provide a network security panacea. The best firewall in the world won't protect your network from other security threats, such as some discussed in Chapter 9. However, they are an important part of network security, particularly for LANs connected to the Internet.

Firewalls come in all shapes and sizes, and range in cost from as little as a few hundred dollars to thousands of dollars. In fact, these days, usually home wireless routers have firewalls built into them. You can also purchase firewall software that can be installed on a computer for around $40.

Different firewall devices have various features, and might encompass both network-based and application-based techniques to protect the network. Firewalls also usually serve as an audit point for the traffic between the two networks, using logging and reporting tools to help the administrator detect and deal with inappropriate network traffic.

Firewalls are discussed in the context of network security in Chapter 9.

Connecting RS-232 Devices with Short-Haul Modems

While some might not consider a short-haul modem to be a true network device, it is a device that your network might require to provide point-to-point connectivity between a workstation or terminal and another device. Short-haul modems (sometimes called *line drivers*) enable you to connect two distant RS-232C devices to one another. Standard RS-232C cables are limited in distance to 15 to 30 meters (50 to 100 feet). Short-haul modems allow the same connection to run as far as five miles using simple telephone-grade twisted-pair cabling.

Short-haul modems can often be perfect solutions when a computer needs terminal access to a remote device. For example, a user might need to access a terminal on a private branch exchange (PBX) telephone system, which uses an RS-232C port. You have two options to provide this remote access:

- Install regular modems on each end and use a telephone connection to connect from the workstation to the PBX.

- Use two short-haul modems and run a twisted-pair cable between the two points.

Depending on how frequently access is needed and how distant the device is, either approach can be good. Generally, short-haul modems are preferred when the two devices often or always need to be connected and running a twisted-pair wire between the locations is not prohibitively expensive or difficult. Short-haul modems are fairly inexpensive, at about $100 each.

In most short-haul modem systems, two pairs of wire connect each short-haul modem, although one-pair variants exist. With the two-pair variety, one pair is used to transmit data and the other to receive data. Most short-haul modems are full duplex, allowing transmission to take place in both directions simultaneously.

To hook up two devices using short-haul modems, you use a standard RS-232C cable to connect each device to its short-haul modem. Then you wire the twisted-pair wire to the short-haul modem, using the instructions that come with the modem. Finally, most short-haul modems require external power, so you need to plug them into a power outlet. Figure 4-5 shows an example of a short-haul modem connection.

Figure 4-5.   Short-haul modem connection

TIP   If you frequently do RS-232C interfacing, you should invest in a device called a *breakout box*. This is a small device that has two RS-232C connectors on each end. In the box, each of the RS-232C pin signals is represented with a light-emitting diode (LED). Special patch posts and switches in the breakout box enable you to reconfigure the RS-232C connection on the fly. Breakout boxes can be invaluable for achieving RS-232C communications between two devices that aren't communicating. They can show what is actually happening with the signals and enable you to try different cable configurations dynamically. Once you use the breakout box to figure out how to make the devices communicate, a permanent cable can then be made to those specifications.

Chapter Summary

In this chapter, you learned about the key pieces of hardware that make up most networks. It is important for you to be familiar with the capabilities of all these types of network hardware, which should form the basis of any network design or performance-tuning efforts. Be aware that you need to know about other types of network hardware as well. Additional important network hardware is discussed in later chapters. In particular, you should also know about remote access hardware, hardware that supports WAN links, and certain network functions that are carried out on different types of network servers.

Chapter 5 discusses the different technologies used to connect networks to other networks, usually over large distances. WAN connections are used to connect to the Internet and also to form part-time or full-time connections between LANs, such as from one company location to another.

CHAPTER 5 | Making WAN Connections

M any companies have multiple locations that need to share network resources. For example, maybe the company's accounting system runs at the headquarters building where the accounting and Information Technology (IT) staff are located, but the warehouse across town still needs access to the accounting system for inventory-picking tickets, data entry, and other order fulfillment and inventory tasks. Or, perhaps the company uses a groupware system such as Lotus Notes that requires regular updates of information and messages from one site to another. In the real world, the situation can become even more complex. Some companies have offices all around the globe, and each office has different requirements both to access and update data in other locations.

All of these are situations in which a *wide area network* (WAN) can be useful. Certainly, in a pinch, multiple offices can exchange data by using Federal Express and identical tape machines, Blu-Ray discs, external Universal Serial Bus (USB) hard disks, or other media. It's possible to simply send the data back and forth like this (assuming the application supports exchanging data in this fashion), but such an arrangement has some drawbacks—the biggest one being that it is pretty slow.

There are many ways to connect local area networks (LANs) in one location to LANs in another location, and making such connections is the subject of this chapter. But before looking into the different WAN technologies, you should assess your networking requirements. Because of the cost and the time required to implement and maintain a WAN, you usually do not want to install one unless it's the only—or best— way to meet your needs.

Determining WAN Needs

WAN links are almost always fairly expensive to maintain. Bandwidth needs increase over time, and these upgrades are costly. Also, WAN links are generally more prone to trouble than LANs because many additional possible points of failure exist. For these reasons, it's important to assess the need for a WAN carefully, and then study the different options available, their costs, and the trade-offs involved.

Costs can vary wildly between different technologies, speeds, and other factors (including your location), so you need to rely heavily on cost and availability data from local providers for your own WAN analysis. Plus, prices and availability change almost every week, so make sure to get current data from your local providers before committing to a particular WAN technology.

TIP   Often, the need for a WAN can be satisfied using a technology called Virtual Private Networks (VPNs) over the Internet. A VPN is called "private" because all of the packets between two points are encrypted, so even though the packets are transmitted over a public network, their information remains secure. And because the Internet provides the transport medium, they're usually much cheaper than dedicated WAN links, and they often can make use of existing Internet connections for two (or more) locations. VPNs are discussed in detail in Chapter 8.

Analyzing Requirements

A company's first WAN is usually driven by a particular application, such as an accounting system. Then once the WAN is operational, the company begins to use the WAN for other applications.

If you fail to take into account all the uses that the company might have for the WAN, you could find that you've invested a lot of money in a solution that doesn't meet all of your needs. Here are some questions to help you determine the requirements for your company's WAN:

- What are the locations that will participate in the WAN and what kind of WAN services are available to them? A sales office in Tahiti, for instance, might have trouble purchasing a Gigabit WAN link.

- How much data needs to be transferred from each site to each other site, and in what timeframe?

- How quickly does the data need to be transferred?

- Does the data transfer need to be synchronous or can it be asynchronous? For example, a warehouse clerk who is entering records directly into an accounting system located at another site requires a synchronous (real-time) connection, while a restaurant that needs to upload sales data to its headquarters at some time each night needs only an asynchronous connection.

- When do the data transfers need to be accomplished? Do they need to occur 24 hours a day, 7 days a week? Or do they need to occur once every 30 minutes, or follow some other schedule?

- What are the budget constraints, and what are the costs of the different available alternatives?

Once you have the answers to these questions, you can determine whether you need a switched or dedicated link, and if it should be public or private. These issues are discussed in the following sections.

Switched or Dedicated?

A *switched* WAN link is one that is not active all the time. For instance, a dial-up modem connection or an Integrated Services Digital Network (ISDN) connection from one location to another is a switched connection. These are connections that are formed only when you need them, and you usually pay for the time the connection is open, rather than the amount of data you're able to transmit over the connection. Figure 5-1 is an example of a switched WAN link.

Switched links can be either connection-based or packet-based. A *connection-based switched link* forms a connection as needed and makes a fixed amount of bandwidth available over that link. A *packet-based switched link* sends data packets into a network cloud in which they can follow a number of paths to their destination and then emerge from the cloud. Packet-switched networks can be more reliable because the data can take many different paths, but you are not guaranteed that each packet will arrive in a certain

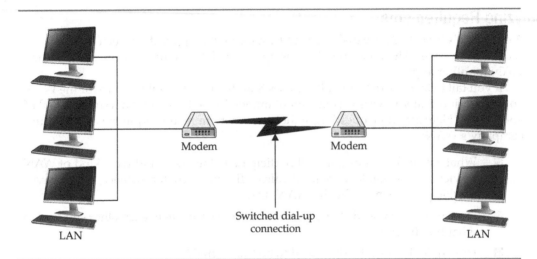

Figure 5-1.   A switched WAN link

amount of time. A connection-based switched link just gives you one "pipe" from your source to your destination, but you can control what goes into the pipe and how long it will take to get to its destination.

A *dedicated* WAN link is one that is always up and running. Examples of dedicated WAN connections are DS1 or DS3 (T-1 or T-3) lines, *x*DSL lines, Ethernet-based telecom links, or fiber-optic telecom links. You use a dedicated connection when you need the connection to be up all the time or when the overall economics show that such a connection is cheaper than a switched link. Figure 5-2 illustrates a dedicated WAN link.

Figure 5-2.   A dedicated WAN link

Private or Public?

A *private network* is one that is run by a particular company. Usually, a private network refers to global networks maintained by large telecom providers, such as AT&T, Verizon, Level3, CenturyLink, XO, and others. It can also refer to a network that is purely private to the company that uses it, such as when you connect buildings in a campus together through cables or wireless connections that you fully control.

The advantages of a private network are that the data is secure, the network usage and capacity can be managed, and you can predict how much bandwidth you have available. A *public network,* such as the Internet, is a network through which many companies' data passes. Public networks are less secure than private networks, but the advantage is that public networks are less expensive to use.

Use a public network under the following conditions:

- You don't care if data occasionally takes longer to reach its destination or if the delay between sites is relatively unpredictable.

- You want the lowest-cost network connection possible.

- The data does not need to be secure or you have the ability to make it secure over the public network. (Technologies such as Virtual Private Networks or some types of data encryption can provide such security.)

WAN Transmission Quality

There are several terms that refer to the quality of WAN network transmissions with which you should be familiar:

- *Latency* refers to the amount of time it takes for any given packet to traverse the network from its source to its destination. Usually, it's quoted as Round-Trip Delay (RTD), in milliseconds.

- *Dropped packets* can result when a router between the source and destination has its buffer fill up. When this happens, packets are "dropped" (discarded).

- *Packet errors* occur when a packet's data becomes corrupted between the source and destination.

- *Jitter* occurs when packets from the same stream of packets arrive at their destination with varying amounts of delay.

- *Out-of-order delivery* occurs when packets arrive out of order at their destination. This can happen, for instance, if the packets take different routes through the network to reach their destination.

Use a private network under these conditions:

- Data security is of utmost concern.
- You have a large, experienced staff to set up and maintain the private network.
- Cost is unimportant relative to the benefits that the network brings.
- You need full, reliable control over the network's bandwidth use.

Comparing WAN Connection Types

Now that you understand some basics of WAN links, the remainder of this chapter provides an overview of the available WAN technologies, ranging from telephone connections to very high-speed, high-bandwidth connections.

Plain Old Telephone Service (POTS)

Plain old telephone service (POTS) is the telephone service everyone knows. While it does not technically qualify as a WAN connection (at least as most people think of WANs), POTS can still serve to link two or more sites together for certain low-bandwidth needs. Although it is among the slowest methods of establishing a network connection, POTS is ubiquitous and easily used throughout the world.

POTS is carried over one set of twisted-pair wires (in other words, just two wires). In some cases, two sets of twisted-pair wires are used, but only the two main wires carry the telephone signal and ring signals. The other two wires are used for other features, such as backlighting a keypad on a phone or providing a message-waiting light with some private branch exchange (PBX) systems. POTS connections currently use RJ-11 telephone jacks, which simply snap into place.

The maximum theoretical speed of basic analog POTS is 33.6 Kbps. Many factors can decrease this speed; chief among them is line quality. Telephone lines with static typically do not connect at the top speed of 33.6 Kbps, and they might lose their connections unexpectedly, lose data being transmitted, or pause for excessive periods of time as bursts of static inhibit the ability to transfer data.

When you are using POTS to establish a network connection, having matched modems at both ends is optimal. Matched modems from the same manufacturer more easily negotiate the highest possible data transmission rates and often can support "step-down" modes, which automatically use a slower speed when line noise unexpectedly becomes a problem.

POTS transmits analog signals, not digital ones. The data sent between systems is converted from digital data to analog data using a modem. The word *modem* is actually an acronym based on the device's function—modulator/demodulator. At each end of the connection, the sending system's modem modulates the digital data into an analog signal and sends the signal over the telephone line as a series of audible sounds. At the receiving end, the modem demodulates the audible analog signal back into digital data for use with the computer.

With much higher-speed Internet connections being ubiquitous these days, POTS is not often used for transmitting data, except in extremely rare cases. However, given its heavy past use and the remote chance that you might run into a system using a POTS connection for some type of data transmission, you should be familiar with it.

Integrated Services Digital Network

ISDN stands for Integrated Services Digital Network. It is a high-speed digital communications network based on existing telephone services. Although it has existed for more than ten years, because of extensive upgrades required at telephone company central offices (COs), it has not become widely available until recently. ISDN connections are still commonly used for voice circuits as well as lower-capacity data circuits, but overall ISDN has been largely eclipsed by *x*DSL and other connection types for data connections.

ISDN comes in two basic forms: the Basic Rate Interface (BRI) and the Primary Rate Interface (PRI). The ISDN-BRI connection is made up of three channels. Two channels are called *bearer channels* and carry data at speeds of 64 Kbps per channel. Bearer channels can also carry voice calls—that is, spoken telephone calls. (Each bearer channel can carry one voice call at a time.) The third channel, called a *data channel*, carries call setup information and other overhead communications necessary to manage the two bearer channels. The data channel carries 16 Kbps of data. Bearer channels are abbreviated as *B-channels;* the data channel is abbreviated as a *D-channel.* Thus, an ISDN-BRI connection is often called a 2B+D connection, which reflects the number and the type of channels it contains.

An ISDN-PRI connection is made up of 24 B-channels and one D-channel. A PRI connection can carry a total of 1.544 Mbps—the same amount as a T-1 line.

NOTE Different flavors of PRI configurations are available in different parts of the world. The configuration named 24B+D is common, and you might also see variations such as 22 B-channels with a 64 Kbps D-channel, 24 56 Kbps B-channels, or even 30 standard B-channels (totaling 1.92 Mbps).

ISDN connections are usually formed as needed—they are switched. For a WAN link, you use on-demand ISDN routers at each end, which can "dial up" the other router when data is pending. Because ISDN has extremely fast call setup times, ISDN connections are formed much more quickly than POTS connections—usually in less than a second.

NOTE Although many systems can also use the Internet or private WAN links for videoconferencing, ISDN is still the mainstay connection type for these types of calls. If you are setting up a videoconferencing system, you should plan on installing at least two BRI connections (three is better) and purchase a videoconferencing system that supports at least 256 Kbps of bandwidth. Videoconferencing calls over a single BRI (128 Kbps) are fairly poor quality; two BRIs (256 Kbps) are much better, and three-BRI (384 Kbps) connections are very good. Note also that both ends of a call need to support the same speed and number of BRIs.

ISDN pricing changes occur regularly. Prices also vary considerably in different parts of the country. Getting full pricing information from your own Regional Bell Operating Company (RBOC) before choosing ISDN is important. Then, using your projected usage data, you should be able to calculate the cost to use ISDN. Generally, the installation of an ISDN-BRI line, assuming no wiring changes are necessary, costs about $150. Some RBOCs might waive the installation charge if you sign an agreement to keep the ISDN line for one to two years.

Monthly ISDN usage charges and long-distance ISDN call charges are similar to POTS charges. But remember that connecting with two B-channels is equivalent to making two separate calls, and whatever charge exists for a single call will double when you use both B-channels.

Digital Subscriber Line

The Digital Subscriber Line (DSL) connection type has become widely available. A number of different flavors of DSL exist. Each of these types begins with a different initial or combination of initials, which is why DSL is often called *x*DSL. The available flavors include the following:

- **ADSL**   Asymmetric DSL is so named because the speed for transmission (called the *upstream direction)* and receiving (called the *downstream direction)* are not the same. ADSL lines almost always provide much higher downstream bandwidth than upstream bandwidth. ADSL lines are very common, particularly for consumer Internet access.

- **HDSL**   High-speed DSL allows higher speeds than ADSL and provides a symmetric connection, meaning that the available upstream bandwidth and downstream bandwidth are the same.

- **RADSL**   Rate-adaptive DSL allows for 600 Kbps to 12 Mbps of data to be received and 128 Kbps to 1 Mbps of data to be sent. RADSL is asymmetric, and its bandwidth can be adjusted by software. For example, if a connection is experiencing noise and lost packets, RADSL can reduce the bandwidth in order to try to improve packet deliverability.

- **SDSL**   Symmetric DSL allows bidirectional rates varying from 160 Kbps to 2.048 Mbps.

- **VDSL**   Very-high-speed DSL allows up to approximately 52 Mbps of downstream bandwidth. VDSL can be either symmetric or asymmetric.

- **IDSL**   ISDN-based DSL speed is about the same as ISDN. IDSL is used for data almost exclusively because it's an always-on connection to a single destination (as discussed earlier, ISDN can be used to place calls to other ISDN connections).

*x*DSL has become ubiquitous, in part because the cost per megabyte of data transmitted is far less than POTS and is even considerably less expensive than ISDN. Presently, *x*DSL is available in most cities in the United States.

In this section, you learn about how *x*DSL works and when you might be able to implement its high-bandwidth capabilities. This discussion focuses on ADSL because it is the most prevalent and the least expensive. For WAN links, however, you should consider SDSL if your WAN data needs are similar in both the downstream and upstream directions.

How *x*DSL Works

The twisted-pair copper wire that carries POTS is capable of carrying signals with up to a 1 MHz spread of frequencies. However, POTS uses only 8 KHz of that potential frequency bandwidth. The RBOC's CO switch contains a card that interfaces with the analog signal that the twisted-pair wire sends to the phone company's digital network. This interface card allows only 4 KHz of signaling frequencies in each direction, even though the wire itself is capable of carrying a far broader frequency range. This limitation exists for standard telephone service because 4 KHz provides reasonable clarity for voice communications, and much of the telephone system is designed around those types of circuits.

*x*DSL works by opening up that 1 MHz maximum capability through the use of new *x*DSL interface cards, which the RBOCs install in their CO switch in place of the cards used for voice lines. The distance from the computer equipment to the CO switch limits the data rate, however. Most *x*DSL implementations function optimally at up to 3,600 meters (12,000 feet, or about 2 miles). In particular, higher-bandwidth versions of DSL can often only operate at peak speeds when they are within 3,600 meters of the CO. Longer distances are possible, but not at that full possible data rate. For instance, running an ADSL connection at 5,500 meters (18,000 feet)—the distance at which 95 percent of telephone locations exist in relation to their CO switch—degrades the performance to about 1.5 Mbps (at best) in the downstream direction. Only an estimated 50 percent of U.S. locations are within 3,600 meters of an RBOC CO switch.

The good news is that newer implementations of *x*DSL have improved these distance limitations. Also, there are extender devices (essentially repeaters) that the RBOCs can install to let them offer DSL connections to more remote rural areas.

Specific implementations of ADSL vary in their data rates. Some of the slower implementations function at only 1.5 Mbps downstream and 256 Kbps upstream. In some cases, this speed might even decrease to 384 Kbps downstream and 64 Kbps upstream.

T-1/T-3 (DS1/DS3) Connections

More than 40 years ago, Bell Laboratories developed a hierarchy of systems that can carry digital voice signals. At the lowest level in this hierarchy is a *DS0 connection* (DS stands for Digital Signal), which carries 64 Kbps of bandwidth. A *DS1* connection aggregates 24 DS0 channels and can carry up to 1.544 Mbps when all channels are in use. The next-common level is called a *DS3,* which carries 672 DS0 channels, for an aggregate total of 44.736 Mbps.

The DS1 connection is commonly called a *T-1 connection,* which actually refers to the system of repeaters that can carry the DS1 traffic over a four-wire twisted-pair

Why Asymmetric DSL?

Many data access needs are asymmetrical. In other words, at any given time, a system often needs to receive more data than it needs to send, or vice versa. Most remote access connections, particularly Internet connections, are asymmetrical. The emphasis is on being able to receive data rapidly rather than on sending data rapidly.

Because of this, ADSL is the most popular among the *x*DSL implementations, simply because it offers more benefits within the same amount of total frequency bandwidth. Many applications will work far better with the data rate being faster downstream than upstream.

Some *x*DSL implementations are symmetric, such as SDSL and HDSL. These connection types are more suited to uses where the exchange of data is roughly equal in both directions, such as two remote LANs that are connected to one another.

connection. DS1 requires only two twisted-pairs, not fiber-optic cable or anything exotic. (For details on how much data can be carried over simple telephone wire, see the preceding section on DSL.)

DS1 connections are commonly used as digital connections between a company's PBX and a point of presence (POP) for a long-distance telephone carrier. They are also commonly used to connect LANs to the Internet. A DS1 connection can handle up to 24 voice calls or as many as 24 data connections simultaneously. Or, using a multiplexer and a DS1, you can form one big 1.544 Mbps connection.

A popular technology called *fractional T-1* also exists, where a full DS1 is installed, but only the number of channels you pay for are turned on and available for use. Fractional T-1 is great because you can buy just the bandwidth you need, and increasing the bandwidth (up to the maximum for a DS1) is just a phone call (and some more money!) away.

At your end of a DS1 connection are two key pieces of equipment: a channel service unit/data service unit (CSU/DSU) that converts the DS1 signals into network signals, and a router that directs data between the DS1 and the LAN.

Asynchronous Transfer Mode (ATM)

Asynchronous Transfer Mode, commonly called just ATM, is a very high-speed technology for transmitting data between locations. ATM is a multiplexed, cell-based networking technology that collects data into entities called *cells* and then transmits the cells over the ATM network connection.

ATM networks can carry both voice and data. ATM is very fast, with speeds ranging from 155 Mbps to 622 Mbps, and in some cases can go as high as 10 Gbps. Usually, ATM is used only by relatively large companies that need ATM's speed for their WAN links, or by companies that need to send enormous amounts of data through a network connection, such as a lot of video data.

Corporate WAN Networking

In this section you'll learn about corporate WAN networking in practice, including the components of a WAN connection, quality of service and class of service, redundant WAN links, and the cost components of WAN network links.

WAN Components

A number of constituent parts make up a company's connection to a WAN. Figure 5-3 illustrates the connections for a single company location, which would be duplicated for all other company locations that connect to the same network. The components parts are described in the following sections.

Local Loop

The connection from a company's building is initially carried over something called a *local loop*, which forms a connection between your building and the local exchange carrier's (LEC) central office building. This connection is often also called the *last mile*, as it usually makes up the last mile (or so) of a circuit. Local loops are usually carried over copper or fiber-optic cable, but in some cases can also be carried using wireless technologies such as microwave transmission.

Within your building, the local loop will be connected to a router, sometimes called customer premise equipment (CPE).

Central Office

In most areas of the world, a single company (sometimes two or three in larger areas) has installed and owns the existing telephony and data cabling. These carriers are called the incumbent local exchange carrier (ILEC, or often just LEC). In the United States, this is frequently AT&T, but there are other companies that are also LECs

Figure 5-3.   The components of an individual WAN link

within various areas, such as Verizon. These local networks originally were installed to support switched voice telephony, but over time they have grown and they now also carry virtually all of the data connections within a given area. When anyone makes a switched telephone call, the signals are carried to the LEC's CO, at which point they are routed to their destination.

In the case of WAN connections, the signals are carried to the CO, at which point they are routed to the main carrier's point of presence.

Point of Presence

A point of presence, usually just called a *POP*, is a building that serves as an edge point of a carrier's private network. Within a POP building are installed various routers and switches that aggregate all of the connections coming in from CO buildings, and that serve as the interface between the carrier's private network and the connections to their customers.

Private Network Cloud

The POP to which a WAN circuit connects is in turn connected to other POPs that are part of the private network cloud. In cases where a carrier has a strong presence in a region, they will often have multiple POPs that connect to each other in a meshed fashion, such that if one particular connection between POPs fails, the data can be routed over redundant connections.

Multiprotocol Label Switching

Large private network clouds almost always make use of a mechanism called Multiprotocol Label Switching (MPLS). MPLS networks encapsulate the data being sent into MPLS packets, which retain within them all of the original packet, but that add short MPLS labels that are used to direct the MPLS packet to the destination POP in a very efficient manner. The advantage to MPLS labels is that they are shorter, and therefore faster, for making routing decisions.

Data that arrives at a POP from a customer end-point is encapsulated into a MPLS packet with an *edge router*. The data then enters the private cloud and is directed to its destination POP, where the edge router there then strips off the encapsulating MPLS data and forwards the data in its original form to the destination endpoint.

Quality of Service and Class of Service

General Internet connections usually work using a *best-effort* class of service. What this means is that the routers between a user and the various servers they are accessing will do their best to forward all of the packets they receive, but if the router gets too busy, it can (and will) drop packets that overflow its internal buffers. For individuals browsing the Web, this is usually no big deal; maybe a page they are loading doesn't load properly, and they hit the Refresh button on the browser, and then the page loads correctly.

However, this sort of behavior would be unacceptable for important data transmissions. For example, you would not want remote users of your company's Enterprise Resource Planning (ERP) system to have to wonder if their transactions got completed normally. Similarly, a voice call that had dropped packets, if very frequent, would make the voice call unusable.

To address this sort of issue, companies implement something called quality of service (QoS), which tags important packets with a QoS label. These labels are then carried along with each data packet, and they indicate to each router that handles those packets how the data should be forwarded. Broadly, the forwarding priorities fall into the following categories:

- **Best effort (BE)**   The lowest priority. When a router's queues are full, best-effort packets will be dropped, and even when not dropped, their forwarding priority is the lowest.

- **Assured forwarding (AF)**   Assured forwarding is made up of four different classes of traffic, each of which has three different *drop priorities.* Used judiciously, the four different classes can be used to prioritize important traffic.

- **Expedited forwarding (EF)**   Expedited forwarding is the highest-priority traffic, and is used for real-time transmissions, such as voice and video. It aims to minimize latency, jitter, and packet loss.

Quality of service can apply to LANs, but usually it becomes most important for data traversing a WAN, and it's important to understand that it's only part of the equation. The other part is something called class of service (CoS), which is specified when you procure data lines from a network carrier. In such cases, when you have critical traffic that you will be transmitting over the WAN, you need to specify the CoS that applies to your data. Typically, these values are stated as percentages of the total bandwidth that the WAN link carries.

For example, say you have a 10 Mbps WAN link between sites, and you expect your traffic to be broken down as follows:

- 10%, or 1 Mbps, will be for voice calls.

- 20%, or 2 Mbps, will be for video conferencing calls.

- 15%, or 1.5 Mbps, will be for mission-critical data.

- 40%, or 4 Mbps, will be for standard business data.

- 15%, or 1.5 Mbps, will be used for nonessential purposes, such as reading e-mail or browsing the company Intranet.

When you order your 10 Mbps WAN link from a carrier, you will specify to them these expected values. They will then sell you (for an additional cost) a CoS package that meets these needs. The CoS package will also include service-level agreements (SLAs) in which they will guarantee these CoS values, and if their network falls short, will credit back to you an agreed-upon amount.

The different carriers have different terminology that they use to describe their CoS offerings. For example, AT&T has a variety of packages (and subpackages) called things like Multimedia High, Multimedia Standard, Business Data, and so forth. Other carriers will divide traffic up into "metals" (Gold, Silver, and Bronze) and will sell CoS packages with those names. Still other carriers will have their own nomenclature. However, if you can describe your usage in terms similar to the breakdown in the preceding bulleted list, the carrier salespeople will be able to translate to their company's specific offerings that match those needs.

WAN Redundancy

For critical WAN links, companies often want to provide some level of redundancy. For example, perhaps a hospital is connected to a remote data center, and its access to patient records and other critical information must be highly assured. Banking is another sector where it is usually vital that the WAN links remain up. And even in industries where a WAN link isn't quite so critical as a bank or hospital, a company's operations can be negatively affected if their WAN links aren't working, such as a company's distribution center, which relies on access to the company's ERP in order to be able to ship its products.

Before designing a redundancy system for a WAN, it's critical that the effects of WAN downtime be quantified in some fashion. What would the effects be if a particular WAN link were down for a few minutes, or a few hours, or a day or more, and what would be the resulting impacts of such downtime? The reason it's important to understand this fully is that WAN redundancy is a complicated area, and usually you have to make trade-off decisions between cost and redundancy.

When considering redundancy for WAN links, it's important to consider all of the different component parts of the WAN link, and then to consider which components should be redundant. Following are some notes about different WAN components that can be made redundant:

- **Customer premise equipment routers**   A WAN link can have a single connection to the WAN, but be supported with two redundant routers. Usually, redundant routers are configured in a failover arrangement, where if the primary router fails, the backup router picks up the routing duties.

- **Local loop**   The local loop, along with the CO to which it connects, is probably the most likely WAN component to experience downtime. Downtime can be due to construction equipment digging a trench and cutting a data line, or can be caused by a failure at the CO. When considering local loop redundancy, it's important that any redundant local loops have what is called *diverse routing*. Diversity in routing means that the redundant local loop does not follow the same path to the CO as the primary local loop. If you had redundant local loops that were not diverse, a failure that cuts off one local loop will almost certainly affect the redundant one simultaneously.

- **Central office (CO)**   When you have local loop redundancy, you will usually also want redundancy in the CO to which the redundant local loop connects. In most business areas, even with a single local exchange carrier, you can make arrangements to have the primary local loop connect to the closest CO, and the redundant local loop to connect to the next closest CO. Bear in mind that, depending on the distance to the alternative CO, the cost of the redundant circuit's local loop will almost certainly be more expensive than the primary circuit's local loop.

- **Point of presence (POP)**   Depending on what region of the world your WAN connection is in, you can often obtain diverse POPs. For example, a business located in Silicon Valley in California might connect its primary circuit to a POP located in San Francisco, and its redundant circuit is connected to a POP in Sacramento (assuming the carrier has POPs in those locations).

- **Network cloud**   Some companies choose to have completely redundant WANs, in which every component of each WAN connection is duplicated with a different carrier.

Diverse network clouds (and therefore POPs) are probably the least important part of a WAN to make redundant. A carrier's network cloud and their POPs are typically built in a "hardened" fashion, with backup power generators and multiple connections to the provider's network cloud. Network cloud failures for the larger carriers are probably, at most, a once-a-decade event, and when they occur, they are usually recovered from rather quickly.

Diverse COs and local loops are more important to make redundant. If you are using a single carrier's network cloud, when you order the redundant circuit, the carrier will tell you if a diverse local loop is available from your location, and should be able to direct that diverse loop to a diverse CO. If you happen to be in a location where diverse routing to an alternative CO is not available, you can explore using some other modality to form your connection to the carrier's network cloud, such as a high-speed wireless connection.

TIP   If you elect to use a single POP (in some regions of the world, depending on the carrier, you may be forced to), it is important to ensure that the carrier has each WAN circuit connected to different provider equipment (PE) within the POP itself. PE routers and switches can fail, and so by ensuring that the carrier has the WAN circuits connected to different equipment, you can mitigate this potential point of failure. Note that not all carriers will automatically ensure that multiple circuits from a single customer are connected to different switches or routers, so be sure to request this and have the carrier confirm it in writing. The good news is that there is not normally an extra charge for equipment diversity.

In addition to determining what WAN components you wish to have redundant, you should consider the overall form of redundancy you wish. For example, if your primary link to a particular site goes down, perhaps the backup circuit can be smaller than the primary circuit. Or, you might divide up a particular location's bandwidth usage between two circuits in a load-sharing arrangement, such that normally each circuit carries half of the bandwidth for the location, and if one fails, the site continues at 50% bandwidth until the failed circuit is restored.

 NOTE Another form of redundancy I have seen is for companies that have a global network, but have two locations relatively close to each other (within 20 to 50 miles). In such cases, what you can do is have each of the nearby locations on a single circuit into the WAN network, but then the two locations additionally have a private line circuit connecting them together. The two LANs are then configured so that if either location's WAN connection goes down, that location's traffic will automatically route through the private line to the other location and then out to the WAN network.

Chapter Summary

In this chapter, you learned about concepts and technologies relating to WANs, including different types of links and different types of connections, as well as how to specify a particular type of WAN technology for a given application. While the number of choices may make this area confusing, it becomes easier when you break the problem down into smaller chunks. Basically, make sure you do a careful and thorough job of identifying your WAN needs, and then work with various WAN providers in your area to analyze how their solutions may meet your needs. You also learned about the main components of WAN networks and some important things to keep in mind when you need redundancy in your WAN network.

The next chapter moves into network protocols, like TCP/IP and IPX/SPX. You learn how these network protocols work, how their packets are constructed, and various characteristics of each type of network protocol. You also learn about some of the other common protocols, particularly those associated with TCP/IP, such as SMTP, HTTP, and WINS.

CHAPTER 6 | Understanding Networking Protocols

A network *protocol* is a set of rules that data communications over a network follow to complete various network transactions. For example, TCP/IP defines a set of rules used to send data from one node on a network to another node. SMTP is a set of rules and standards used to transfer e-mail and attachments from one node to another. Dynamic Host Configuration Protocol (DHCP) is a set of rules and standards used to allocate IP addresses dynamically for a network, so they do not need to be set manually for each workstation.

Many protocols are used in networking. In fact, in a sense, almost *every* activity on a network follows a protocol of one sort or another. Some protocols function at a low level in the OSI network model, others operate at a high level, and some operate in between.

In this chapter, you learn about the essential networking protocols used to transmit and receive data across a network.

Understanding TCP/IP and UDP

As its name suggests, TCP/IP is actually two protocols used in concert with one another. The Internet Protocol (IP) defines how network data is addressed from a source to a destination and in what sequence the data should be reassembled at the other end. IP operates at the network layer in the OSI model. The Transmission Control Protocol (TCP) operates one layer higher than IP, at the transport layer. TCP manages connections between computers. TCP messages are carried (encapsulated) in IP datagrams.

The User Datagram Protocol (UDP) serves the same role as TCP but offers fewer features. Both TCP and UDP packets are carried within IP packets, but the only reliability feature that UDP supports is the resending of any packets not received at the destination. (UDP is called a *connectionless* protocol.) The chief advantage to UDP is that it is much faster for trivial network communications, such as sending a web page to a client computer. Because UDP doesn't offer many error-checking or error-handling features, it should be used only when it isn't that important if data occasionally gets mangled between points and needs to be resent, or when an application program provides its own extensive error-checking and error-handling functions.

DEFINE-IT! Datagrams, Frames, and Packets

A *packet* is any collection of data sent over a network, and the term is usually used generically to refer to units of data sent at any layer of the OSI model. For instance, people talk about *IP packets*, even though technically the correct term is *IP datagrams*. In this book, *packet* is used generically. The persnickety definition of packet applies only to messages sent at the top layer of the OSI model, the application layer.

Network layer units of data, such as those carried by IP, are called *datagrams*. Units of data carried at the data-link layer (Layer 1) are called *frames*.

All of these terms to refer to a collection of data that is transmitted as a single unit.

TCP and UDP Ports

Both TCP and UDP support the concept of *ports*, or application-specific addresses, to which packets are directed on any given receiving machine. For example, most web servers run on a server machine and receive requests through port 80. When a machine receives any packets that are intended for the web server (such as a request to serve up a web page), the requesting machine directs those packets to that port number. When you request a web page from a web server, your computer sends the request to the web server computer and specifies that its request should go to port 80, which is where Hypertext Transfer Protocol (HTTP) requests are directed.

Hundreds of different ports have standardized uses. Defining your own ports on a server for specific applications is easy. A text file called SERVICES defines the ports on a computer. An example of a portion of a Windows SERVICES file follows. (Only selected entries are shown due to space constraints; the following is not a complete SERVICES file, but it illustrates what the file contains.)

```
# Copyright (c) 1993-2004 Microsoft Corp.
#
# This file contains port numbers for well-known services defined by IANA
#
# Format:
#
# <service name>   <port number>/<protocol>   [aliases...]    [#<comment>]
#
echo             7/tcp
echo             7/udp
systat          11/tcp     users               #Active users
systat          11/udp     users               #Active users
daytime         13/tcp
daytime         13/udp
ftp-data        20/tcp                         #FTP, data
ftp             21/tcp                         #FTP. control
ssh             22/tcp                         #SSH Remote Login Protocol
telnet          23/tcp
smtp            25/tcp     mail                #Simple Mail Transfer
                                               Protocol
time            37/tcp     timserver
time            37/udp     timserver
nameserver      42/tcp     name                #Host Name Server
nameserver      42/udp     name                #Host Name Server
domain          53/tcp                         #Domain Name Server
domain          53/udp                         #Domain Name Server
tftp            69/udp                         #Trivial File Transfer
gopher          70/tcp
finger          79/tcp
http            80/tcp     www www-http        #World Wide Web
kerberos        88/tcp     krb5 kerberos-sec   #Kerberos
kerberos        88/udp     krb5 kerberos-sec   #Kerberos
```

pop2	109/tcp	postoffice	#Post Office Protocol - Version 2
pop3	110/tcp		#Post Office Protocol - Version 3
nntp	119/tcp	usenet	#Network News Transfer Protocol
ntp	123/udp		#Network Time Protocol
netbios-ns	137/tcp	nbname	#NETBIOS Name Service
netbios-ns	137/udp	nbname	#NETBIOS Name Service
netbios-dgm	138/udp	nbdatagram	#NETBIOS Datagram Service
netbios-ssn	139/tcp	nbsession	#NETBIOS Session Service
imap	143/tcp	imap4	#Internet Message Access Protocol
snmp	161/udp		#SNMP
snmptrap	162/udp	snmp-trap	#SNMP trap
bgp	179/tcp		#Border Gateway Protocol
irc	194/tcp		#Internet Relay Chat Protocol
ipx	213/udp		#IPX over IP
ldap	389/tcp		#Lightweight Directory Access Protocol
https	443/tcp	MCom	#HTTP over TLS/SSL
https	443/udp	MCom	#HTTP over TLS/SSL
who	513/udp	whod	
cmd	514/tcp	shell	
syslog	514/udp		
printer	515/tcp	spooler	
timed	525/udp	timeserver	
dhcpv6-client	546/tcp		#DHCPv6 Client
dhcpv6-client	546/udp		#DHCPv6 Client
dhcpv6-server	547/tcp		#DHCPv6 Server
dhcpv6-server	547/udp		#DHCPv6 Server
ftps-data	989/tcp		#FTP data, over TLS/SSL
ftps	990/tcp		#FTP control, over TLS/SSL
telnets	992/tcp		#Telnet protocol over TLS/SSL
imaps	993/tcp		#IMAP4 protocol over TLS/SSL
ircs	994/tcp		#IRC protocol over TLS/SSL
nfa	1155/tcp		#Network File Access
nfa	1155/udp		#Network File Access
wins	1512/tcp		#Microsoft Windows Internet Name Service
wins	1512/udp		#Microsoft Windows Internet Name Service
pptp	1723/tcp		#Point-to-point tunnelling protocol
remote-winsock	1745/tcp		
remote-winsock	1745/udp		

As you can see, most of the Internet services that you might be familiar with actually work through the use of TCP and/or UDP ports, such as HTTP (port 80) for the Web, SMTP (port 25) for e-mail, Network News Transfer Protocol (NNTP) (port 119) for Usenet, and so forth. The use of ports ensures that network communications intended for a particular purpose are not confused with others that might also be arriving at the same machine.

Ports allow the receiving machine to direct arriving data appropriately. An example is a server that hosts web pages and also receives and processes e-mail. Packets arriving at port 80 will be sent to the web-serving software, while those that arrive at port 25 will go to the e-mail software. Other services on the machine, such as Telnet and FTP, can also function concurrently through this mechanism.

IP Packets and IP Addressing

IP packets include addresses that uniquely define every computer connected to the Internet (see Figure 6-1). These addresses are used to route packets from a sending node to a receiving node. Because all the routers on the Internet know the network addresses to which they are connected, they can accurately forward packets destined for a remote network.

In addition to carrying its data, each IP packet contains a number of fields, which are organized in the following order:

- **Version**   This field indicates the version of the IP protocol being used.

- **Header length**   This field indicates the length of the header information before the data begins in the packet.

- **Type of service**   This field is used for different purposes by different vendors. It can be used for features such as requesting high-priority routing, requesting highest possible reliability, and so forth.

- **Total length**   This field indicates the total length of the packet.

- **Identification, flags, and fragment offset**   These three fields are used to reassemble an IP packet that was disassembled at some point during transmission. They include all the information necessary for the correct reassembly of the packet at the receiving end.

- **Time to live**   This field (called "Time" in Figure 6-1) defines how many network hops the packet can traverse before it is declared dead and the routers stop forwarding it to other routers. This number is set when the packet is sent, and each router that handles the packet decrements the value by one. When the number reaches zero, the packet is dead and is no longer transmitted. If there is a routing configuration error on the path to the destination that causes the packet to go into an endless loop between routers, this is the feature that will stop it after a period of time.

Version (4 bits)
Header length (4 bits)
Type of service (8 bits)

Total length (16 bits)

Identification (16 bits)

Flags (4 bits)

Fragment offset (12 bits)

Time (8 bits)

Protocol (8 bits)

Header checksum (16 bits)

Source IP address (32 bits)

Destination IP address (32 bits)

Options (26 bits)

Padding (6 bits)

Data (variable number of bytes)

Figure 6-1.   A schematic showing the layout of an IP packet

- **Protocol**   This field indicates whether the IP packet is contained within a TCP or a UDP packet.

- **Header checksum**   The header checksum is used to help ensure that none of the packet's header data (the fields discussed in this list) is damaged.

- **Source IP address**   This field contains the address of the sending computer. It is needed in case a packet must be retransmitted to tell the receiving node (or, in some cases, a router) from which node to request a retransmission.

- **Destination IP address**   This field contains the address of the receiving node.

- **Options and padding**   These final two fields of the header of the IP packet are used to request any required specific routing instructions or to specify the time that the packet was sent.

- **Data**   The final field of an IP packet is the actual data being sent.

IP addresses are 32 bits long, allowing for a theoretical maximum number of addresses of 2^{32}, or about 4.3 billion addresses. To make them easier to work with and to help route them more efficiently, they are broken up into four *octets*, which are each 1 byte long. Thus, in decimal notation, IP addresses are expressed as *xxx.xxx.xxx.xxx*, where each *xxx* represents a base-10 number from 0 to 255. The numbers 0, 127, and 255 are usually reserved for special purposes, so they are typically unavailable for assignment to nodes. The remaining 253 unique addresses are available for assignment in each octet.

Addresses on the Internet are guaranteed to be unique through the use of an address registration service, presently administered by the Internet Corporation for Assigned Names and Numbers (ICANN). Actual registrations of domain names and addresses are handled through one of many *registrars*, which include companies such as InterNIC, Network Solutions, and many others. ICANN is the overall authority.

Help! We're Almost Out of Addresses!

The current implementation of IP, called IP version 4 (IPv4), is approaching the point where running out of addresses is becoming a real possibility. In 1994, a proposal was issued to address this limitation. Called IP Next Generation (IPng, now IP version 6, or IPv6), the new version of IP takes care of the addressing limitation by bumping up the address length from 32 bits to 128 bits. This allows 3.4×10^{38} (34 followed by 37 zeros, or around 340 trillion, trillion, trillion) unique addresses, which should leave plenty of room for all anticipated Internet addresses, even allowing for refrigerators, toasters, and cars to have their own IP addresses!

ICANN assigns three major classes of addresses, called Class A, B, and C, as follows:

- For a Class A address, ICANN assigns the owner a number in the first octet. The owner is then free to use all possible valid combinations in the remaining three octets. For example, a Class A address might be 57.*xxx*.*xxx*.*xxx*. Class A addresses enable the owner to address up to around 16.5 million unique nodes.

- Class B addresses define the first two octets, leaving the remaining two open for the address's owner to use. For instance, 223.55.*xxx*.*xxx* would be a valid Class B address assignment. Class B addresses enable the holder to have about 65,000 unique nodes.

- Class C follows this progression, defining the first three octets and leaving only the last octet available for the Class C owner to assign. The owner can assign up to 255 unique addresses.

An Internet Service Provider (ISP) might own either a Class A or a Class B address, and then can handle a number of Class C addresses within its own address structure. Changing ISPs, even for a company that has a valid Class C address, means changing the company's address from a Class C address available through the first ISP to a Class C address available from the new ISP.

As mentioned earlier, the addresses 0, 127, and 255 are reserved. Usually, address 0—as in 123.65.101.0—refers to the network itself, and the router that connects the network to other networks handles this address. The address 127 is a special *loopback address* that can be used for certain kinds of testing. The address 255 refers to all computers on the network, so a broadcast message to address 223.65.101.255 would go to all addresses within 223.65.101.*xxx*.

IP addresses are made up of two main components. The first, or leftmost, is the *network ID*, also called the *netid*. The other is the *host ID*, usually referred to as *hostid*. The netid identifies the network, while the hostid identifies each node on that network. (In IP parlance, every node is called a *host*, regardless of whether it's a server, client computer, printer, or whatever.) For a Class C address, for instance, the netid is set in the first three octets, and the hostids use the fourth octet. For a Class B address, the first two octets are the netid, and the final two octets are hostids. These address parts are important for subnetting, as described next.

IP Subnetting

Suppose that a company has three networks in three different buildings, all connected by an Ethernet link. Each network has about 25 nodes. Each building has its own set of servers and printers for the workers in that building. The Ethernet link between the networks is necessary to transmit information between buildings, such as e-mail messages or accounting transactions. How should the company assign IP addresses in this situation?

The company could request a single Class C set of addresses and then assign those addresses across the three networks in some fashion. This seems like a simple solution, but it's actually a poor idea for a couple of reasons. Typically, a lot of network traffic is sent to each hostid within a single netid. The slow Integrated Services Digital Network (ISDN) link between the buildings would become a tremendous bottleneck in this situation, and the entire network would function very poorly.

Another idea is to use separate Class C addresses (netids) for each building. This is a relatively simple solution, and it would work just fine, except that the ISP might not be able to assign three separate Class C addresses. Also, it would be terribly wasteful of the available pool of IP addresses. In this situation, each building would be wasting more than 200 addresses for no good reason.

What if there were a way to divide a Class C address so that each building could have its own *virtual* netid? Such a solution is what subnetting is all about. *Subnetting* allows you to subdivide a *hostid* range (usually that of a Class C address, but such subnetting can also be done with Class A or B addresses) across two or more networks. Subnetting is done through the use of subnet masks, which are discussed in the next section.

NOTE   To understand subnetting, you first need to understand the binary representation of IP addresses. For a quick overview of how binary numbers work, see Chapter 1.

IP Addresses: Public or Private?

The IP addresses administered by ICANN are for the public Internet. Most companies only have—or need—a few of the public addresses, even if they have hundreds of computers on their local area network (LAN).

Public IP addresses are those that computers need to be able to reach over the public Internet. So, for example, a small company might need just a few— for example, one for the company's overall Internet connection, one for the company's public-facing web server, and one for the company's e-mail system. Larger companies may need somewhat more, but basically it won't be a very large quantity for most companies.

All of the other computers, servers, and other devices within a company that need an IP address usually use a private address, which is only reachable within the company's LAN. These addresses usually begin with 10.xxx.xxx.xxx or 192.168.xxx.xxx. These ranges are defined as private IP address ranges, and they are not routable over public Internet routers. Within a particular private network, however, they are routable and can still be subnetted, as described in the following section.

If your home computer is connected to a wireless router, it will be using a private IP address. In Windows, you can open a command prompt and type the command IPCONFIG to learn exactly what address your computer is using.

Subnet Masks

If you look at a computer's IP configuration, you'll see that the computer always has both an IP address (such as 205.143.60.109) and a *subnet mask* (such as 255.255.255.0). The subnet mask defines which part of the computer's IP address is the netid and which part is the hostid. To see this clearly, you need to represent the addresses in binary form:

```
Computer IP Address (Dec):        205        143        60         109
Computer IP Address (Bin):        11001101   10001111   00111100   01101101
Subnet mask (Dec):                255        255        255        0
Subnet mask (Bin):                11111111   11111111   11111111   00000000
```

The netid of an address, defined by the subnet mask, is whatever portion of the address has a binary 1 set in the corresponding subnet mask. In the preceding example, the netid is the full first three octets (the first 24 bits), and the hostid is the last octet (the last 8 bits). Now you can see why 255 (decimal) is used so frequently in subnet masks: 255 corresponds to having all bits set to 1 in an 8-bit number.

NOTE   Subnet masks should always use contiguous 1's, starting from the left and working to the right. The hostid portion of the subnet mask should contain all contiguous 0's, working backward from the right to the left. While it is theoretically possible to build subnet masks that have interspersed 1's and 0's, it is never done in practice because it would quickly become too complicated to manage properly and because there's no real reason to do so. Also, the portion of the hostid address that is subnet-masked cannot consist of all 0's or all 1's. While certain implementations of IP do allow all 0's, such a configuration is not part of the accepted standard IP rules, and thus using such a hostid address is risky because some devices on the network might not understand it.

Let's now return to the example of the company with three buildings. What if the company could divide a single Class C address so that each building could use its own portion, and the routers connecting the buildings would understand which transmissions should be forwarded to the other buildings and which ones should not? Such a configuration is where subnet masks are useful.

A subnet mask allows you to "borrow" some bits from your hostids and then use those bits to create new netids. For the example, you would need to borrow three bits from the Class C address (the fourth octet) and use that address to create four separate netids. Examine how this configuration would work in binary format:

```
Subnet mask (Bin):       11111111   11111111   11111111   11100000
Bldg. 1 IP addresses:    11001101   10001111   00111100   100xxxxx
Bldg. 2 IP addresses:    11001101   10001111   00111100   011xxxx
Bldg. 3 IP addresses:    11001101   10001111   00111100   101xxxxx
Subnet mask (Dec):       255        255        255        224
Bldg. 1 IP addresses:    205        143        60         129 - 158
Bldg. 2 IP addresses:    205        143        60         97 - 126
Bldg. 3 IP addresses:    205        143        60         161 - 190
```

Binary Mask	Decimal Equivalent	Number of Subnets	Number of Hostids per Subnet
00000000	0	1	254
10000000	128	2	126
11000000	192	4	62
11100000	224	8	30
11110000	240	16	14
11111000	248	32	6
11111100	252	64	2
11111110	254	N/A	N/A
11111111	255	N/A	N/A

Table 6-1.   Common Subnet Masks

Using this configuration, the company can create up to 6 netids, and each building can be provided with 30 available hostid addresses. By using subnetting to designate each separate netid, the company can program the routers to send packets between networks only when the packets are supposed to be routed.

Because subnet masks should always be created using contiguous bits for the mask itself, only nine subnet masks are possible, as shown in Table 6-1.

In Table 6-1, some configurations are marked as N/A, for not applicable. These subnet masks would result in no available addresses because of the rule that the subnet portion of the netid cannot be all 0's or all 1's. For example, consider the subnet mask of 224, which uses three hostid bits for the subnetid. In theory, this configuration should result in eight subnets. However, the subnets represented by 000 and 111 are not valid. Likewise, 128 is not a valid subnet mask because that one bit would always be either a 1 or a 0.

 TIP   If you need to implement subnets, you should initially work through the project with an experienced network engineer, who can help you avoid pitfalls (which were not explicitly described in the preceding section). You might also want to learn more about TCP/IP through resources devoted to detailed coverage of the concepts introduced here. One good book is *CompTIA Network+ All-in-One Exam Guide, Fifth Edition (Exam N10-005)* (McGraw-Hill Education, 2012).

Understanding Other Internet Protocols

Quite a few other protocols used on the Internet either rely on or make use of TCP/IP. In this section, you learn about these different protocols.

Domain Name System (DNS)

If you had only IP address numbers to address computers over the Internet, trying to keep track of them and using their correct addresses might make you a little crazy. To go to the web site for Google, for example, you would need to remember to type their main address, like http://209.85.171.100. To solve this problem, a system called the Domain Name System (DNS) was developed.

DNS enables people to register domain names with ICANN—or a valid DNS registrar governed by ICANN—and then use them to access a particular node over the Internet. Therefore, DNS is the service that allows you to open a web browser and type http://www.google.com to connect to a particular computer over the Internet. In this case, google.com is the domain name.

NOTE   Domain names are given out on a first-come, first-served basis. However, ICANN gives preference to a holder of a valid registered trademark if a conflict develops. Upon being presented with valid trademark information and notice of the domain name that infringes on that trademark, ICANN goes through a process to assess the truth of the claim and, if necessary, takes a domain name away from its present holder and transfers the name to its rightful owner.

Domains are organized in a tree arrangement, like a directory tree on a disk drive. The top level defines different *domain types,* called *top-level domain names* (TLDs). The most common is the .com domain type, usually used with for-profit commercial entities. The following are other common domain types:

- .edu for educational institutions
- .gov for governmental entities
- .mil for military entities
- .net for Internet-related entities
- .org for nonprofit entities
- *.xx* for different countries, such as .it for Italy and .de for Germany (Deutschland)

NOTE   In recent years, a number of other TLDs have been added to the system, such as .biz, .info, and .name. You can find a complete list of the TLDs at http://www.icann.org.

Within a domain name, entities are free to add other names before the beginning of the domain name, and these usually refer to a particular host or server, or sometimes to a particular type of service for that domain. For example, if you had the domain bedrock.gov, you would be free to create additional names, such as quarry.bedrock.gov and flintstone.bedrock.gov.

As a matter of standards, the first portion of a domain name preceding the actual domain name indicates what type of service is being connected. For instance, www .bedrock.gov would be used for a World Wide Web server for the domain bedrock.gov, and ftp.bedrock.gov would be used for an FTP server. The standards for service types within the domain name are usually followed, but not always. The owners of domain names are free to invent their own service type names that meet their particular needs. For example, some domain name holders refer to their e-mail servers as smtp.domain.org; others might prefer to use mail.domain.org, and still others might even use mercury .domain.org (Mercury being the Roman god of, among other things, messaging).

Domain names are resolved to IP addresses through the use of *domain name servers* (DNS), which are servers that accept the typed domain name, perform a database query, and then return the actual address that should be used for that domain name. Generally, each ISP maintains its own DNS (and many companies and organizations maintain their own DNS as well). Any changes are propagated throughout all the Internet's DNS rapidly, usually within about an hour.

NOTE   Changes to DNS entries used to take up to several days to propagate throughout the Internet, but updates to the system now allow changes to propagate much more quickly—often within minutes of the change being posted.

Dynamic Host Configuration Protocol

In the early days of TCP/IP-based networks, administrators defined each node's address in a text file or dialog box. From then on, the address was fixed unless someone changed it. The problem was that administrators occasionally would mistakenly put conflicting addresses into other nodes on the network, causing a network's version of pandemonium. To resolve this problem and to make it easier to assign TCP/IP addresses, a service called Dynamic Host Configuration Protocol (DHCP) was invented.

DHCP services run on a DHCP server, where they control a range of IP addresses called a *scope*. When nodes connect to the network, they contact the DHCP server to get an assigned address that they can use. Addresses from a DHCP server are said to be *leased* to the client that uses them, meaning they remain assigned to a particular node for a set period of time before they expire and become available for another node to use. Often, lease periods are for just a few days, but network administrators can set any time period they want.

DHCP servers assign most addresses using *dynamic allocation*, where addresses are assigned automatically from a pool of available addresses, and in which the address assigned might change for a particular computer from time to time. DHCP servers can also assign addresses using *static allocation*, where you pair the MAC address of a particular computer with a specific IP address, and that particular computer then always has the same address.

You should not use DHCP dynamic allocation for nodes that provide network services, particularly for servers that provide services over the Internet. This is because changing a TCP/IP address would make reliably connecting to those computers impossible. Instead, use DHCP dynamic allocation to support client workstations that do not need to host services for other nodes, and use static allocation for IP addresses that should remain fixed for a given device.

> **DEFINE-IT! Host**
>
> You might think a *host* is a server, and in some networking contexts, you would be right. However, in the jargon of Internet names and addresses, every computer that has an IP address is called a *host*, thus the name Dynamic Host Configuration Protocol. Remembering that every computer is called a host is particularly important in the UNIX and Linux worlds, where the term is much more common than in the Windows or Macintosh worlds.

Hypertext Transfer Protocol

The World Wide Web is made up of documents that use a formatting language called Hypertext Markup Language (HTML). These documents are composed of text to be displayed, graphic images, formatting commands, and hyperlinks to other documents located somewhere on the Web. HTML documents are displayed most often using web browsers, such as Mozilla Firefox or Microsoft Internet Explorer.

A protocol called Hypertext Transfer Protocol (HTTP) controls the transactions between a web client and a web server. HTTP is an application-layer protocol. The HTTP protocol transparently makes use of DNS and other Internet protocols to form connections between the web client and the web server so the user is aware of only the web site's domain name and the name of the document itself.

HTTP is fundamentally an insecure protocol. Text-based information is sent "in the clear" between the client and the server. To address the need for secure web networking, alternatives are available, such as HTTP Secure (HTTPS) and Secure Sockets Layer (SSL).

Requests from a web client to a web server are connection-oriented, but they are not persistent. Once the client receives the contents of an HTML page, the connection is no longer active. Clicking a hyperlink in the HTML document reactivates the link, either to the original server (if that is where the hyperlink points) or to another server somewhere else.

File Transfer Protocol

The acronym FTP stands for two things: File Transfer Protocol and File Transfer Program (which makes use of the File Transfer Protocol). It's sort of like, "it's a dessert topping *and* a floor polish," (from the *Saturday Night Live* TV show). Because FTP (the program) makes use of FTP (the protocol), it can become confusing to know which is being discussed. This section discusses the protocol. (When I'm referring to the program, I'll say so.)

FTP is an application-layer protocol used to send and receive files between an FTP client and an FTP server. Usually, this is done with the FTP program or another program that can also use the protocol (many are available). FTP transfers can be either text-based or binary-based, and they can handle files of any size.

When you connect to an FTP server to transfer a file, you log in to the FTP server using a valid user name and password. However, some sites are set up to allow *anonymous FTP,* where you enter the user name *anonymous* and then enter your e-mail address as the password. For example, Mozilla maintains an FTP site you can use to download development builds of the Firefox web browser and other products, located at ftp.mozilla.org, which allows anonymous FTP.

To use the FTP program, on most platforms you type the command **ftp** followed by the address to which you want to connect. So, to use the Mozilla example, you would type **ftp ftp.mozilla.org**, press ENTER, and then log in. Then you can use all of the FTP commands—PUT, GET, MGET, and so forth. Most FTP program implementations have online help to assist you with the various commands. Type **?** or HELP to access this feature.

TIP   Recent versions of Windows also support FTP connections using Internet Explorer. Just open Internet Explorer and instead of entering an http:// address in the address bar, type an address preceded by ftp://. For example, to connect to Mozilla's FTP server, you would use the address ftp:// ftp.mozilla.org. This trick also works in most other current web browsers, such as Mozilla Firefox. Note that for FTP sites that require a login, the browser must support logging in. In Internet Explorer, a Logon As option is available on the File menu after you browse to an FTP site.

Network News Transfer Protocol

Usenet (NetNews) is a set of discussion groups devoted to an extremely wide variety of topics. There are well over 100,000 such groups in existence. Usenet conversations are posted to Usenet servers, which then echo their messages to all other Usenet servers around the world. A posted message can travel to all the Usenet servers in a matter of hours and then be available to users accessing any particular Usenet server.

Usenet discussion groups are loosely organized into the branches of a tree. The following are some of the main branches:

- Alt, for discussions about alternative lifestyles and other miscellaneous topics
- Comp, for computer-oriented discussions
- Gov, for government-oriented discussions
- Rec, devoted to recreational topics
- Sci, for science-based discussions

Usenet groups can either be public, which are echoed to other Usenet servers, or private, which are usually hosted by a particular organization and require the user to enter appropriate login credentials before reading and posting messages.

The Network News Transfer Protocol (NNTP) protocol is what makes Usenet possible. It allows for a connection between a Usenet reader (also called a *news reader*) and a Usenet server. It also provides for message formatting, so messages can be text-based or can also contain binary attachments. Binary attachments in Usenet postings are usually encoded using Multipurpose Internet Message Encoding (MIME), which is also used for most e-mail attachments. Some older systems use different methods to encode attachments, including one method called UUEncode/UUDecode and, on the Macintosh, a method called BinHex.

Telnet

Telnet defines a protocol that allows a remote terminal session to be established with an Internet host, so remote users have access similar to using a terminal connected directly to the host computer. Using Telnet, users can control the remote host, performing tasks such as managing files, running applications, or even (with appropriate permissions) administering the remote system. Telnet is a session-layer protocol in the OSI model.

For Telnet to work, Telnet software must be running on both the server and client computer. You run the program Telnet on a client computer and run the program Telnetd on the server computer to allow the connection. Telnet is specific to the TCP protocol and typically runs on port 23 (although it can run on any port that has been enabled on the server system). Once users connect using Telnet, they must log in to the remote system using the same credentials they would use if they were working from a directly connected terminal.

Simple Mail Transfer Protocol

E-mail had a somewhat rocky start on the Internet, with early e-mail programs sharing few standards with other e-mail programs, particularly in the handling of attached binary data. The good news is that the situation is now resolved, and all current e-mail software supports all the widely accepted standards.

The Simple Mail Transfer Protocol (SMTP) is used to send and receive e-mail messages from one e-mail server to another. The SMTP protocol defines a dialog between a sending system and a receiving system.

An SMTP dialog starts when a sending system connects to port 25 of a receiving system. After the connection is established, the sending system sends a HELO command, followed by its address. The receiving system acknowledges the HELO command along with its own address. The dialog then continues, with the sending system issuing a command indicating that the system wants to send a message and identifying the recipient for whom the message is intended. If the receiving system knows of the recipient, it acknowledges the request, and then the sending system transmits the body of the message along with any attachments. Finally, the connection between the two systems is terminated once the receiving system acknowledges that it has received the entire message. Figure 6-2 illustrates this process.

TIP   Details on SMTP can be found in RFC 821 (http://www.faqs.org/rfcs/rfc821.html).

Voice over IP

An important emerging set of IP protocols concerns the transmission of voice and facsimile information over IP-based networks, called *Voice over IP,* or *VoIP* for short

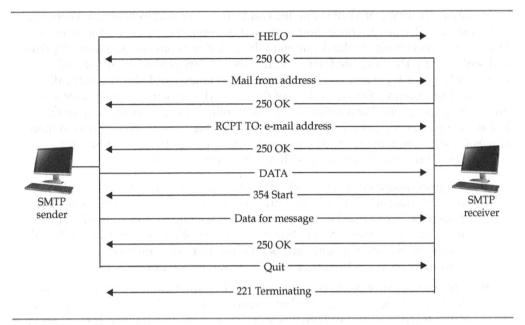

Figure 6-2.   Part of an SMTP dialog between systems

(pronounced "voyp"). VoIP is a protocol that allows analog voice data—for telephone calls—to be digitized and then encapsulated into IP packets and transmitted over a network. VoIP can be used to carry voice telephone calls over any IP network, such as a company's local area network (LAN) or wide area network (WAN), or the Internet.

Sending voice data over IP networks has some very attractive possible payoffs. One is more efficient use of available connections.

Consider a large company with two main offices. At any given time, hundreds of voice conversations might be occurring between those two offices. Each traditional voice connection consumes one DS0 line (a telephone line that can carry one telephone call at a time), capable of carrying up to 56 Kbps of data if the line were used digitally. Each conversation does not use all of the available bandwidth on the line. Part of this is because most conversations have a lot of silent spaces—time between words or sentences, time where one party stops speaking and the other starts, and so forth. Plus, most conversations, were they encoded digitally, could be significantly compressed. Add all of this up, and each voice conversation is likely to use only one-third to one-half of the available bandwidth on a single DS0 circuit.

If you were able to carry all of these voice conversations digitally, much less bandwidth would be required. Instead of 200 DS0 lines for 100 two-person conversations, for example, the same conversations might use up only the equivalent of 25 to 33 DS0 lines if they were digitally packaged. Moreover, instead of consuming switched phone connections, these conversations could be carried as part of larger data connections, or even over the Internet. Many companies can save a significant amount of money by using VoIP.

Another advantage of VoIP is that the connections are packet-oriented. When the user places a call, a single connection is formed between the caller and the receiver. This connection is static for the duration of the call. If the conversation were digitized and sent over a packet-oriented network, however, many possible paths would be available for each packet, and much more redundancy would be automatically available. For instance, if some portion of the network between the two points went down, the packets could still arrive at their destination through an alternative route, just as data packets do over the Internet. Also, available circuits would be used more efficiently, allowing more calls to be routed within a particular geographic area.

VoIP also has some disadvantages that you need to consider:

- **No guaranteed delivery**   VoIP does not guarantee delivery of IP packets over the Internet. For a digital transmission of data, this is no big deal; if a packet isn't confirmed as being received, it is simply retransmitted. For a real-time voice conversation, however, the loss of packets directly inhibits the conversation, and you can't go back in time to retransmit missing packets. (Over a private WAN, however, delivery can be guaranteed.)

- **Out-of-sequence packets**   Not only can IP packets simply fail to arrive at their destination on occasion, but sometimes they arrive out of sequence due to other Internet traffic and other reasons. This is fine for transmitting things such as files, because the packets can be reassembled on the other end in the proper sequence once they are all received. For a real-time application such as voice, however, having packets arrive out of sequence results in a hopelessly jumbled, and thus useless, transmission.

- **QoS not widely implemented**   Real-time uses of the Internet, such as VoIP or multimedia streaming and time-sensitive transmissions, should be given priority over transmissions that are not particularly time-sensitive, such as the transmission of an e-mail message. Fortunately, IP has a quality of service (QoS) field that enables the user to prioritize traffic for such reasons. However, QoS is not widely implemented on the Internet. Instead, QoS usually requires a private WAN connection between points in order to be guaranteed.

VoIP is a hot emerging technology that is virtually certain to become an important part of the Internet and most companies' networks. However, there is still much work to be done toward actually implementing this technology widely and solving the problems outlined in this section. In other words, if you're learning about networking, you should be aware of VoIP—what it is and what it does.

NOTE   There are a number of companies offering VoIP services for residential customers, including AT&T, Vonage, Verizon, and many cable television providers. These companies provide packages that allow virtually unlimited calling over an existing high-bandwidth Internet connection for as little as $30 additional per month. They often package the necessary VoIP hardware with a subscription agreement.

Comparing Important Proprietary Protocols

While Microsoft-based, Novell-based, and Apple-based networks can work with TCP/IP and all the previously discussed protocols, each type of network got its start supporting proprietary protocols unique to the company, and each of these protocols can still be found in current networks. All these companies have embraced TCP/IP and support it fully, both for servers and for network clients.

Novell networks originally used the Internetwork Packet Exchange/Sequenced Packet Exchange (IPX/SPX) protocols. These are not the same as TCP/IP, but they are comparable. IPX is analogous to IP, and SPX is analogous to TCP.

Microsoft networks were originally based on an IBM-developed protocol called Network Basic Input/Output System (NetBIOS). NetBIOS is a relatively high-level protocol that, in essence, extends the functionality of DOS to a network. Microsoft also used IBM's NetBIOS Extended User Interface (NetBEUI), an enhancement to NetBIOS.

Apple Macintosh computer networks originally supported only AppleTalk. The protocol was designed expressly for the purpose of sharing Apple LaserWriter printers within small workgroups using a low-bandwidth (230 Kbps originally) network media called LocalTalk. Over time, Apple extended AppleTalk somewhat to enable file sharing and other network functions. However, AppleTalk is still an extremely inefficient network protocol that, even over Ethernet (called EtherTalk in Apple's implementation), works slowly.

Novell's IPX/SPX

Novell's IPX/SPX protocol was originally a derivative of the Xerox Network Systems (XNS) architecture and closely resembles it. While IPX/SPX can be used on any of the popular network media (Ethernet, Token Ring, and so forth), it was originally designed for Ethernet networks and works best with that media. In fact, the IPX/SPX protocol depends on Ethernet MAC addresses for part of its own addresses. IPX/SPX addresses are dynamic and are automatically negotiated with the server at login, rather than being statically set, as is the case with TCP/IP without DHCP services.

An IPX/SPX network address is composed of both a 32-bit network address and a 48-bit node address. In addition, another 16 bits are used for a connection ID, which allows up to 65,000 unique connections between a client and a server. The address design of IPX/SPX theoretically allows for about 281 trillion nodes on each of 16 million networks.

IPX/SPX was originally designed only for LANs, but it has been enhanced to support WAN connections. While typically considered a "chatty" protocol that requires a lot of send/acknowledgment transactions, IPX/SPX has been enhanced with burst-mode capabilities, which increase the size of packets destined for a WAN and decrease the number of back-and-forth communications required. IPX/SPX can be routed, but only if the network includes an IPX/SPX-capable router.

NetBIOS and NetBEUI

IBM originally developed NetBIOS and NetBEUI to support small networks. Microsoft adopted the protocols as part of LAN Manager, a network operating system built on top of early versions of the OS/2 operating system.

Neither protocol is routable, so each is suitable only for small LANs that do not rely on routers between different LAN segments. However, NetBIOS can be encapsulated within TCP/IP packets on Windows networks using a service called NetBIOS over TCP/IP (abbreviated as NBT).

Microsoft LANs prior to Windows 2000 rely on a NetBIOS service called NetBIOS Names to identify each workstation uniquely. In a simple NetBIOS implementation, names are registered with all workstations through a broadcast message. If no computer has already registered a particular name, the name registration succeeds. In a more complex Windows-based network that also uses TCP/IP, however, the NetBIOS names resolve to TCP/IP addresses through the use of Windows Internet Name Service (WINS). The names can also be resolved using static name definition entries contained in a file called LMHOSTS (for LAN Manager HOSTS).

Because some older networking applications still use NetBIOS Names, either WINS or LMHOSTS allows such applications to continue to function in a TCP/IP-only network. As far as the application is concerned, it is still working with NetBIOS, while TCP/IP performs the actual work in the background.

AppleTalk

AppleTalk has been extended into AppleTalk Phase 2, which now allows routing of AppleTalk packets (assuming an AppleTalk Phase 2-capable router). The Phase 2 variant can run over Ethernet, Token Ring, or Apple's LocalTalk media. Under Ethernet, AppleTalk uses a variant of the 802.2 frame type called Ethernet Subnetwork Access Point (SNAP).

AppleTalk has an important history for Apple Macintosh networking, but Apple now fully supports and recommends TCP/IP for its computers.

Chapter Summary

This chapter is built on the knowledge you gained in earlier chapters, delving into various important protocols involved in virtually all networks, including the Internet. You learned primarily about the TCP/IP protocol, which has essentially displaced older protocols such as IPX/SPX and NetBIOS/NetBEUI (although these older protocols are still used in some circumstances). You also learned about some specific application-layer Internet protocols, such as SMTP, DHCP, and HTTP. It is vital that any networking professional understand these protocols.

It would be nice if the protocols discussed in this chapter were all you had to contend with, but, unfortunately, many more protocols exist. Some are specific to certain functions, such as remote access to a network, and are discussed in appropriate chapters within this book. Others are still being developed and are not a factor now but may be in the near future. You will certainly want to stay up-to-date with emerging protocols that may become important to networking.

The next chapter is about directory services, which make complex networks easier to use and administer.

CHAPTER 7 | Exploring Directory Services

In the early days of local area networks (LANs), finding server resources was simple. Most organizations started with just a file server and a print server or two, so knowing which files, printers, and other services were in which locations on the LAN was easy.

These days, the situation is considerably more complex. Even relatively small organizations might have multiple servers, all performing different jobs—storing different sets of files and providing different Internet or intranet services, such as e-mail servers, web hosting, database servers, network services, and so forth.

Directory services work to bring organization to this far-flung network clutter. In this chapter, you learn about what directory services do and how they work. You also learn about the directory services in use today and those slated for use in the near future. With directory services becoming more and more central to the administration of networks, learning this information becomes an increasingly important part of designing, deploying, and managing networks.

What Is a Directory Service?

In most networks, you optimize the function of different services by hosting them on different computers. Doing so makes sense. Putting all your services on one computer is a bit like placing all your eggs in one basket—if you drop the basket, you'll break all your eggs. Moreover, you can achieve optimal performance, more reliability, and higher security by segregating network services in various ways.

Most networks have quite a few services that need to be provided, and often these services run on different servers. Even a relatively simple network now offers the following services:

- File storage and sharing
- Printer sharing
- E-mail services
- Web hosting, both for the Internet and an intranet
- Database server services
- Specific application servers
- Internet connectivity
- Dial-in and dial-out services
- Fax services
- Domain Name System (DNS) service, Windows Internet Naming Service (WINS), and Dynamic Host Configuration Protocol (DHCP) services
- Centralized virus-detection services
- Backup and restore services

This is only a short list. Larger organizations have multiple servers sharing in each of these functions—with different services available through different means in each building or location—and might have additional services beyond those listed here.

All this complexity can quickly make a network chaotic to manage. If each one of the individual servers required separate administration (with, for instance, separate lists of users, passwords, groups, printers, network configurations, and so on), the job would become virtually impossible in no time.

Directory services were invented to bring organization to networks. Basically, directory services work just like a phone book. Instead of using a name to look up an address and phone number in a phone book, you query the directory service for a service name (such as the name of a network folder or a printer), and the directory service tells you where the service is located. You can also query directory services by property. For instance, if you query the directory service for all items that are "printers," it can return a complete list, no matter where the printers are located in the organization. Even better, directory services enable you to browse all the resources on a network easily, in one unified list organized in a tree structure.

One important advantage of directory services is that they eliminate the need to manage duplicates of anything on the network because the directory is automatically shared among all of the servers. For example, you don't need to maintain separate user lists on each server. Instead, you manage a single set of user accounts that exists in the directory service and then assign them various permissions to particular resources on any of the servers. Other resources work the same way and become centrally managed in the directory service. Not only does this mean that you have only one collection of objects to manage, but also that users have a much simpler network experience. From the users' perspective, they have only one network account with one password, and they don't need to worry about where resources are located or keep track of multiple passwords for different network services or servers.

NOTE In this chapter, the term *network resource* refers to any discrete resource on a network, such as a user account, security group definition, e-mail distribution list, storage volume, folder, or file. The term *directory* refers to the directory that a directory service uses, rather than a directory on a hard disk.

To provide redundancy, directory services usually run on multiple servers in an organization, with each of the servers having a complete copy of the entire directory service database. Because a directory service becomes central to the functioning of a network, this approach lets the network as a whole continue to operate if any single server with directory services on it crashes. Servers that do not actually host a copy of the directory still make use of it by communicating with the directory servers. For instance, if a user tries to open a file hosted on a server that doesn't actually host the directory service, the server will automatically query the directory service on another server to authenticate the user's access request. To the user, this happens behind the scenes.

You should know about five important directory services: Novell eDirectory, Microsoft's Windows NT domains, Microsoft's Active Directory, X.500 Directory Access Protocol, and Lightweight Directory Access Protocol. These are described later in this chapter.

Forests, Roots, Trees, and Leaves

One thing common to all directory services is a tree-based organization (with the tree usually depicted upside-down with the root at the top), somewhat similar to the organization of directories on a hard disk. A *forest* is a collection of trees managed collectively. At the top of each directory tree is the *root* entry, which contains other entries. These other entries can be containers or leaves. A *container object* is one that contains other objects, which can also include more containers and leaves. A *leaf object* represents an actual resource on the network, such as a workstation, printer, shared directory, file, or user account. Leaf objects cannot contain other objects. Figure 7-1 shows a typical directory tree.

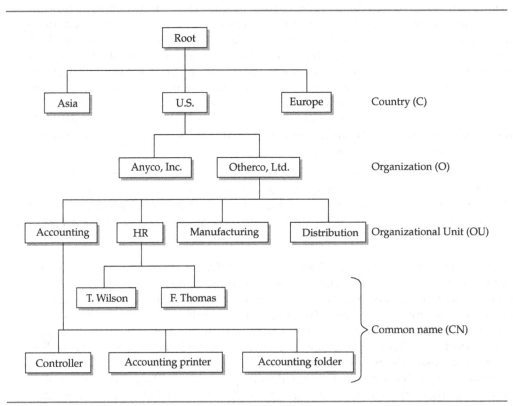

Figure 7-1. A typical directory tree

All the objects in a directory tree have *attributes* (sometimes called *properties*), which vary depending on the type of object to which the attribute is attached. For example, a *printer leaf object* might contain attributes that describe the printer, who can administer the printer, what the printer's name is on the network, and so forth. A *user account leaf object* might contain attributes that include the full name of the user account, its password, and resources that the user can access. The details of what attributes attach to what leaf or container objects vary among all the directory services, although they generally use similar attributes.

Department of Redundancy Department

Keeping directory services running is essential for any network that relies on them. Because they contain all details about accounts, resources, and security, the absence of directory services means the network won't work—at all! Since the directory service becomes so important to a network, you must protect them with some degree of redundancy. As mentioned earlier, keeping duplicate copies of the directory on multiple servers provides the necessary redundancy. This is done using one of two approaches:

- ■ In the *primary/backup model*, a single primary database contains the primary (or "real") directory on one server, while other servers hold one or more backup copies. If the primary copy stops working for some reason, the backups can continue to provide directory services to the network without the user even knowing that the primary copy isn't available. Windows NT domains use a primary/backup approach.

- ■ In the *multimaster model*, multiple directory servers exist, but they are all peers to one another. If one goes down, the other peers continue to operate normally. The advantage of the multimaster model is that each directory server can fully participate in doing the work of the directory service. Active Directory in Windows 2000 Server and later uses the multimaster approach.

Directory servers—whether they use the primary/backup or multimaster approach—must keep in sync with changes on the network. The separate databases are kept synchronized through a process called *replication*, in which changes to any of the individual directory databases are transparently updated to all the other directory service databases.

A potential problem exists with any replication process, though: If two changes are made to the same leaf object on two different directory servers and the changes are different, what does the system do when the changes "collide" during replication? The various directory services handle this problem in slightly different ways. In the case of Novell eDirectory, the timestamps of the changes drive which of two conflicting changes will win. (Because of this, servers running eDirectory must carefully keep their time synchronized; this synchronization is also handled during replication.) Microsoft's Active Directory doesn't use timestamps, but instead uses sequence numbers in a clever scheme that avoids the potential problems of a timestamp approach.

(Even though eDirectory servers synchronize their time, their time can still become out of sync between synchronizations.)

Some directory services also allow a concept called *partitioning*, in which different directory servers keep different parts of the entire directory tree. In this case, a controlling directory server usually manages the entire tree (called the *global catalog* in Active Directory), and then other directory servers can manage smaller pieces of the total tree. Partitioning is important for networks with multiple LANs connected by a wide area network (WAN). In such cases, you want to host a partition that relates to a particular LAN locally, yet still allow access to the entire tree for resources accessed over the WAN. Each LAN hosts its own partition, but can still access the total tree when needed. You arrange the partitions (and set the scheduled replication times) to make the best use of the WAN's performance, which usually is slower than that of a LAN.

Learning About Specific Directory Services

Quite a few different directory services are available. Choosing one usually goes hand in hand with choosing a main network operating system, although this isn't always the case. Both eDirectory and Active Directory can handle non-Novell and non-Microsoft servers, respectively. Consequently, even a network that currently uses mostly Windows servers might still rely on eDirectory for some things. Using a single directory service with different network operating systems often happens because an organization starts out favoring a particular network operating system and then later finds itself forced to support additional ones, but the organization still wants to maintain a coherent, single directory service to manage the network operating systems.

The following are the main directory services:

- *Novell eDirectory* (previously called Novell Directory Services, or NDS) is the network directory service that has been available for the longest time. eDirectory runs on NetWare 4.*x* and later servers, and is also available for other server operating systems (such as Solaris, Linux, and Windows), enabling you to use eDirectory as a single directory service for managing a multivendor network.

- *Windows NT domains* (introduced with Windows NT 4) are not actually complete directory services, but they provide some of the features and advantages of directory services.

- *Microsoft's Active Directory* debuted with the Windows 2000 Server line of products. This is a true directory service, and it brings the full features of a directory service to a network predominantly built using Windows servers. Active Directory is probably the most prevalent directory service in use today.

- *X.500 Directory Access Protocol* (DAP) is an international standard directory service that is full of features. However, X.500 provides so many features that its overhead makes deploying and managing it prohibitive. Consequently, X.500 is in an interesting position: It is an important standard, yet, paradoxically, it is not actually used.

■   The *Lightweight Directory Access Protocol* (LDAP) was developed by a consortium of vendors as a subset of X.500 to offer an alternative with less complexity than X.500. LDAP is in wide use for e-mail directories and is suitable for other directory service tasks. The most recent versions of eDirectory and Active Directory are compatible with LDAP.

These are the predominant directory services that you will encounter, although others exist. For instance, a number of companies offer different software that provides LDAP-compliant directory services on different platforms.

eDirectory

Novell eDirectory has been available since 1993, introduced as NDS as part of NetWare 4.*x*. This product was a real boon and was rapidly implemented in Novell networks, particularly in larger organizations that had many NetWare servers and desperately needed its capabilities. eDirectory is a reliable, robust directory service.

eDirectory uses a primary/backup approach to directory servers and also allows partitioning of the tree. In addition to running on Novell network operating systems, eDirectory is available for Windows, Solaris, AIX, and Linux systems. The product's compatibility with such a variety of systems makes it a good choice for managing all these platforms under a single directory structure.

You manage the eDirectory tree from a client computer logged in to the network with administrative privileges. You can use a graphical tool designed to manage the tree, such as Novell Identity Manager, or other tools that mimic the look and feel of the operating system on which they run and that are also available from Novell.

The eDirectory tree contains a number of different object types. The standard directory service types—countries, organizations, and organizational units—are included. The system also has objects to represent NetWare security groups, NetWare servers, and NetWare server volumes. eDirectory can manage more than a billion objects in a tree.

Windows NT Domains

The Windows NT domain model breaks an organization into chunks called *domains*, all of which are part of an organization. The domains are usually organized geographically, which helps minimize domain-to-domain communication requirements across WAN links, although you're free to organize domains as you wish. Each domain is controlled by a *primary domain controller* (PDC), which might have one or more *backup domain controllers* (BDCs) to kick in if the PDC fails.

All changes within the domain are made to the PDC, which then replicates those changes to any BDCs. BDCs are read-only, except for valid updates received from the PDC. In case of a PDC failure, BDCs automatically continue authenticating users. To make administrative changes to a domain that suffers PDC failure, any of the BDCs can be *promoted* to PDC. Once the PDC is ready to come back online, the promoted BDC can be *demoted* back to BDC status.

Windows NT domains can be organized into one of four domain models:

- **Single domain**   In this model, only one domain contains all network resources.

- **Master domain**   The master model usually puts users at the top-level domain and then places network resources, such as shared folders or printers, in lower-level domains (called *resource domains*). In this model, the resource domains trust the master domain.

- **Multiple master domain**   This is a slight variation on the master domain model, in which users might exist in multiple master domains, all of which trust one another, and in which resources are located in resource domains, all of which trust all the master domains.

- **Complete trust**   This variation of the single-domain model spreads users and resources across all domains, which all trust each other.

You choose an appropriate domain model depending on the physical layout of the network, the number of users to be served, and other factors. (If you're planning a domain model, you should review the white papers on Microsoft's web site for details on planning large domains, because the process can be complex.)

Explicit trust relationships must be maintained between domains using the master or multiple master domain model, and must be managed on each domain separately. Maintaining these relationships is one of the biggest difficulties in the Windows NT domain structure approach, at least for larger organizations. If you have 100 domains, you must manage the 99 possible trust relationships for each domain, for a total of 9,900 trust relationships. For smaller numbers of domains (for example, fewer than 10 domains), management of the trust relationships is less of a problem, although it can still cause difficulties.

Active Directory

Windows NT domains work relatively well for smaller networks, but they can become difficult to manage for larger networks. Moreover, the system is not nearly as comprehensive as, for example, eDirectory. Microsoft recognized this problem and developed a directory service called Active Directory, which is a comprehensive directory service that runs on Windows 2000 Server and later. Active Directory is fully compatible with LDAP (versions 2 and 3) and also with the Domain Name System (DNS) used on the Internet.

Active Directory uses a peer approach to domain controllers; all domain controllers are full participants at all times. As mentioned earlier in this chapter, this arrangement is called *multimaster* because there are many "master" domain controllers but no backup controllers.

Active Directory is built on a structure that allows "trees of trees," which is called a *forest*. Each tree is its own domain and has its own domain controllers. Within a domain, separate organizational units are allowed to make administration easier and more logical. Trees are then aggregated into a larger forest structure. According to Microsoft, Active Directory can handle millions of objects through this approach.

Active Directory does not require the management of trust relationships, except when connected to Windows NT 4.*x* servers that are not using Active Directory. Otherwise, all domains within a tree have automatic trust relationships.

X.500

The X.500 standard was developed jointly by the International Telecommunications Union (ITU) and the International Standards Organization (ISO). The standard defines a directory service that can be used for the entire Internet. Because of its broad applicability, the X.500 specification is too complex for most organizations to implement. Also, because of its design, it is intended to publish specific organizational directory entries across the Internet, which is something most companies would not want to do. Just the same, the X.500 standard is extremely important, and most directory services mimic or incorporate parts of it in some fashion.

The X.500 directory tree starts with a root, just like the other directory trees, and then breaks down into country (C), organization (O), organizational unit (OU), and common name (CN) fields. To specify an X.500 address fully, you provide five fields, as in the following:

```
CN=user name, OU=department, OU=division, O=organization, C=country
```

For example, you might configure the fields as follows:

```
CN=Bruce Hallberg, OU=Networking Books, OU=Computer Books, O=McGraw-Hill,
C=USA
```

LDAP

To address the complexity problems involved with full X.500 DAP, a consortium of companies came up with a subset of X.500, called LDAP. LDAP's advocates claim that it provides 90 percent of the power of X.500, but at only 10 percent of the processing cost. LDAP runs over TCP/IP and uses a client/server model. Its organization is much the same as that of X.500, but with fewer fields and fewer functions.

LDAP is covered predominantly by RFC 1777 (for version 2) and RFC 2251 (for version 3). (Some other RFCs also describe aspects of LDAP.) The LDAP standard describes not only the layout and fields within an LDAP directory, but also the methods to be used when a person logs in to a server that uses LDAP, or queries or updates the LDAP directory information on an LDAP server. (Because directory services might fulfill many simultaneous authentications, run simultaneous queries, and accept simultaneous updates, it is important that these methods be clearly defined to avoid collisions and other potentially corrupting uses of the directory by client applications and administrative tools.)

NOTE Many of the standards on the Internet are controlled by documents called Requests for Comments (RFCs). These are documents that describe a proposed standard and are submitted to the Internet Engineering Task Force group. You can read more about this group, as well as peruse any of the networking RFCs you see mentioned in this book (or elsewhere), on the group's home page at http://www.ietf.org.

An LDAP tree starts with a root, which then contains entries. Each entry can have one or more *attributes*. Each of these attributes has both a *type* and *values* associated with it. One example is the common name (CN), which contains at least two attributes: FirstName and Surname. All attributes in LDAP use the text string data type. Entries are organized into a tree and managed geographically and then within each organization. The following four basic models describe the LDAP standard:

■ **Information model**   This model defines the structure of the data stored in the directory. It describes a number of aspects of the directory, including the schema, classes, attributes, attribute syntax, and entries. The directory's *schema* is the template for the directory and its entries. *Classes* are categories to which all entries are attached. *Attributes* are items of data that describe the classes, such as CN and OU. The *syntax* for the attributes specifies exactly how attributes are named and stored, and what sort of data they are allowed to contain (such as numbers, string text, dates and times, and so forth). Finally, *entries* are distinct pieces of data, like objects, that can be either a container or a leaf.

NOTE Microsoft uses nomenclature to describe LDAP that differs from the terms defined in the RFCs. Most notably, Microsoft calls an *entry* an *object*, and calls an *attribute* a *property*. These names refer to the same things, and you should be aware of this when reading the RFCs or other documents about LDAP and comparing the information to that found in documents from Microsoft.

■ **Naming model**   This model describes how to reference and organize the data. It defines the names that serve as primary keys for entries in the directory: *distinguished names* (DNs), which are full names of entries, as well as *relative distinguished names* (RDNs), which are components of DNs. Each component of the DN—such as the CD, OU, or O entries—is an RDN. The following is an example of an LDAP DN:

```
CN=Bruce Hallberg, OU=Networking Books, OU=Computer Books,
O=McGraw-Hill, C=USA.
```

■ **Functional model**   This model describes how to work with the data. It defines how LDAP accomplishes three types of operations: authentication, interrogation, and updates. *Authentication* is the process by which users prove their identity to the directory. *Interrogation* is the process by which the information in the directory is queried. *Updates* are operations that post changes to the directory.

■ **Security model** This model defines how to keep the data in the directory secure. For most implementations of LDAP, a security protocol called Simple Authentication and Security Layer (SASL) is used. RFC 2222 describes SASL.

One nice feature of LDAP is that an organization can build a global directory structure using a feature called *referral,* where LDAP directory queries that are managed by a different LDAP server are transparently routed to that server. Because each LDAP server knows its parent LDAP server and its child servers, any user anywhere in the network can access the entire LDAP tree. In fact, the users won't even know they are accessing different servers in different locales.

Chapter Summary

In this chapter, you learned about both the importance of directory services and the factors driving that importance. You also learned how directory services work, what they accomplish, and those common features found in almost all directory services. Finally, the most important directory services were each reviewed, including Novell's eDirectory, Microsoft's domain service, and Active Directory service.

The next chapter continues the discussions about essential network technologies and services by teaching you about remote access services, in which far-flung users can access LANs from anywhere in the world. Implementing a good remote access system that everyone is happy with is one of the most difficult things to do—especially for large organizations with many different needs—so a variety of approaches are discussed.

CHAPTER 8 | Connections from Afar: Remote Network Access

In the preceding chapters, you learned about networking systems together through a local area network (LAN) and through a wide area network (WAN), and about the technologies that go into both types of networks. You also need to know about another important type of network connection: remote access to a network. With today's travel-happy corporate cultures, and with companies needing to support such things as working from home and small remote offices, remote access has become more important than ever. Unfortunately, it can be a difficult part of a network to get right, as you will see in this chapter.

One of the big problems with remote access is that it can seem as though all the remote users have different requirements, the various solutions address different needs, and none of those solutions takes care of *all* the needs. Finding solid solutions that meet those needs is usually nontrivial and requires a fair amount of time and effort. This chapter describes how you might analyze your company's needs and then discusses the remote access technologies that can provide a solution (or solutions) for your network.

Determining Remote Access Needs

Every company has a different mix of remote users, and their specific needs may vary from company to company. Moreover, even when needs are identical, the solutions you employ might change based on other criteria. For instance, you might handle access to an accounting system from a remote location differently, depending on whether it's a client/server or a monolithic application.

Understanding Application Implications for Remote Access

Client/server applications consist of processes (programs) that run on both the server side and the client side, and work in concert. For example, a database server performs queries for the client and then transmits to the client only the results of that query. The client's job is just to display the results and maybe format them for printing.

A monolithic application, on the other hand, performs all of its work on one computer, typically the client computer. The server for a monolithic application serves up only the files needed for the application to run and the data files that the application manipulates.

Generally, client/server applications require much less bandwidth to work at acceptable speeds than monolithic applications. A slow network connection might be adequate for a client/server application, such as an accounting system, whereas that connection would be totally inadequate for that same application designed to be monolithic.

What Types of Remote Users Do You Need to Support?

Users who require remote access generally fall into one of the following four categories:

- Broad traveler
- Narrow traveler
- Remote office user
- Remote office group

Each category of remote user has different needs, and different technologies and remote access solutions are often required to satisfy these needs completely. Your first step in finding a remote access solution is to determine which categories of remote users you must support. So, let's look at each of these remote access user categories.

The *broad traveler* is the most common type of remote access user. This is someone who normally is based in an office that has LAN access, but also travels on business. Travel takes this person to virtually any place in the world, so the traveler must contend with different telephone systems, long-distance carriers, and other geographic challenges (see Figure 8-1). Often, this type of user mostly needs e-mail access, with occasional access to stored or e-mailed files. The user might normally use a desktop computer on the LAN but have a notebook computer for traveling, might use a single notebook both on the LAN and when traveling, might check out notebook computers from a shared pool when travel needs arise, or might even rent a notebook computer for an occasional travel need. These different approaches further complicate providing services to the broad traveler.

The *narrow traveler* is someone who travels to relatively few locations, such as from corporate headquarters to the company's manufacturing plants or distribution centers. Since you can predict the sites from which the user might need to access data, local

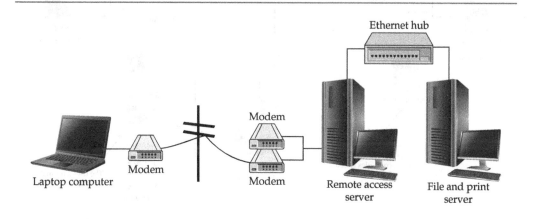

Figure 8-1.   A typical remote access session

support may be available to help. For instance, you might have a way for the user to log in to the distribution center's LAN and access e-mail and files at the headquarters location through an existing WAN link, as shown in Figure 8-2. This type of user needs e-mail, file access, and possibly access to centralized applications, such as an accounting system.

The *remote office user* is in a single location and needs access to the corporate LAN for e-mail and application access (see Figure 8-3). This person usually does not need file access, except to send files through the e-mail system, because this person maintains local file storage. This user is in a single location, so you can pursue certain high-speed links that may not be feasible for the travelers. A person telecommuting from home would fall into the category of remote office user.

Sometimes a small group (two to five people) stationed in a remote location needs certain services from the corporate LAN. These services are not cost-effective for this group to have locally, yet these users have a small local LAN for printer and file sharing, as illustrated in Figure 8-4. These users fall into the *remote office group* category, which needs a combination of services. They combine aspects of both remote LAN users and remote office users. They usually require a mixture of both types of solutions for proper support.

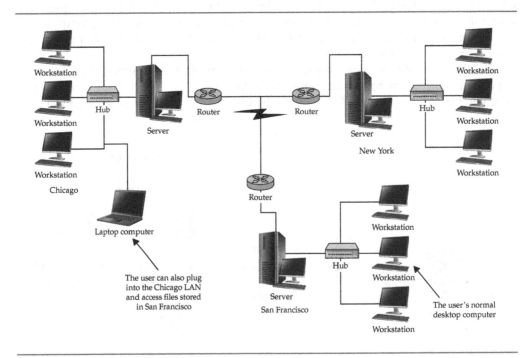

Figure 8-2.   A WAN used by a "narrow traveler"

Figure 8-3.   A remote office user's network setup

Figure 8-4.   Supporting a small remote office that requires LAN access

You generally need different strategies to support these various types of users. Of course, if you're working in a small company, you likely won't have to support all these categories right off the bat.

What Types of Remote Access Are Required?

Before implementing any remote access system, you must define clearly the types of remote access required by the users in the company. The following are some examples of remote access needs:

- Easy remote access to e-mail and to files stored in e-mail
- Remote access to stored private or shared files on the LAN
- Remote access to a centralized application, such as an accounting system or a sales order system
- Remote access to groupware programs or custom applications
- Internet access
- Intranet/extranet access, including any hosted web-based applications on those systems
- Remote access to any of the previous features from a fixed location, such as a remote sales office
- Remote access to any of the previous features from anywhere in the world

To understand your specific remote access support needs, interview all the potential users (or at least a representative subset) and find out how to categorize them, as described in the previous section. Chances are that you must support remote access through more than one mechanism. How you categorize the users and their needs will suggest which mechanisms make sense.

When you interview the users, carefully probe all possible needs. For example, if you ask them if they need remote access to the files stored in their LAN directories and they reply, "Not really," that's not an adequate answer. You need to pin them down by asking questions such as, "Will you *ever* need remote access to files? What if you had only e-mail access? Could your assistant e-mail you any needed files?"

Once you have come up with different remote access needs in your company, try to survey the users in writing to inquire about their specific needs. Not only should you get less ambiguous answers, but you also get important documentation to justify the expenses and effort in acquiring and setting up the remote access systems needed.

How Much Bandwidth Do You Need?

When examining remote access needs, you need to estimate bandwidth requirements and tolerances for the different users. This is important for planning and also for appropriately setting user expectations. For example, if salespeople want minute-to-minute access to a sales-tracking system and also frequently want to download large file packages to use for quotations, you might need to explain the possible bandwidth limitations for the method they are using to obtain those services to set their expectations. Or you can find different solutions that are consistent with the amount of bandwidth you can offer.

You can estimate a particular application program's bandwidth requirements by actually measuring the amount of bandwidth that application uses. On the LAN, you can monitor the amount of data being sent to a particular node that uses the application in the way it would be used remotely. You can measure the data in a number of ways. For a Windows PC, you can run System Monitor or Performance Monitor on the client and look at the network traffic that the PC is consuming (see Figure 8-5). You can also measure the volume of data from the server. For a Windows server, you can use Performance Monitor to measure bytes transmitted to and from the client.

If the bandwidth requirements of an application are simply too great to handle over the type of remote connection that you have available (such as a slow cellular modem connection), you need to explore other alternatives. These include using a remote control solution (discussed later in this chapter) or using the application in a different way. For example, you might load the application's program files onto the remote computer rather than use it across the LAN. Also, perhaps the user does not need the data to be updated so frequently, and you can set up a procedure whereby the user receives weekly data updates on a CD-R disc or an overnight download.

The ways that you can satisfy remote access needs are virtually limitless. However, the key is to assess those needs carefully and to work creatively, given your available or proposed remote access technologies.

Figure 8-5.   Using Windows System Monitor to look at the bandwidth that an application is using

Learning Remote Access Technologies

A variety of different ways exist to accomplish remote access connections for users. Sometimes these different technologies are appropriate for some users but not for others. Sometimes the choices you have are restricted by how the remote user needs to access the data. For example, a remote user at a single location can fairly easily set up a high-speed link to the corporate LAN, while a traveling remote user might be limited to using cellular modems and even dial-up telephone connections in some parts of the world.

The following sections discuss different techniques and technologies, along with the pros and cons of each. The ones you implement depend on the needs you've identified, your budget, and the existing infrastructure of your network.

Remote Node vs. Remote Control

Remote users can connect to a network in two basic ways: remote node and remote control. A *remote node connection* is one in which the remote computer becomes a node on the network. Data flows between the remote node and the network much as it would for a LAN-connected user, albeit usually at much slower rates. When you connect to an Internet Service Provider (ISP) to access the Internet, you are using a remote node connection.

A *remote control connection* is one in which a remote user takes control of another computer directly connected to the LAN, with only the screen, keyboard, and mouse information being transmitted through the connection. Because the computer hosting the remote control service is directly connected to the LAN, its network performance is just as fast as that of any other LAN workstation. The information actually transmitted—the screen information, keyboard data, and mouse data—usually doesn't require much bandwidth. (One exception to this rule is a highly graphical application, such as a computer-aided design program.) Remote control connections also have ways to transfer files back and forth from the remote computer to the controlled computer, so files can still be downloaded from the LAN to the remote computer and vice versa.

Remote control is accomplished using special applications designed for this purpose. You run the remote control software on both the LAN-connected computer and the remote computer. The connection is established over a dial-up line or through the Internet.

Two types of remote control applications are available. The first runs on a single computer and supports a single remote computer at a time. pcAnywhere and GoToMyPC are examples of this type. Another type allows multiple sessions to run on a single computer, so you can allow more than one user making use of a single computer connected to the LAN. Windows NT Terminal Server, Windows Terminal Services, and Citrix XenServer are examples of this type. The multiuser solutions use the LAN computer's multitasking capabilities to construct multiple virtual PCs, windows, and desktops, sort of like a mainframe with multiple terminal sessions.

Any of the remote connection technologies can work with both remote node and remote control. You can connect to a remote control system through modems connected directly to the remote control computer, through Integrated Services Digital Network (ISDN) lines, over the Internet, or even over a LAN or WAN link.

How do you know whether to choose remote node or remote control connections? Consider these points:

- When a remote user needs only LAN file access and e-mail access, a remote node connection can meet these needs and is often simpler to set up and maintain on both sides of the connection.

- If a remote user needs to run an application that is LAN-connected, choose remote control. A few applications might be able to run reasonably well over a remote node connection, provided the application itself is already installed on the remote computer and the application must access only relatively small amounts of data through the remote link. For example, accessing e-mail through Microsoft Outlook works fine over a remote node connection, provided the remote users already have Outlook installed on their local computer.

- Many applications are now web-enabled, so a remote user can use a web browser to access and use such applications. These types of applications run equally well—more or less—over a remote node or remote control connection. For example, Microsoft Exchange Server supports a number of connection types, including web access to mailboxes and calendars, through a feature called Outlook Web Access. Many client/server accounting systems are also starting to implement web access.

- If you need to maintain an application directly for the users, remote control might be the way to go because it leaves the application on the LAN-connected machine, where you can easily access it to make configuration changes or perform other maintenance. The remote user runs only the remote control software and instantly benefits from any work you do on the LAN-connected machine. This capability can provide a real advantage if your network's users are not comfortable doing their own maintenance or troubleshooting on the software. With such a connection, you can more easily handle any problems that arise, without needing to travel to some remote location or requiring users to ship their computers to you for repair or maintenance.

Remote control is the best bet when the remote users need to access applications that don't work well over lower-bandwidth connections. And because most applications don't run well over slower connections, remote users will usually find that a LAN-connected application works better with remote control than with remote node.

Whether you choose remote node or remote control, you then must determine how the users will connect to the LAN. Almost always, this is done through a Virtual Private Network connection, discussed in the next section.

Virtual Private Networks

A Virtual Private Network (VPN) is a network link formed through the Internet between the remote user—who is directly connected to an ISP—and the company LAN. A VPN connection is carried over a shared or public network—which is almost always the Internet.

VPNs use sophisticated packet encryption and other technologies, so the link from the user to the LAN is secure, even though it may be carried over a public network. VPN connections cost much less than dedicated connections, such as the WAN technologies discussed in Chapter 5, because they take advantage of the cost efficiencies of the Internet without compromising security.

VPN solutions range from simple ones that can be implemented on a Windows server essentially for free—using the Remote Access Service (RAS) included with Windows NT Server or the equivalent Routing and Remote Access Service (RRAS) in Windows 2000 Server or later—to stand-alone specialized VPN routers that can support hundreds of users. Figure 8-6 shows how a VPN connection works.

NOTE   Windows Server 2008 and 2012 also include a feature for remote access called DirectAccess. It requires that the remote computer be a member of the Active Directory domain. In Windows Server 2008, RRAS and DirectAccess cannot coexist on the same server in the domain. However, Windows Server 2012 brought a host of improvements to DirectAccess, including a new unified RRAS and DirectAccess server role that can run on a single server and simplifies administration.

Figure 8-6.   A typical VPN connection

VPN connections are used in two important ways:

- To form WAN connections using VPN technology between two networks that might be thousands of miles apart but that each have some way of accessing the Internet. These are usually called site-to-site VPN connections, and are configured on a capable router on each end.

- To form remote access connections that enable remote users to access the company's network through the Internet.

The emphasis in this chapter is on remote access, but it's important to know that VPNs support WAN connections in much the same way as they support a remote access connection. The main difference for a WAN VPN connection is that it connects two networks together, rather than a user and a network, and relies on different hardware (typically) than a remote access connection uses. A WAN VPN connection takes advantage of the existing Internet connection for both LANs and might run virtually 24 hours a day. A remote access connection, on the other hand, is usually formed when needed and uses less expensive hardware on the remote side, such as a dial-up modem or perhaps a higher-speed Internet connection, such as *x*DSL, ISDN, or cable modem.

TIP   In some circumstances, a VPN might even be an appropriate way to segregate users in a single location from other users by using the company's intranet to host the VPN tunnel. Such a scheme might be appropriate, for example, if one group of users accesses data that is so sensitive that it must be separated from the rest of the company in some fashion. In such cases, the sensitive network can be separated from the corporate LAN, except for a firewall that allows VPN connections from the sensitive LAN to the corporate LAN, but not vice versa. This configuration would still allow users on the sensitive LAN to access general corporate network services.

A VPN connection has several requirements:

- Both sides of the VPN connection must be connected to the Internet, usually using the Point-to-Point Protocol (PPP). (Other public or private networks can also carry VPNs, but this discussion will stick with the Internet because it's the most frequently used network for this purpose.)

- Both sides must have a networking protocol in common. This protocol is usually TCP/IP, but can also be IPX, NetBEUI, or AppleTalk.

- Both sides must establish a tunnel through their existing PPP connections through which their data packets will pass. The tunnel is formed using a tunneling protocol.

- Both sides must agree on an encryption technique to use with the data traversing the tunnel. A variety of different encryption techniques are available.

So, both sides of a VPN connection must be running compatible VPN software using compatible protocols. For a remote access VPN solution, the software you install depends on the VPN itself. Dedicated VPN solutions also sell client software that you can distribute to your users. Usually, this software carries a per-copy charge, typically around $25 to $50 per remote computer supported. (Some VPN solutions include unlimited client licenses, but the VPN device is licensed to accept only a certain number of connections at a time.)

If you are using a Windows server and RRAS service on the server, and some version of Windows on the remote computer, you can take advantage of the VPN software included for free with those network operating systems. However, this software must still be set up on each client computer.

VPN Protocols

The three most popular tunneling protocols used for VPNs are Point-to-Point Tunneling Protocol (PPTP), Layer 2 Tunneling Protocol (L2TP), and Internet Protocol Security (IPSec). PPTP is a Microsoft-designed protocol that can handle IP, IPX, NetBEUI, and AppleTalk packets. PPTP is included with Windows, starting with Windows 95, and is also supported by Windows RRAS (a free upgrade to RAS) and by later versions of Windows servers. For a Windows-oriented network, PPTP is the way to go.

L2TP is a newer protocol that is an Internet Engineering Task Force standard. It will probably become the most widely supported tunneling protocol because it operates at Layer 2 of the OSI model, and thus can handle all Layer 3 protocols, such as IP, IPX, and AppleTalk.

IPSec, while probably the most secure tunneling protocol, seems to be most popular for LAN-to-LAN VPNs and for UNIX-oriented VPNs, due to its reliance on IP. IPSec is a Layer 3 protocol and is limited to handling only IP traffic.

NOTE   While IPSec works only with IP packets, an L2TP VPN can also carry the resulting IPSec packets because they can be handled like the other major Layer 3 packets, such as IP, IPX, and AppleTalk packets.

Types of VPNs

Four major types of VPNs are in use today. One type uses a router with added VPN capabilities. VPN routers not only can handle normal routing duties, but they can also be configured to form VPNs over the Internet to other similar routers located on remote networks. This method is used to create VPN WAN links over the Internet, usually between multiple company locations.

Another major type of VPN is one built into a firewall device. Most popular firewalls, such as Check Point's Firewall-1, Cisco's ASA product line, or WatchGuard's Firebox, serve not only as firewall devices, but also as VPN hosts. Firewall VPNs can be used both to support remote users and to provide WAN VPN links. The benefit of using a firewall-based VPN is that you can administer your network's security—including both standard firewall security and VPN security—entirely within the firewall. For example, you could configure the firewall to allow connections to the network only when they are made as part of a valid VPN connection.

The third major type of VPN includes those offered as part of a network operating system. The best examples of this type are Windows RRAS and Novell's BorderManager software. These VPNs are most often used to support remote access, and they are generally the least expensive to purchase and install.

The fourth major type is the SSL VPN, a relatively new category. This is actually my overall favorite for remote access support. An SSL VPN takes advantage of the Secure Sockets Layer (SSL) encryption technology built into most web browsers to offer VPN services through the web browser. SSL is the same technology used to encrypt information in web pages that use the "https://" prefix, such as for shopping or online banking web sites.

SSL VPNs bring a number of attractive benefits to supporting remote access users:

- No client software needs to be installed on the remote computer, except for usually an ActiveX or Java add-in that installs into the browser automatically.

- There is essentially no configuration or management required on the remote system. This is an important point, because most VPN client software can be problematic for helpdesk workers to support.

- Provided the users know the web address of the SSL VPN server and have the correct information to authenticate (log in) to the system, they can log in from almost any Internet-connected computer in the world and access a wide range of network services through simple web pages.

- Because many common functions, such as file management, can be performed using web pages, SSL VPNs work much better over lower-bandwidth connections than other VPN alternatives. HTML was designed to be stingy in its use of network bandwidth, so many tasks that are slow over a traditional VPN connection are much faster with an SSL VPN.

- Most SSL VPNs, in addition to their web-based access features, allow the user to start a remote node connection on demand, and this remote node connection runs using automatically installed and configured browser plug-ins.

SSL VPNs are typically offered as an appliance—a rack-mountable piece of equipment that contains all of the hardware and software needed to run the VPN. They can vary quite a bit in price, depending on the number of simultaneous users they can support.

At the time of this writing, there are a number of SSL VPN vendors. The pioneer in this space is the NetScreen product family from Juniper Networks (which acquired a product originally launched by a company called Neoteris, which pioneered SSL VPNs). Another leader is the FirePass line of products from F5 Networks. AEP Networks, SonicWALL, and Nokia are some other firms that offer SSL VPNs. Since this product area is evolving rapidly, you should conduct a careful search for products that meet your needs.

To give you an idea of how an SSL VPN looks to a remote access user, some screens of a demo version of F5 Network's FirePass 4000 are shown in this section. Figure 8-7 shows a typical login screen after browsing to the SSL VPN's URL. (If you deploy an SSL VPN, this screen would be customized with your own company's logo and other information.)

SSL VPNs can authenticate users through a variety of different techniques, including the following:

■ Through user names and passwords defined in the SSL VPN for each user.

■ Through integration with an existing authentication system, such as Windows Active Directory. Choosing this option lets remote users use their normal network user name and password, and the SSL VPN then integrates with the preexisting authentication system on the network.

Figure 8-7.   An SSL VPN login screen

■ Through the integration of a two-factor authentication system. Two-factor authentication systems usually include a small device for each user that displays a number that changes every minute or so. Users log in by typing the number on the device at the time they are logging on, plus an additional number that is known only to them (sort of like an ATM PIN). Two-factor authentication systems are extremely secure, because the devices use a randomized sequence of numbers known only to a secure server installed in the network.

Once users log in to an SSL VPN, they are shown a home page that displays all of the connection options available to them, such as the example shown in Figure 8-8. The choices available to a remote user may include the following:

■ Access to a remote node connection through the SSL VPN

■ Access to other web servers on the company's network, such as a corporate intranet site, which are not normally accessible through the Internet

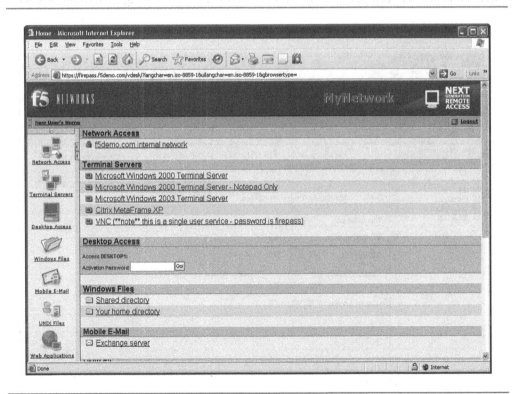

Figure 8-8.   A sample user's home page on the SSL VPN

- Access to e-mail, either through an application like Web Outlook or through a web-enabled e-mail client provided by the SSL VPN

- The ability to perform web-based file management through the SSL VPN; files that are managed might be hosted on Windows- or UNIX-based servers

- Access to shared corporate applications that have been set up to work through the SSL VPN, such as an accounting system

- Access to Windows Terminal Services or Citrix sessions via the SSL VPN

- Access to mainframe terminal sessions

While many of these choices are important for companies, the mainstay of remote access is letting remote users access e-mail and files stored on the network. SSL VPNs provide web-based access to many different types of e-mail servers. They also include the ability to manage files and directories through a web interface, such as the one shown in Figure 8-9. In this example, the user can select files in the left pane and can then choose to download, add to a download cart, view within the web browser, rename, or even delete files. The user can also manage folders and upload new files. All file access follows network permissions granted to the user that is logged in to the SSL VPN.

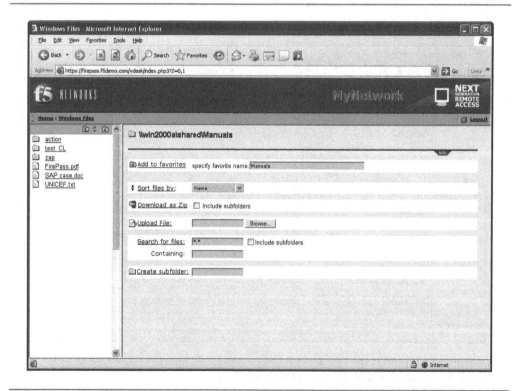

Figure 8-9.   A folder containing several files that can be managed

Chapter Summary

Most network administrators would agree that supporting remote access is one of the trickiest parts of managing any network. Many factors come together to make this so. You can support remote connections in a number of ways. Most remote connection speeds have lower bandwidth than remote users would like. Many remote users are often important people in the company, and various problems are introduced with any connection made over a distance. Still, remote access is an important network service, and its benefits to the company justify most levels of effort to make it reliable and work right.

Use the information you learned in this chapter to assess your own company's remote access requirements, to learn what your users actually need, and to start searching among different possible solutions for the ones that make the most sense for your situation. You should also consider whether you need to support more than one type of solution.

The next chapter talks about technologies and techniques that can keep a network's information safe and from falling into the wrong hands. Network security, when done right, shouldn't require much of your time to maintain. However, you do need to spend enough time and effort when you set up a network to ensure the network's security is strong from the beginning.

CHAPTER 9 | Securing Your Network

Most networking tasks are relatively straightforward. Do you want a new file and print server? You install it and set it up, and it either works or it doesn't. If it doesn't work, you proceed to troubleshoot it, fix any issues, and ultimately complete the task. Network security, on the other hand, is a horse of a different color. You can *never* really finish the project of securing a network, and you can *never* be certain that a network is completely secure. How much money you invest in securing a network, how much time you devote to the job, and how much fancy security hardware and software you install doesn't matter—no network is ever completely secure. Having said that, network security is one of the most important jobs facing any network administrator. Good network security helps prevent the following:

- Company secrets, such as proprietary designs or processes, falling into the wrong hands (both internally and externally)
- Personal information about employees falling into the wrong hands
- Loss of important information and software
- Loss of use of the network itself or any part of the network
- Corruption or inappropriate modification of important data

These are just some of the more important losses that network security should try to prevent. If you spend any time thinking about all the information that is stored on and that flows through the networks with which you work (and you *should* spend time thinking about this), you'll probably come up with additional dangers to avoid.

This chapter provides an overview of the subject of network security. Its aim is to familiarize you with important network security ideas and concepts, as well as various technologies involved in network security. If you are responsible for a network's security, you should pursue more detailed information, and you should also seriously consider hiring a specialist on this subject to help you secure your network. Even if you don't have the primary responsibility of keeping your network secure, the security of the network is everyone's job. If you're an IT professional, security is an even more important part of your job.

Understanding Internal Security

Internal security is the process of securing your network from internal threats, which are generally much more common than external threats. Examples of internal threats include the following:

- Internal users inappropriately accessing information such as payroll records, accounting records, or business development information.
- Internal users accessing other users' files to which they should not have access.
- Internal users impersonating other users and causing mischief, such as sending e-mail under another person's name.

- Internal users accessing systems to carry out criminal activities, such as embezzling funds.

- Internal users compromising the security of the network, such as by accidentally (or deliberately) introducing viruses to the network. (Viruses are discussed in their own section later in this chapter.)

- Internal users "sniffing" packets on the network to discover user accounts and passwords.

To deal with threats such as these, you need to manage the network's security diligently. You should assume that in the population of internal users, at least some exist who have the requisite sophistication to explore security holes in the network and that at least a few of those might, at some point, try to do so.

 NOTE One of the more unpleasant parts of managing security is that you need to expect the worst of people, and then you must take steps to prevent those actions you expect. In other words, a certain amount of paranoia is required. It's not a pleasant mindset, but it is required to do a good job in the security arena. Remember, too, that you're likely to get better results if you hire an outside firm to help manage the network's security. Not only should the outside firm have a higher skill level in this area, but its workers will be used to thinking as security people, and they will have invaluable experience gained from solving security problems at other companies. Perhaps even more important, using an external firm doesn't put employees in the position of being in an adversarial relationship with other employees.

Account Security

Account security refers to the process of managing the user accounts enabled on the network. A number of tasks are required to manage user accounts properly, and the accounts should be periodically audited (preferably by a different person than the one who manages them daily) to ensure that no holes exist. Following are a number of general steps you should take to manage general account security:

- Most network operating systems start up with a user account called Guest. You should remove this account immediately because it is the frequent target of crackers (a *hacker* is a person who likes to explore and understand systems, while a *cracker* is a person who breaks into systems with malicious intent). You should also avoid creating accounts that are obviously for testing purposes, such as Test, Generic, and so forth.

- Most network operating systems start up with a default name for the administrative account. Under Windows server operating systems, the account is called Administrator; under NetWare, it is called either Supervisor or Admin (depending on which version you are using). You should immediately rename this account to avoid directed attacks against it.

TIP   As a safety measure, also create a new account to be a backup of your administrative account. Call it whatever you like (although less obvious names are better), give the account security equivalence to the administrative account, and safely store the password. If something happens that locks you out of the real administrative account, you can use the backup account to regain access and correct the problem.

- You should know the steps required to remove access to network resources quickly from any user account and be sure to explore *all* network resources that might contain their own security systems. For example, accounts will be managed on the network operating system (and possibly on each server) and also in specific applications, such as database servers or accounting systems. Make sure that you find out how the system handles removed or deactivated accounts. If you delete a user account in order to remove access, some systems don't *instantly* deny access to that user; instead, the user just cannot log back in again, but any current sessions may continue, at least for a period of time.

- Work closely with the human resources (HR) department. Make sure that the HR staff is comfortable working with you on handling security issues related to employee departures, and develop a checklist to use for standard employment changes that affect IT. The HR department might not be able to give you much—if any—advance notice, but it needs to understand that you need to know about any terminations *immediately* so you can take proper steps. Along the same lines, you should develop a set of procedures on how you handle accumulated e-mail, files, and other user access—both for friendly departures and terminations. Your relationship with the appropriate people in the HR department is crucial in being able to handle security well, so make sure that you establish and maintain mutual trust.

- Consider setting up a program whereby new users on the network have their assigned permissions reviewed and approved by their supervisor. This way, you won't mistakenly give people access to things they shouldn't have.

- For publicly traded companies, the advent of the Sarbanes-Oxley Act of 2002 (discussed in Chapter 1) means you will likely need to set up a system to document how users of the network are added, modified, and removed from the system. This type of system usually involves a set of request forms initiated by the appropriate department (HR, accounting, and so on), signed by the individual's supervisor and any other parties that need to authorize access to certain systems, and then documents the IT staff's actions. These forms are then filed and will be examined by the company's auditors.

Password Security

Another important aspect of account security is account password security. Most network operating systems enable you to set policies related to password security. These policies control how often the system forces users to change their passwords, how long their passwords must be, the complexity of the password (alphanumeric, capital letters, or symbols), whether users can reuse previously used passwords, and so forth. At a minimum, consider these suggestions for password policies:

- Require users (through network password policy settings) to change their main network password every 90 to 180 days. (Actually, 30 days is a common recommendation, but this might be too frequent in most environments.)

- Set the reuse policy so that passwords cannot be reused for at least a year.

- Require passwords that are *at least* eight characters long. For case-insensitive passwords that do not allow special characters, this yields potentially 36^8 possible permutations, or almost 3 trillion possibilities. And if the network operating system uses case-sensitive passwords, the possibilities are much larger: 62^8 (218 trillion). For systems that allow special characters to be part of the password (characters like a space, comma, period, asterisk, and so forth), the number of possible combinations is even higher still.

NOTE Even 2 billion possible combinations for passwords is a lot. If crackers were able to try one password a second, they would need to spend 63 years to try that many permutations. Or, with an optimized program that can try 5 million possibilities a second, it would take about a year to crack an eight-character mixed-case password using brute force.

- Encourage users to create passwords that are not words in any language or, if they are words, that they have numbers and other nonalphanumeric characters inserted somewhere in the word so a "dictionary attack" won't work as easily. (Many password-cracking programs rely on dictionaries of common words and names to reduce dramatically the number of possibilities they need to try.) Also, for networks that support mixed-case passwords, encourage users to use these.

- Make sure that you turn on any policies that monitor for and deal with people entering in wrong passwords. Often called *intruder detection*, this type of policy watches for incorrect password attempts. If too many attempts occur within a set period of time, the system can lock out the user account, preventing further attempts. I usually set this type of feature to lock an account any time five incorrect passwords are entered within an hour, and then lock the account until it's reset by the administrator. This way, if users enter a large number of incorrect passwords, they will need to talk with the administrator to reopen the account. Usually, this occurs when users forget their passwords, but someone else may be trying to guess passwords, so it deserves to be examined. Many companies also set up intruder detection to lock the account for a set period of time if too many incorrect passwords are entered, where the account will be locked for an hour before the user can try to log in again.

- Windows servers enable you to establish limits on when and where a user can log in to the network. You can establish times of day that a user is allowed to log in, and you can also restrict a user account to particular network computers.

Doing so for all users on the network is usually overkill, but you might want to consider restricting the administrative account to several different workstations so someone at a different workstation (or coming in through a WAN connection) cannot log in to the account, even if that person somehow knows the password.

There's an interesting catch-22 concerning network security policies: If you make them *too* strict, you can actually *reduce* the security of your network. For example, suppose that you set the network to require 12-character passwords to force a password change once a week and to disallow the reuse of passwords. Most users will be unable to remember from week to week what password they're using, and they will naturally resort to writing down their password somewhere in their office. Of course, a written password is much less secure than a remembered password. The trick with network security is to strike a balance between security and usability.

Are There Alternatives to Passwords?

There are a number of emerging alternatives to passwords that should make networks more secure, and also make network security easier on the users. The first alternative is something called two-factor identification. This is a system whereby the user carries around a small electronic device called a fob, which is about the size of a Universal Serial Bus (USB) key. (Newer systems also have apps for smartphones that serve the same purpose.) The fob displays a constantly changing set of numbers that are specific to that particular fob. The user remembers just a four-digit PIN. When users log in to the system, they enter in whatever number is currently displayed on the fob, plus their PIN. Because the network side of the system has a matching inventory of fobs and their sequence of numbers, and also has a way to authenticate the user's PIN, the user can be very securely identified. If a fob is lost, it can be easily deactivated in the system and a new one issued. Two-factor identification is often used for remote access identification.

Some web systems are also starting to offer two-factor identification. These systems usually work by sending a Short Message Service (SMS) message to the user's phone with a PIN after the user logs in with their user name and password. The user then enters this PIN as an additional authentication to validate their identity. Another emerging alternative to passwords is the use of biometric data, such as fingerprint readers. Some notebook computers now come with integrated fingerprint readers that can quickly scan users' fingerprints and log them in to a system. Other companies sell similar stand-alone devices. However, usually the vendors specifically state that they are not intended for corporate use. So, although such devices are not yet suitable for corporate use, security is rapidly moving in this direction. I believe the day is not far off when computers will routinely come equipped with fingerprint readers, and users will only have to touch their thumb to the reader to securely identify themselves to their systems.

File and Directory Permissions

Another type of internal security that you need to maintain for information on your network involves the users' access to files and directories. These settings are actually a bit tougher to manage than user accounts, because you usually have at least 20 directories and several hundred files for every user on the network. The sheer volume of directories and files makes managing these settings a more difficult job. The solution is to establish regular procedures, follow them, and then periodically spot-audit parts of the directory tree, particularly areas that contain sensitive files. Also, structure the overall network directories so that you can, for the most part, simply assign permissions at the top levels. These permissions will "flow down" to subdirectories automatically, which makes it much easier to review who has access to which directories.

Network operating systems allow considerable flexibility in setting permissions on files and directories. Using the built-in permissions, you can enable users for different roles in any given directory. These *roles* control what the user can and cannot do within that directory. Examples of generic directory roles include the following:

- **Create only**   This type of role enables users to add a new file to a directory, but restricts them from seeing, editing, or deleting existing files, including any they've created. This type of role is suitable for allowing users to add new information to a directory to which they shouldn't otherwise have access. The directory becomes almost like a mailbox on a street corner: You can only put new things in it. Of course, at least one other user will have full access to the directory to retrieve and work with the files.

- **Read only**   This role enables users to see the files in a directory and even to pull up the files for viewing on their computer. However, the users cannot edit or change the stored files in any way. This type of role is suitable for allowing users to view information that they should not change. (Users with read privileges can copy a file from a read-only directory to another directory and then do whatever they like with the copy they made. They simply cannot change the copy stored in the read-only directory itself.)

- **Change**   This role lets users do whatever they like with the files in a directory, *except* give other users access to the directory.

- **Full control**   Usually reserved for the "owner" of a directory, this role enables the owners to do whatever they like with the files in a directory and to grant other users access to the directory.

These roles are created in different ways on different network operating systems. Chapter 15 provides more details on how Windows server operating systems handle directory permissions.

Just as you can set permissions for directories, you can also set security for specific files. File permissions work similarly to directory permissions. For specific files, you can control a user's ability to read, change, or delete a file. File permissions usually override directory permissions. For example, if a user has change access to a directory, but you set their permission to access a particular file in that directory to read-only, they would have only read-only access to that file.

 TIP For a network of any size, I recommend avoiding the use of file-specific network permissions except in very rare cases. It can quickly become an unmanageable mess to remember to which files each user has special permissions and to which files a new hire needs to be given specific permission.

Practices and User Education

The most insecure part of any network is the people using it. You need to establish good security practices and habits to help protect the network.

It's not enough to design and implement a great security scheme if you do not manage it well on a daily basis. To establish good practices, you need to document security-related procedures, and then set up some sort of process to make sure that the employees follow the procedures regularly. In fact, you're far better off having a simple security design that is followed to the letter than having an excellent but complicated security design that is poorly followed. For this reason, keep the overall network security design as simple as possible while remaining consistent with the needs of the company.

You also need to make sure—to the maximum extent possible—that the users are following prudent procedures. You can easily enforce some procedures through settings on the network operating system, but you must handle others through education. The following are some tips to make this easier:

- Spell out for users what is expected of them in terms of security. Provide a document that describes the security of the network and what they need to do to preserve it. Examples of guidelines for the users include choosing secure passwords, not giving their passwords to anyone else, not leaving their computers unattended for long periods of time while they are logged in to the network, not installing software from outside the company, and so forth.

- When new employees join the company and are oriented on using the network, make sure that you discuss security issues with them.

- Depending on the culture of the company, consider having users sign a form acknowledging their understanding of important security procedures that the company expects them to follow.

- Periodically audit users' security actions. If the users have full-control access to directories, examine how they've assigned permissions to other users.

- Make sure that you review the security logs of the network operating system you use. Investigate and follow up on any problems reported.

 TIP It's a good idea to document any security-related issues you investigate. While most are benign, occasionally you might find one in which the user had inappropriate intent. In such cases, your documentation of what you find and what actions you take might become important.

While it's important to plan for the worst when designing and administering network security, you also need to realize that most of the time, security issues arise from ignorance or other innocent causes, rather than malicious intent.

Understanding External Threats

External security is the process of securing the network from external threats. Before the Internet, this process wasn't difficult. Most networks had only external modems for users to dial in to the network, and it was easy to keep those access points secure. However, now that nearly all networks are connected to the Internet, external security becomes much more important and also much more difficult.

At the beginning of this chapter, I said that no network is ever totally secure. This is especially true when dealing with external security for a network connected to the Internet. Almost daily, crackers discover new techniques that they can use to breach the security of a network through an Internet connection. Even if you were to find a book that discussed all the threats to a specific type of network, the book would be out of date soon after it was printed.

Three basic types of external security threats exist:

- **Front-door threats**   These threats arise when a person from outside the company somehow finds, guesses, or cracks a user password and then logs on to the network. The perpetrator could be someone who had an association with the company at some point or could be someone totally unrelated to the company.

- **Back-door threats**   These are threats where software or hardware bugs in the network's operating system and hardware enable outsiders to crack the network's security. After accomplishing this, the outsiders often find a way to log in to the administrative account and then can do anything they like. Back-door threats can also be deliberately programmed into software you run.

- **Denial of service (DoS)**   DoS attacks deny service to the network. Examples include committing specific actions that are known to crash different types of servers or flooding the company's Internet connection with useless traffic (such as a flood of ping requests).

 NOTE   Another type of external threat exists: computer viruses, Trojan horses, worms, and other malicious software from outside the company. These threats are covered in their own section later in the chapter.

Fortunately, you can do a number of things to implement strong external security measures. They probably won't keep out a determined and extremely skilled cracker, but they can make it difficult enough that most crackers will give up and go elsewhere.

DEFINE-IT! Important Network Security Devices

Here are some important security devices you should be familiar with:

- A *firewall* is a system that enforces a security policy between two networks, such as between a local area network (LAN) and the Internet. Firewalls can use many different techniques to enforce security policies.

- A *proxy server* acts as a proxy (an anonymous intermediary), usually for users of a network. For example, it might stand in as a proxy for browsing web pages so that the user's computer isn't connected to the remote system except through the proxy server. In the process of providing proxy access to web pages, a proxy server might also speed web access by caching web pages that are accessed so that other users can benefit from having them more quickly available from the local proxy server, and might also provide some firewall protection for the LAN.

- Usually built into a router or a firewall, a *packet filter* enables you to set criteria for allowed and disallowed packets, source and destination IP addresses, and IP ports.

Front-Door Threats

Front-door threats, in which someone from outside the company is able to gain access to a user account, are probably the most likely threats that you need to protect against. These threats can take many forms. Chief among them is the disgruntled or terminated employee who once had access to the network. Another example is someone guessing or finding out a password to a valid account on the network or somehow getting a valid password from the owner of the password.

Insiders, whether current or ex-employees, are potentially the most dangerous overall. Such people have many advantages that some random cracker won't have. They know the important user names on the network already, so they know what accounts to go after. They might know other users' passwords from when they were associated with the company. They also know the structure of the network, what the server names are, and other information that makes cracking the network's security easier.

Protecting against a front-door threat revolves around strong internal security protection because, in this case, internal and external security are closely linked. This is the type of threat where all the policies and practices discussed in the section on internal security can help to prevent problems.

An additional effective way to protect against front-door threats is to keep network resources that should be accessed from the LAN separate from resources that should be accessed from outside the LAN, whenever possible. For example, if you never need to provide external users access to the company's accounting server, you can make it nearly impossible to access that system from outside the LAN.

NOTE There's a great story about a company that hired an outside security firm to try to breach their network to test their security. They had the latest firewalls, intrusion detection systems, proxy servers, and so forth, and really challenged the outside firm to try to break in. They were amazed when the outside firm was able to gain access to the network within a day. How did they do it? They dropped a few USB memory keys in the parking lot that had a program on it that allowed remote control from outside the network. Some curious employee noticed one of these and put it into their computer in order to try to identify who they should return it to, and that was all it took.

You can separate network resources through a number of measures. You can set up the firewall router to decline any access through the router to that server's IP address. If the server doesn't require IP, you can remove that protocol. You can set up the server to disallow access outside normal working hours. Depending on the network operating system running on the server, you can restrict access to Ethernet media access control (MAC) addresses for machines on the LAN that should be able to access the server. You can also set the server to allow each user only one login at a time. The specific steps that you can take depend on the server in question, the server applications it runs, and its operating system, but the principle holds true: Segregate internal resources from external resources whenever possible.

Here are some other steps you might take to stymie front-door threats:

- Control which users can access the LAN from outside the LAN. For example, you might be running Virtual Private Network (VPN) software for your traveling or home-based users to access the LAN remotely through the Internet. You should enable this access only for users who need it and not for everyone.

- Consider setting up remote access accounts for remote users who are separate from their normal accounts, and make these accounts more restrictive than their normal LAN accounts. This might not be practicable in all cases, but it's a strategy that can help, particularly for users who normally have broad LAN security clearances.

- If employees with broad access leave the company, review user accounts where they might have known the password. Consider forcing an immediate password change to such accounts once the employees are gone.

NOTE An important aspect of both internal and external security is physical security. Make sure that the room in which your servers are located is physically locked and secure.

People trying to access the network who have not been associated with the company at some point often try a technique euphemistically called *social engineering*, which is where they use nontechnological methods to learn user accounts and passwords inside the company. These techniques are most dangerous in larger companies, where not all the employees know each other. An example of a social engineering technique is calling an employee and posing as a network administrator who is trying to track down a problem and who needs the employee's password temporarily. Another example is to sort through a company's trash looking for records that might help the culprit crack a password. Make sure to instruct your company's employees carefully to never give out their password to anyone over the telephone and also that IT people usually never need to ask anyone's password.

Back-Door Threats

Back-door threats are often directed at problems in the network operating system itself or at some other point in the network infrastructure, such as its routers. The fact is that all network operating systems and most network components have security holes. The best thing you can do to prevent these problems is to stay current with your software and any security-related patches that are released. You should also periodically review new information about security holes discovered in the software you use.

TIP   Don't rely on just the vendor's web site for the best information about software security holes. A good web site to use to stay current on security holes is the one maintained by the Computer Emergency Response Team (CERT), located at www.cert.org. Aside from finding advisories on security holes, you can also discover much valuable security information on the site.

Web servers are a frequent target for crackers. Consider the following tips to help protect against threats to web servers:

- You're better off if you can host the company's web site on an external server, such as an Internet Service Provider's (ISP's) system, rather than on your own network. Not only is an ISP better able to provide the service for the server for 24 hours a day, 7 days a week, but it also probably has better security. Also, you don't need to worry about allowing web server access to your LAN from outside the company, which can sometimes leave open other holes.

- Make sure that you implement a strong firewall router for your network. Firewall routers are discussed in more detail in Chapter 4. You should also have someone knowledgeable about the specific firewall and web server you implement test your configuration or help with the configuration. Remember that firewalls also need to have their software kept current.

- Make absolutely certain that you've carefully reviewed the security settings appropriate for your web server and have implemented all of them, and that you audit these settings occasionally.

- Consider placing a web server designed for people outside the company outside your firewall (in other words, between the firewall and the router that connects you to the Internet—this area is called a *demilitarized zone*, and most firewalls have a specific Ethernet port for this purpose). This way, even if crackers are able to break into the web server, they won't have an easy time getting to the rest of your network.

- Safely guard your e-mail traffic. E-mail is one of the most commonly used means to get viruses or Trojan horse programs into a company. Make sure you run virus-scanning software suitable for your e-mail server and that the virus signatures are updated at least *daily*—hourly is better.

DEFINE-IT! Demilitarized Zone

When you place computers between your firewall (on the other side of the firewall from your network) and your connection to an external network, such as the Internet, the area between those two devices is called the demilitarized zone, or DMZ for short. Usually, an organization will place its public web server in the DMZ, and that computer will not have any sort of confidential information on it. This way, if the security of that computer is broken, the attacker hasn't gained entry to the network itself.

DoS Threats

DoS attacks are those that deny service to a network resource to legitimate users. These are often targeted at e-mail servers and web servers, but they can affect an entire network. DoS attacks usually take one of two forms: They either deny service by flooding the network with useless traffic or they take advantage of bugs in network software that can be used to crash servers. DoS attacks against an e-mail server usually flood the server with mail until the e-mail server either denies service to legitimate users or crashes under the load placed on it.

Here are few ways to help prevent DoS attacks:

- Make sure to keep your various network software programs current.

- Use settings on your firewall to disallow Internet Control Message Protocol (ICMP) traffic service (which handles ping requests) into the network.

- Deny access to servers from outside the LAN that do not need to be accessed from outside the LAN. For example, the company's accounting system server probably does not need to be accessed from outside the LAN. In such a case, you would configure the firewall or packet-filtering router to deny all outside traffic to or from that server's IP address.

Viruses and Other Malicious Software

Unfortunately, an increasing array of malicious software is circulating around the world. Many different types of this software exist, including the following:

- **Viruses** A computer *virus* is a program that spreads by infecting other files with a copy of itself. Files that can be infected by viruses include program files (COM, EXE, and DLL) and document files for applications that support macro languages sophisticated enough to allow virus behavior. (Microsoft Word and Excel are common targets of macro-based viruses.) Sometimes even data files like JPEG image files can be infected by sophisticated viruses.

- **Worms**   A *worm* is a program that propagates by sending copies of itself to other computers, which run the worm and then send copies to other computers. Sometimes, worms have spread through e-mail systems around the world like wildfire. One way they spread is by attaching to e-mail along with a message that entices the recipients to open the attachment. The attachment contains the worm, which then sends out copies of itself to other people defined in the user's e-mail address book, without the user knowing that this is happening. Those recipients then have the same thing happen to them. A worm like this can spread rapidly around the world, through the Internet, in a matter of hours.

- **Trojan horses**   A *Trojan horse* is a program that purports to do something interesting or useful and then performs malicious actions in the background while the user is interacting with the main program.

- **Logic bombs**   *Logic bombs* are malicious pieces of programming code inserted into an otherwise normal program. They are often included by the program's original author or by someone else who participated in developing the source code. Logic bombs can be timed to execute at a certain time, erasing key files or performing other actions.

There are an enormous number of known viruses, with more being written and discovered daily. These viruses are a major threat to any network, and an important aspect of your network administration is protecting against them.

To protect a network from virus attacks, you need to implement some sort of antivirus software. Antivirus software runs on computers on the network and "watches" for known viruses or virus-like activity. The antivirus software then either removes the virus, leaving the original file intact, quarantines the file so it can be checked by an administrator, or locks access to the file in some other fashion.

Antivirus software can be run on most network computers, such as file servers, print servers, e-mail servers, desktop computers, and even computerized firewalls. Antivirus software is available from a number of different vendors.

Your best bet is to make sure you run antivirus software on all your servers and set up the software so that it is frequently updated (at least daily). (You can set up most server-based antivirus software to update its list of known viruses securely over an Internet connection automatically.) Also, because e-mail is the chief mechanism of transmission for computer viruses these days, make especially sure that you run antivirus software on your e-mail server. I recommend updating virus signatures on an e-mail server hourly, if possible. This is because new e-mail–borne viruses can spread throughout the world very rapidly—in a matter of hours. By having your antivirus software on your e-mail server update itself hourly, you're a little more likely to get a necessary update before the virus hits your network.

TIP Consider using antivirus software from different companies for different parts of your network. For example, you might use one company's antivirus software for your e-mail server and some other company's software for your other computers. While rare, I have seen cases where one antivirus company's virus database does not detect certain viruses, while a different company's database does, or where new viruses are added much more quickly to one database versus others.

You should also run antivirus software on your workstations, but you shouldn't rely on this software as your primary means of prevention.

Chapter Summary

In this chapter, you learned about common security threats and read advice that can help you formulate and implement good security practices. You should seriously consider retaining an outside security consultant to help you set up your security plans and to review and audit them on a regular basis.

Even in an entire book devoted to the subject of network security, you can't learn all you need to know to make a network as secure as possible. New threats are discovered constantly, and the changing software landscape makes such information quickly obsolete. If you're responsible for network security, you should know it's a job that never sleeps, and you can never know enough about it. You need to spend time learning more of the ins and outs of network security, particularly for the operating systems that you use on your network. The following books can help further your network security education:

- *Network Security: A Beginner's Guide, Third Edition,* by Eric Maiwald (McGraw-Hill Education, 2012)

- *Hacking Exposed 7: Network Security Secrets & Solutions, Seventh Edition,* by Stuart McClure, Joel Scambray, and George Kurtz (McGraw-Hill Education, 2012)

- *Information Security: The Complete Reference* by Mark Rhodes-Ousley (McGraw-Hill Education, 2013)

You also might want to read *Internet Firewalls and Network Security, Second Edition,* by Chris Hare and Karanjit Sayan (New Riders Publishing, 1996). This is an older book, but has an excellent explanation of true "security" (that is, Department of Defense levels). The book also describes how to develop network security policies in a company and explains packet filtering and firewall technology.

Finally, *The Happy Hacker: A Guide to (Mostly) Harmless Computer Hacking, Fourth Edition,* by Carolyn P. Meinel (American Eagle Publishing, 2002), is an excellent introduction to hacking. The book applies a "how-to" approach and teaches both novices and moderately experienced network security persons what to look for on a daily basis.

CHAPTER 10 | Network Disaster Recovery

Network servers contain vital resources for a company in the form of information, knowledge, and invested work product of the company's employees. If they were suddenly and permanently deprived of these resources, most companies would not be able to continue their business uninterrupted and would face losing a lot of money, both in the form of lost data and the effects of that loss. Therefore, establishing a network disaster recovery plan and formulating and implementing the network's backup strategy are—in my opinion—the two most important jobs in network management.

In this chapter, you learn about the issues that you should address in a disaster recovery plan, and also about network backup strategies and systems. Before getting into these topics, however, you should read about the City of Seattle's disaster recovery experiences.

Notes from the Field: The City of Seattle

The technical editor of the first through third editions of this book, Tony Ryan, had a personal experience with network disaster recovery. Tony worked in the IT department for the City of Seattle. On February 28, 2001, Seattle experienced an earthquake that caused the city's disaster recovery plans to be tested. What follows is Tony's discussion about the City of Seattle's disaster recovery operations and how it handled the problems that occurred in the wake of the earthquake. This is an excellent example of why you need a disaster recovery plan that encompasses all possible events that could occur during a disaster.

Notes on the Seattle 2001 Earthquake and Its Disaster Recovery
By Tony Ryan
Seattle has seen some very unusual and attention-grabbing events over the past few years. Notable among them were the World Trade Organization (WTO) conference of 1999 and the violent demonstrations that accompanied it, which were broadcast worldwide on television and the Internet. Also, riots broke out during Mardi Gras celebrations in 2000. However, nothing compared to the potential and realized damage wrought by the 6.8 magnitude earthquake that struck Wednesday, February 28, 2001.

The EOC Situation
The City of Seattle has an Emergency Operations Center, or EOC, which is activated during any event or crisis that has a potential impact on public safety, or that might otherwise affect any number of services provided by the city to its citizens. Sometimes that EOC can be activated ahead of time; for example, for

(continued)

the Y2K event and the anniversary of the WTO demonstrations. Looking at the preparation made for those events and comparing it to what happens during unplanned events such as the earthquake helps to illustrate some important principles about IT disaster recovery and disaster preparedness.

Never Assume

During the preparation for Y2K, members of my staff were asked to augment the staff normally assigned to support the EOC's desktop and laptop PCs and printers. The staff members who normally support the EOC are from a different IT organization than ours, and as can be expected, their way of doing things differed from ours for a number of valid reasons. However, once my staff members had a chance to look at the EOC's environment, they were able to share some new perspectives and methods that were welcomed and adopted by EOC support staff, and all involved had a new idea of what would be expected to be the "standard" way of configuring EOC PCs. Examples ranged from hard-coding certain models of PC network interface cards (NICs) to run better on the switches in their wiring closet to developing and implementing a base image for all the laptops to be deployed in the building. The Y2K event, as a result, was lauded as an example of ideal cooperation between IT groups and excellent preparation overall. It was a very calm Saturday morning!

Change Management?

Between events, however, there was a great deal of time and opportunity for things to change. The facility might have been used for other business purposes; equipment such as laptops might have been loaned out, or customers could have come in and used the equipment; and other IT groups besides ours might have assisted the staff and performed alterations to the configurations that went undocumented or were not communicated to all involved.

The Results

Whatever it was that might have happened remains unknown. What we did discover following the earthquake was that when customers who normally use the EOC in emergency situations went to use the equipment, in some cases, the machines did not work as expected. Software could not be loaded on this PC; that laptop would not connect to the network anymore; some PCs were not the same or had been swapped for less powerful processors. Things had changed, and the result was that some of the emergency work IT professionals such as web support technicians had to perform took more time than we had anticipated. Ironically, the Web played a crucial role in our overall communications "strategy." The impact of that equipment not immediately working was not yet evident; however, the following events illustrate how they might have been.

(continued)

A few minutes after the earthquake struck, several of the downtown buildings in which City of Seattle employees worked were evacuated due to fear of structural damage. No one was injured, and amazingly only two keyboards were broken throughout all the buildings in which we provide support. But imagine a couple thousand very frightened and concerned people streaming onto the sidewalks and streets, flooding cellular telephone networks in frantic attempts to contact loved ones and looking for any possible focus for communication—especially managers such as myself and other supervisory staff, all possessing varying levels of training in disaster preparedness.

Luckily, the mayor's office had sent representatives to the gathering sites indicated for staff to walk to in such events and informed everyone in the core buildings that were directly affected that they were to go home. With that announcement, the chief technical officer (CTO) announced to all to "check the Web" for information, meaning the city's internal web site. But what if the EOC PC had been swapped out, let's say, for a Pentium 133 with 64MB RAM and that PC could not run Microsoft's FrontPage 2000? If that web site had to be updated with news and official information on a routine basis, the results could have been at best inconvenient and confusing.

Contingency and Costs

Because we are a publicly funded entity, we are very careful about how we spend our customers' money, as it is subject to great scrutiny (and rightfully so). Customers often do not have the funds to afford both modern PC equipment to run the latest version of Windows and a spare PC to sit in the closet, "just in case." After the earthquake, a couple of buildings were temporarily unavailable for occupancy until inspectors had a chance to examine the damage to see if the buildings were safe for employees. One of those buildings actually houses a lot of our IT staff, and as a result, not only were we trying to find "spare PCs" for our customers to use while they looked for office space, but as IT support staff, we found ourselves doing the same thing. The direct impact was that we found it difficult in a few cases to support our customers as quickly as our service-level agreements (SLAs) required, especially since we could not immediately reenter our building to gather our PCs or other necessary equipment.

Lesson Learned: Keep Spares ... At Least a Few

So it seems that you either pay up front or pay later. It makes sense to keep a percentage of PCs available for these rainy-day events; 10 to 15 percent of replaceable inventory should work. Consider that businesses of any kind are obligated in such situations to perform a kind of "triage" as to which of their business functions are most critical and which can be postponed—until their entire stock of equipment can be reconnected or replaced—and 10 to 15 percent is justified.

(continued)

Have a Plan for Communications and How You Will Communicate

Following the CTO's announcement, some asked, "What about those who don't have web access at home?" As IT staff, we asked, "What if the web servers themselves had all been destroyed?" (In fact, ceiling debris in the room in which they were housed fell very close to them, but the servers were not damaged and the service was never down.) Still others asked, "What about those who missed the message and don't know to check the Web?" These questions, as well as "What to do in the event of …?" could be addressed with a clear, ever-ready communications plan. Ironically, such plans had been developed down to the last detail for other events, but in the case of a real "emergent" event, we as a department had not identified a plan to follow. A priority for our department now is to reexamine that situation and develop a plan, using communications plans developed for the Y2K event and the like as models.

Another point: As previously mentioned, our staff is not responsible for supporting the EOC on a routine basis. We are more than happy to be directed to assist in that support, and as evidenced, have done so on a few occasions. Almost immediately following the earthquake, I received a page indicating that I was to dispatch technicians to the EOC to support the city officials who report there during emergencies. While our team was under no agreement with the EOC to provide support, even "on demand," I immediately asked two of my senior technicians, who had worked at the EOC in the past, to respond. They reported for duty there and supported the facility until the assigned staff arrived. There was never a doubt that we would pitch in whenever asked, but I made it a point to ask our divisional director if developing some clearer expectations, or even an SLA, between our staff and the EOC would be appropriate, and he agreed. I did find out that those in the EOC are granted power by legislation to use "all" city resources in the event of an emergency, but a clear agreement could also permit me to identify a rotating on-call staff person who could be proactive and call the EOC in such instances.

I must point out that none of these preparations can substitute for dedicated, intelligent people. The shining example is one of my technicians who supports programmers responsible for the city's payroll application. He had the presence of mind to come early to work the day after the quake, and he somehow persuaded the construction crew and inspectors to permit him access to the building. He walked up 13 flights of stairs, picked up a PC and peripherals, carried it back down the stairs and to another building, and configured it to work on the segment in the new building. This made it possible for the programmer to run the operations necessary for the city's payroll run that weekend, and employees received their checks on time, as expected. You cannot ask for more than that.

Disaster Recovery Plans

A *disaster recovery plan* is a document that explores how a network recovers from a disaster that either imperils its data or stops its functioning. A company's external financial auditors often require annual disaster recovery plans because of the data's importance to the business and the effect that such a network failure would have on a company. Moreover, disaster recovery plans are also important because they force the manager of the network to think through all possible disaster scenarios. By taking these scenarios into account, the manager can make more effective plans to protect the network's data from loss and to restore full operations of the business as quickly as possible. As mentioned at the beginning of this chapter, planning for disaster recovery and managing the company's backup systems are a network manager's two most important jobs.

Most companies do not have extremely long disaster recovery plans. For a single network of up to several hundred nodes and 15 or so servers, such a plan usually consists of about 10 to 20 pages or fewer, although its length varies depending on the complexity of the company's network operations. Fortune 500 companies, for instance, may have disaster recovery plans that are several hundred pages long, when all sites are considered in aggregate.

One strategy to keep disaster recovery plans concise and to maximize their usefulness is to focus on problems that, while remote, are at least somewhat likely to occur. Alternatively, you can focus on disaster results—what happens—rather than trying to cover disaster causes—why it happened. Focusing your plan on disaster results means contemplating problems such as loss of a single server, loss of the entire server room, loss of all of the customer service workstation computers, and so forth, without worrying about the possible disasters that might cause those results.

The following sections discuss the minimum key issues that a disaster recovery plan should address. Depending on your own company, your plan may need to address additional issues.

Assessing Disaster Recovery Needs

Before drafting the actual plan, you should first assess the needs that the plan must meet. These needs will vary depending on who requires input into the disaster recovery planning process and what issues these people want the plan to address. Consider these types of needs:

- Formally planning for contingencies and ensuring that all possible disasters have been considered, and defining countermeasures in the plan

- Assuring the company's external accounting auditors that the company has considered and developed plans to handle disasters

- Informing the company's top management about the risks that exist for the network and its data in different situations, and how much time you expect to need to resolve any problems that occur

- Soliciting input from top management of the company as to recovery priorities and acceptable minimum requirements to reestablish services

- Formally planning with the key areas of your company's business (for example, manufacturing, customer service, and sales) considerations surrounding different types of computer-related disasters or serious problems

- Assuring customers of the firm that the firm's data operations are safe from disaster

Identifying these needs will not only give you a clear vision of what the plan must address, but also which other people from the different parts of the company should be involved in the planning process.

Considering Disaster Scenarios

You should start your planning process by considering different possible disaster scenarios. For example, consider the following disasters:

- A fire in your server room—or somewhere else in the building—destroys computers and tapes.

- Flooding destroys computers and backup batteries low enough to the server room floor to be affected. Remember that floods may be caused by something within the building itself, such as a bad water leak in a nearby room or a fire that activates the fire sprinklers.

- An electrical problem of some kind causes power to fail.

- Some problem causes total loss of connectivity to the outside world. For example, a critical wide area network (WAN) or Internet link may go down.

- A structural building failure of some kind affects the network or its servers.

- Any of the preceding problems affects computers elsewhere in the building that are critical to the company's operations. For example, such an event may happen in the manufacturing areas, in the customer service center, or in the telephone system closet or room.

While none of these events is very likely, it is still important to consider them all. The whole point of disaster recovery planning is to prevent or minimize serious losses, and the process is much less useful if you consider only those disasters that you think are the most likely.

After considering disasters such as those mentioned, you should next consider serious failures that could also affect the operations of the network. Here are some examples:

- The motherboard in a business-critical server fails, and the vendor cannot get a replacement to you for three or more days.

- Disks in one of your servers fail in such a way that data is lost. If you are running some kind of redundant array of independent disks (RAID) scheme (discussed in Chapter 11), plan for failures that are worse than the RAID system can protect. For example, if you use RAID 1 mirrored drives, plan for both sides of the mirror to fail in the same time frame. If you are using RAID 5, plan for any two drives failing at the same time. Both of these failures will mean that you will need to restore from backup.

- Your tape backup drive fails and cannot be repaired for one to two weeks. (While this doesn't cause a loss of data in and of itself, it increases your exposure to such an event.)

You should plan how you would respond to these and any other possible failures. If the motherboard in a critical server fails, you may want to move its drives to a compatible computer temporarily. To address disk failure, you should design a plan under which you can rebuild the disk array and restore data from your backups as rapidly as possible. Regarding your tape backup drive, you will likely want to find out how quickly you can acquire an equivalent drive or whether the maker of the tape drive can provide reconditioned replacement drives quickly in exchange for your failed drive.

For all of these failures, you will also want to consider the cost of keeping spare parts, or even entire backup servers, available so that you can restore operations as rapidly as possible. You should consider and investigate all of the following types of possible responses:

- Should you carry a maintenance contract? If so, make sure you thoroughly understand its guarantees and procedures.

- Should you stock certain types of parts on hand so that they are readily available in case of failure?

- Are other computers available that might work as a short-term replacement for a key server? What about noncomputer components that are important, such as routers, hubs, and switches?

- If you need to take temporary measures, are the affected employees trained to do their jobs with the replacement, or even with no system at all, if necessary? For example, if a restaurant's electronic systems are down, can the restaurant (and the food servers, kitchen staff, cashiers, and so on) still operate the business manually until the system is repaired?

- Should you maintain a cold or hot recovery site? A "cold" recovery site is a facility maintained by your company and near the protected data center. The cold site has all of the power, air conditioning, and other facility features needed to host your site should the data center experience some disaster. A "hot" site is the same as a cold site, except that it also has all of the necessary computer equipment and software to duplicate the processing of the data center. Hot sites usually synchronize their data on a real-time basis with the main data center so that they can literally take over the work of the main site in seconds. Companies with very sensitive, mission-critical data operations often maintain cold or hot recovery sites.

The process of considering possible problems, such as disasters or failures of key pieces of equipment, and then making plans for handling them is certainly the meat of disaster recovery planning. However, your written plan should also discuss or address other issues, which are covered in the following sections.

Handling Communications

An important part of any disaster recovery plan concerns how you will handle communications. Without effective communications, your attempts at handling the disaster will be hampered, and other people will not be able to do their jobs as well as they might otherwise.

Start by listing all of the different parties who may need to be notified of a problem, its progress toward resolution, and its final resolution. Your list might look something like this:

- The board of directors
- The chief executive officer or president
- The vice presidents of all areas
- The vice president or head of an affected area
- Your supervisor
- Employees affected by the problem

For each of these parties—and any others you may identify—you next need to consider what level of problem requires their notification. The board of directors, for example, might not need to know about a disaster unless it is likely that it will have a material effect on the company's performance. Your supervisor, on the other hand, probably wants to be notified about every problem, and certainly any affected employees need to be notified.

Once you have listed the parties to notify and what they need to be informed about, you should then decide *how* you will inform them. If you're the primary person resolving the disaster, it's best to delegate notification to someone else who is less directly involved so that you can focus on resolving the problem as quickly as possible. For example, the job of communicating with the appropriate people should be delegated to your supervisor or to an employee who works in your department and is free to handle this job. Whoever has this job should be clear on the communication procedures and should have access to the necessary contact information—such as home phone numbers, pager numbers, cell phone numbers, and so forth—for situations that require notification after working hours. You may also want to consider setting up a telephone tree for rapid notification. Finally, for your environment and for different types of disasters, you may need to specify the order in which people are notified, which may not match their order in the company's organization chart.

TIP   I'm not suggesting that it's your responsibility to directly inform, for example, the company's board of directors. Instead, it's your responsibility to address in the plan how communications and the decisions surrounding them work, and to make sure that people in the chain are aware of the plan. Your communication responsibility to upper management may only include notifying your direct supervisor, and it's then their responsibility to decide to inform the next level of management, and so forth.

The written disaster recovery plan should include all of the preceding information.

Planning Offsite Storage

Offsite storage is an important way of protecting some of your backup tapes in the event that a physical disaster, such as a fire, destroys all of your onsite copies. Because offsite storage is such an important aspect of disaster protection, it should be discussed in your disaster recovery plan.

NOTE   If you do not yet have an offsite storage procedure, you should seriously consider adopting one. While fireproof file cabinets can protect tape media from small fires, they are not necessarily invulnerable to very large or hot fires. Plus, tapes are more sensitive to smoke and heat than the papers that a fireproof file cabinet is designed to protect.

Companies that provide offsite storage of files often also offer standardized tape-storage practices. These usually work on a rotation basis, where a storage company employee comes to your office periodically—usually weekly—and drops off one set of tapes and picks up the next set of tapes. The companies typically use stainless steel boxes to hold the tapes, and the network administrator is responsible for keeping the boxes locked and safeguarding the keys. You need to decide which tapes you should keep onsite and which ones to send offsite. One rule of thumb is always to keep the two most recent complete backups onsite (so that they're available to restore accidentally deleted files rapidly) and send the older tapes offsite. This way, you keep on hand the tapes that you need on a regular basis, and you minimize your exposure to a disaster. After all, if a disaster destroys your server room and all of the tapes in it, you probably won't be too worried about losing just a few days' worth of data.

NOTE   The amount of data that you can accept exposing to a disaster will vary widely depending on the nature of your company's business and the nature of the data. Some operations are so sensitive that the loss of even a few minutes' worth of data would be catastrophic. For example, a banking firm simply cannot lose any transactions. Businesses that need to protect supersensitive data sometimes enlist a third-party vendor to provide offsite online data storage. Such a vendor replicates a business's data onto the vendor's servers over a high-speed connection, such as an Ethernet connection purchased from a telecom carrier (which can range up to Gigabit speeds). These vendors usually also offer failover services, where their computers can pick up the jobs of your computers should your computers fail. Alternatively, if a business runs multiple sites, it might set up software and procedures that enable it to accomplish the same services using its own sites.

Describing Critical Components

Your plan should describe the computer equipment and software that will be required to resume operations if the entire building is lost. This list should roughly estimate the cost of the equipment and how it can be procured rapidly. By preparing such a list, you can reduce the time required to resume operations in a temporary facility. Also, if your company purchases insurance against business interruptions, you will need these estimates for that insurance policy.

Network Backup and Restore Procedures

A network disaster recovery plan is worthless without some way of recovering the data stored on the server. This is where network backup and restore procedures come in. If you're a network administrator, or aspire to become one, you should already know about the importance of good backups of the system and of important data. If you don't know this, then it's probably the most important lesson that you can take away from this book. Making regular backups is a requirement when using computers—period.

You don't need to work with computers for very long before you observe firsthand the importance of good backups. Computers can and do fail, and they sometimes fail in ways that render the data stored on them unrecoverable. Also, some turn of events may cause certain important files to be deleted or corrupted. In cases such as these, jobs are saved or lost based on the quality of the backups in place and the ability to restore that important data.

Assessing Backup Needs

Before designing network backup procedures, you must understand the company's backup and restoration needs. Questions such as the following may help in assessing the needs that you must meet:

- How dynamic is the data stored on the servers? How often does it change, and in what ways does it change?

- How much data needs to be backed up, and at what rate is the amount of data growing?

- How much time is available to make the backup? Make sure that you avoid situations where you need to back up terabytes of data using a system that can handle only megabytes per hour.

- If a partial or complete restoration from a backup is required, how quickly must it take place? As a rule of thumb, restoring data takes about twice as long as backing it up, although in some cases the times may be approximately equal. In other words, if it takes your backup system 10 hours overnight to back up the entire network, it will take 10 to 20 hours to restore that data—and this estimate doesn't include the time required to resolve whatever problem made it necessary to restore data in the first place.

■ How coherent does the backed up data need to be? In other words, does a collection of data files need to be handled as a single unit? For example, a directory containing a bunch of word processing files isn't terribly coherent; you can restore one, many, or all of them without much concern about how those restorations will affect other files. On the other hand, a collection of database files for a high-end database is often useless unless you can restore *all* of the files in the set from *exactly* the same point in time. (High-end databases— such as Oracle's—that require this kind of backup will have their own detailed instructions for how backups must be made, and usually include utilities that can be used to create special backup files, often without even needing to make the database unavailable.)

■ What is the required trade-off between cost and recoverability? You can design backup systems that operate minute-to-minute so that if something fails, the systems will not lose any data, and management can place a high degree of confidence in this fact. (A bank, for instance, requires this kind of high-end backup system.) However, such backup systems cost a lot of money and require a lot of administration. Most companies would gladly trade that sort of extreme cost for some lower degree of recoverability, such as nightly backups of the system. What does your company need and what is it willing to pay for?

■ How many levels of redundancy does the company need in its backups? Most backups are made onto tapes and support servers that use RAID arrays, so the tapes are actually a *secondary* level of protection. In some cases, multiple tapes may be required, each with a separate copy of the backup. Or another way to proceed for maximum redundancy is to copy backups to an offsite storage company over some sort of network connection.

When making your assessment, it is important to involve the senior management of your company in the process. At a minimum, you should present your findings and seek management's agreement or input.

Acquiring Backup Media and Technologies

Once you have some idea of your backup needs, you can then proceed to acquire the necessary hardware and software to create and manage your backups.

If you need to purchase new backup hardware for a system, you can choose from a number of proven, good systems, depending on your actual needs. When choosing a backup technology, consider the following factors:

■ Reliability of the hardware and the media

■ Cost of the hardware and the media

■ Storage capacity

■ Likely frequency of restorations

■ The importance of fitting the entire backup onto a single piece of media

Table 10-1 reviews different types of backup technologies, their approximate costs, and the relative pros and cons of each. Note that the prices of drives, media, and costs per megabyte in Table 10-1 are approximations.

If your company can afford digital linear tape (DLT) or linear tape-open (LTO) systems and can make use of their capacities, you should definitely look into purchasing this technology. DLT and LTO tapes are rock solid, can be used a rated million times, and are said to have a shelf life of 30 years. Moreover, the drives are fast for both backups and restorations. Finally, robotic autochangers are available for DLT and LTO drives, which means that there is plenty of head room if you outgrow the size of your drive. Also, the robotic systems are relatively inexpensive and range from small systems that can hold five tapes up to large libraries that can hold tens or hundreds of tapes.

Some newer backup technologies, such as Super DLT S4 (800GB per tape) and LTO-6 (2,500GB per tape), promise to up DLT's ante. For larger networks, these emerging technologies may make sense. Both DLT and LTO are reliable tape formats with a lot of support from various computer equipment vendors.

Type	Approximate Cost of Drive	Approximate Cost of Media	Media Capacity	Pros and Cons
DVD-ROM/RW drives	$50 ($10/GB)	$1 ($0.2/GB)	5GB	+ Random access + Large capacity −Slow speed
Blu-ray (BDXL)	$100 ($1/GB)	$50 ($0.5/GB)	100GB	
Digital linear tape (DLT V4)	$500 ($1.6/GB)	$50 ($0.16/GB)	320GB	+ Very reliable + Very fast + High per-tape capacities + Extremely low media cost/MB
Super DLT (SDLT 600)	$3,000 ($5/GB)	$50 ($0.08/GB)	600GB	+ Very reliable + Very fast + High per-tape capacities + Extremely low media cost/MB
Linear Tape-Open (LTO-2 to LTO-6)	$1–4,000 ($1.6–5/GB)	$30–100 ($0.04–0.15/GB)	200GB–2.5TB	+ Very reliable + Very fast + High per-tape capacities + Extremely low media cost/MB

Table 10-1.   Types of Backup Technologies

Choosing Backup Strategies

After acquiring all the necessary information, you can plan a backup rotation strategy, which addresses how backup media is rotated. Backup rotations are designed to accomplish the following goals:

- Rebuild the system with the most recent data possible, in case of a catastrophic failure.

- Restore files from older tapes that may have been accidentally erased or damaged without anyone noticing the potential loss of data immediately.

- Protect against backup media failure.

- Protect the data from an environmental failure, such as a fire, that destroys the original system and data.

Most network operating systems maintain special bits for each file on the system. One of these is called the *archive bit,* which indicates the backup status of the file. When a user modifies a file, its archive bit is set to on, indicating that the file should be backed up. When the backup is accomplished, the archive bit is cleared. Using this archive bit and your backup software, you can make the following types of backups:

- A *full backup,* where all selected directories and files are backed up, regardless of their archive bit state. Full backups clear the archive bit on all of the backed-up files when they are finished.

- An *incremental backup,* where only files with their archive bit set are backed up. This backs up all files changed since the last full or incremental backup. Incremental backups clear the archive bit of the backed-up files; those files will not be backed up during the next incremental backup unless they are modified again and their archive bits are reset to the on state. Incremental backups generally minimize the amount of time needed to perform each daily backup, but they take longer to restore and pose a greater risk of media failure.

- A *differential backup,* which is similar to the incremental backup in that it backs up only files with their archive bits set. The key difference with a differential backup is that the archive bits are left turned on. Subsequent differential backups will back up those same files again, plus any new ones that have been modified. Differential backups take longer to make, but reduce the time required to restore and reduce the risk of media failure.

In a perfect world, it would be nice always to perform full backups. If the system were to fail, then you would need only the most recent backup tape to restore the system fully. However, for a number of reasons, performing a full backup may not always be feasible. For one thing, perhaps there is inadequate time to perform a full backup each day. Another reason is to extend the life of your media and tape drive by reducing the amount of work that they do. You need to weigh these concerns against the increased time it takes to restore from a combination of full and incremental or differential backups, and the increased possibility of being unable to restore backups properly using a combination approach. (For example, if a full restoration required a full backup from the previous week, plus four incremental backups since then, you're counting on having all five tapes be perfectly good, and you're somewhat more exposed to a bad tape.)

One common way to mix these types of backups is to perform a full backup of the system once a week and perform only incremental or differential backups each day of the week. Examine the following examples:

- **Full backup Friday nights and incremental backups Monday–Thursday** If the system fails Monday morning before any data is entered, you need to restore only the full backup from the previous Friday night. If the system fails on Thursday morning, you need to restore four tapes sequentially in order to retrieve all of the data: the full backup from the previous Friday, then the incremental tapes from Monday, Tuesday, and Wednesday nights. Moreover, to guarantee the integrity of the data, you must be able to restore *all* of those tapes, and in their proper sequence. Otherwise, you run the risk of ending up with mismatched data files. In this scenario, you have four media-based points of failure, which might entail more risk than you care to take.

- **Full backup Friday nights and differential backups Monday–Thursday** In this scenario, if the system fails Monday morning, you just restore the tape from the previous Friday night. However, if the system fails on Thursday morning, you need to restore only two tapes: the last full backup from Friday night, plus the differential backup from Wednesday night. Because differential backups back up all changed files since the last full backup, you never need to restore more than two tapes, thereby reducing the number of possible points of media failure.

To determine the best backup scheme for your system, you need to balance the nature of the data and the amount of risk you're willing to take against the cost of each backup, the capacity of the tapes, and the amount of time it takes to make each regular backup.

The most common backup rotation scheme is called grandfather-father-son (GFS). A common way to implement this scheme is to use at least eight tapes. You label four of the tapes as "Monday" through "Thursday," and four others "Friday 1," "Friday 2," "Friday 3," and "Friday 4." Every Monday through Thursday, you use one of those labeled tapes, replacing the data stored the previous week. Each Friday tape corresponds to which Friday in the month you are on: for the first Friday, you use Friday 1, and so forth. Finally, on the last day of each month, you prepare a month-end tape, which you do not reuse, but instead keep offsite in case an environmental failure destroys the system and all locally stored tapes.

There are three main variations of the GFS scheme. In the first, you simply make a full backup of the system each time you perform a backup. This variation offers the greatest amount of media redundancy and the minimum amount of restoration time. In the second, you perform a full backup on each of the Friday tapes and the monthly tape, but perform only incremental backups during the week. In the third, you do much the same thing, but use differential backups instead of incremental backups.

> **TIP** If your data is extremely critical and not easily reconstructed, you can often perform full backups every night and also squeeze in a quick incremental backup midday. This way, you can't lose more than a half-day's worth of data.

You can also choose rotation schemes that are simpler than GFS. For instance, you may use just two or three tapes and then rotate them in sequence, overwriting the old data each time you do so. This lets you restore any of the previous three days' data. The shortcoming of this scheme is that you may need to go back further in time to restore data that was erased or damaged without anyone immediately noticing. You can combat this problem by using several tapes that you rotate weekly or monthly.

One factor to keep in mind when considering different tape rotation schemes is the *granularity* of your backups. Generally, granularity refers to the flexibility that you retain to recover data from earlier tapes. In the standard GFS scheme, where full backups are made all the time, you could restore a file from any given day for a week's time, for any given end of the week (Friday) for a month's time, or for any given month for a year's time. You could not, however, restore a file that was created three months ago in the middle of the month and erased (or damaged) before the month was over because a clean copy wouldn't exist on *any* of the backup tapes.

The best advice for choosing a rotation scheme for important data is that unless there are reasons to do otherwise (as already discussed), use the GFS scheme with full backups. This maximizes the safety of your data, maximizes your restoration flexibility, and minimizes the risk of media failure. If other factors force you to choose a different scheme, use the discussions in this chapter to arrive at the best compromise for your situation.

Granularity and Data Corruption: A Tricky Balance

One reason to consider granularity carefully is the possibility of data becoming corrupted and the situation not being noticed. For instance, I once worked with a database file that had been corrupted several weeks earlier, but had continued to function and seemed normal. After problems started to develop, however, the database vendor's technical support staff discovered that a portion of the database that wasn't regularly used had become lost and wasn't repairable. The problem was caused by a bad sector on the database's hard disk. The only way that the support people could recover the database and ensure that it was clean was to restore backups, going further and further back in time, until they found a copy of the database that didn't have the damage. They then reentered the data that had been added since the nondamaged copy was made. Because of the increasing time span between backups as the support people dug further and further back in time, the amount of data that we needed to reenter grew rapidly.

(continued)

Near-Line Backups

Many companies these days, particularly those running larger networks, are turning to backup solutions that back up the company's data to disk storage on a daily (or more frequent) basis. There are a number of providers of such solutions, such as EMC's Avamar and Commvault. These solutions typically employ compression and de-duplication technology in order to store the backed-up data far more compactly than it normally is, and they can usually keep several weeks' worth of data backed up, including multiple versions (when the data is modified) from each time the backup routine is run.

Such systems have many benefits on a day-to-day basis, and they are much faster to back up and to restore data, compared to tapes. However, when employing such a solution, it is important to keep in mind the exposure of the company data to location-based disasters. For example, if your servers and your backup system are all housed in a single data center, the company's data is exposed to a disaster that occurs at that data center, such as a fire or flood.

There are two ways to mitigate the risks of location-based disasters:

- Disk-based backup systems usually have a "tape-out" function, whereby the backup contents can be written to tapes, which can then be stored at secure offsite storage. This option is probably the more economical of the two mitigation strategies.

- Your company can house its backup solution in a *colocation* facility, which is a remote data center where your company rents space, and which provides electricity and data connections for your device. Then, you make your backups over a data connection between your data center and the colocation facility. This option is likely much more expensive, particularly if your company has a lot of data that it backs up regularly, because WAN links between your data center and the colocation facility are likely to be very expensive and probably require quite a lot of bandwidth.

Chapter Summary

You can be the most proficient person at networking in the world, but if you don't create and carefully manage an appropriate disaster recovery program for your company, you're not doing your job. The importance of this area cannot be overstated. In addition to this chapter, you should study material covering specific backup and restore instructions for your network operating systems and databases, as well as the documentation for your backup hardware device and the backup software you select.

The next chapter discusses key information that you should know about selecting, installing, and managing servers. Servers are the heart of any network, and selecting reliable, productive servers not only will eliminate potential trouble spots for your network, but can also help you avoid needing to actually use the disaster recovery plans and strategies that you have put in place.

CHAPTER 11

Network Servers: Everything You Wanted to Know But Were Afraid to Ask

$\mathbf{M}$ any different *types* of servers exist: file and print servers, application servers, web servers, communications servers, and more. What all servers have in common, though, is that multiple people rely on them and they are usually integral to some sort of network service. Because servers are used by tens or hundreds (or thousands!) of people, the computers you use for servers need to be a cut—or two—above just any old workstation. Servers need to be much more reliable and serviceable than workstations. Plus, they need to perform in different ways from workstations.

This chapter covers network server hardware. You learn what distinguishes a server from a workstation, different server hardware configurations, and preparing a server for use in your network.

What Distinguishes a Server from a Workstation?

With high-performance desktop computers selling for $750 to $1,500, it can be hard to see how a computer with the same processor can cost in excess of $7,000 just because it's designed as a "server." Server computers truly are different from workstations, however, and they incorporate a number of features not found in desktop computers. These features are important to a server's job, which is to serve up data or services to a large number of users as reliably as possible.

Server Processors

Much of the performance of a server derives from its *central processing unit*, or CPU. While servers are also sensitive to the performance of other components (more so than a desktop computer), the processor is still important in determining how fast the server can operate.

Servers can run using one processor or many processors. How many processors you choose for a server depends on various factors. The first is the network operating system (NOS) you use. You need to carefully research how many processors are supported on your proposed NOS if you wish to use multiprocessing.

If you plan to use one of the Windows family of servers, you can use multiple processors, depending on which version and edition you plan to run. Windows Server 2012 can handle from 1 processor (Foundation Edition) up to 64 processors (for Standard and Datacenter Editions).

NOTE   These days, most processors have multiple processor cores on the same chip. The values given for the number of allowed Windows server processors are for the number of processor chips (in other words, the *sockets* on the motherboard).

If you plan to use UNIX, then it depends—some versions of UNIX support multiple processors; others do not.

Another factor to consider is the job that the server does and whether the server's tasks are presently bottlenecked by the processor. File and print servers may not need multiple processors. While they benefit from fast processors, the advantage is not as great as you might think. It's far more important for a file and print server to have a lot of random access memory (RAM) and a fast disk subsystem. Database servers, on the other hand, are processor-hungry and definitely benefit from as many processors as possible running at the fastest possible speed. (It's also important for the database server software to be configured in such a way that it can make optimal use of multiple processors.) Web servers tend to be modest in their processor requirements—they rely on fast busses, fast network connections, a lot of RAM, fast disks, and that's about it. A fast processor (or multiple processors) is nice on most web servers, but it also might be overkill.

Managing multiple processors requires a lot of overhead work on the part of the operating system. Because of this, having twice as many processors in a computer doesn't double its processing capability; instead, doubling the processors might improve the computer's speed by only about 50 to 70 percent. Depending on your operating system, there is also a point of diminishing returns, past which additional processors won't give you much additional performance. Part of this has to do with how the operating system handles multiple processors. Another part has to do with the number of threads doing work in the operating system. (Threads cannot be shared between processors, so if only two main threads are doing all the work on the system, more than two processors won't improve your performance by any meaningful amount.)

DEFINE-IT! What's a Thread?

Operating systems that multitask often do so using a mechanism called a *thread*. In fact, all modern operating systems use threads, including Windows (from Windows 95 on up), NetWare, and some versions of UNIX. In operating systems that make use of threads, each running program runs as a *process*, which has its own memory resources and is kept separate from other processes in the computer. However, the process is divided into different units of work, called *threads*. These threads have access to all the resources of the process in which they run and are the actual "agents of work" within the process. For example, a word processor such as Microsoft Word might have a thread that accepts typed input from the user and displays it on the screen, another that handles any printing chores, and others that constantly check spelling and grammar in the background as the user works. In this example, the application Word is a single process with multiple threads. In a multithreaded operating system, every process always has at least one thread.

To determine the number of processors you should use for any given task, you should consult with the maker of both the NOS you plan to use and makers of the primary applications you plan to run on the server. You might also want to discuss these issues with other companies that are performing similar work with the proposed server application. For instance, for a database server for an accounting system that supports hundreds of users, you should talk to people at other sites that use the same software and have roughly the same number of users to learn about their experiences and suggestions. It's vital to double-check your proposed server configurations in this way because different uses of a server might require far more—or far fewer—hardware resources than you might estimate. If you can find another company doing about the same thing and with approximately the same load, you can drastically improve your confidence in a proposed server hardware configuration's ability to meet your needs.

The Intel Pentium Family

Intel's Pentium family has a variety of different processors, ranging from the basic Pentium all the way up to the Pentium Xeon processor. Current server-class computers usually ship with Pentium Xeon processors. The Xeon series of processors are optimized for server-type duties and are more amenable to running in a multiprocessor system.

Pentium Xeon processors are currently available in speeds ranging up to 3.80 GHz with up to ten cores on a single chip. The design of the Xeon processor allows for up to 8 processors in a Pentium Xeon system (and up to 256 processors in certain third-party system designs). For certain applications, having such a large number of processors can be an advantage.

NOTE   You cannot generally compare the clock speed of processors from one processor family with the clock speeds of processors from another family to get an idea of their relative performance. Processors in different families and from different manufacturers work in very different ways from one another. What takes one processor family four to six instruction cycles to perform might take another processor family only one instruction cycle. Instead, use clock speeds to get an idea of the relative speed difference only among processors within a single processor family.

Intel Clones

Advanced Micro Devices (AMD) makes the Opteron line of processors, which essentially emulates the functioning of the Intel family of processors. AMD has been successful in producing processors that emulate Intel's, and in some cases, they can outperform them.

The problem with clone chips such as AMD's is that, despite claims to the contrary, they won't ever be 100 percent compatible with Intel's processors. Because software vendors *usually* certify their software against only Intel processors, such vendors are likely to be slow to respond to any problems that crop up with the clones. Because of this issue, clone chips are not typically used in server-class machines, where reliability and serviceability are of paramount importance.

TIP Before choosing any server hardware, ensure that the maker of the NOS you plan to use certifies the entire system, including the processor. It is also wise to make sure that the maker of any applications you plan to run on the server certifies the hardware you are choosing. (Most server application makers insist only that the hardware be certified for the operating system, but it's wise to double-check.)

PowerPC

Originally, Motorola, IBM, and Apple teamed up to design and use the PowerPC processor, a reduced instruction set computer (RISC)-based processor that is actually manufactured by Motorola, but based largely on IBM's design. The PowerPC was used in Apple Macintosh computers (Macs now use Intel processors) and some UNIX-based servers from IBM and Motorola.

Bus Capabilities

For most servers, the name of the game is moving data—usually, a *lot* of data. File and print servers might need to serve up hundreds of files simultaneously to hundreds of users and to coordinate and handle the data needs of all those users. Database servers might manage databases that are many gigabytes or terabytes in size, and they must be able to retrieve large chunks of data from their databases and provide it to users within milliseconds. Application servers might perform both processor-intensive and disk-intensive operations while providing application services to users.

Just as networks often have fast backbone segments connecting many slower segments together, a computer relies on its bus to do the same sort of work. A *bus* is the data transfer "backbone" of a computer system, to which the processor, memory, and all installed devices connect.

At any given time, a server might be moving gigabytes of data from its disks to the network cards, to the processor, to the system's memory, and back to the disks as it performs its tasks. All these components are connected together by the system's bus, so optimizing that portion of the computer as much as possible makes sense. The bus might handle about five times more data than any single component in the system, and it needs to do so quickly. While it's true that a conventional Peripheral Component Interconnect (PCI) bus can handle 33 MHz at 32 bits, this just isn't enough in a high-end server. Many servers must handle multiple network interface cards (NICs) (each running at speeds up to 10 Gbps) and multiple disk controllers running at speeds up to 9.6 Gbps. If those devices are busy at the same time, even a PCI bus will quickly get saturated.

Thus, server manufacturers need to get around bus speed limitations. The manufacturers use several schemes to do so. One way is by using multiple busses in a single system. For example, some servers use three PCI busses that can all run at full speed simultaneously. Just by using a little planning in placing certain peripherals on the different busses, you can greatly increase the system's overall speed.

RAM

Another important part of any server is its installed memory. Servers cache data from the network and from the server's disks to achieve the best possible performance, and they rely heavily on their RAM to do this. For example, most NOSs cache the entire directory of files they store for quick access. They also keep requested files in the cache for an extended period of time in case the data from the file is needed again. They also buffer writes to the system's disk through write caches in RAM and perform the actual disk writes asynchronously, so the disks are not as much of a bottleneck as they otherwise would be.

For most servers, 4 to 8GB of RAM should be considered a bare minimum. For heavy-duty database servers supporting hundreds of users, you almost certainly will want multiple gigabytes of RAM to achieve the best possible performance. (Some high-end servers can support up to 768GB of RAM).

TIP   How much RAM do you really need for your server? This is hard to say because a lot depends on how the server is used. The good news is that the Windows family of servers provide statistics showing how the memory in the system is used. You can use this information to help determine when more memory would be beneficial. For the Windows family of server operating systems, use Performance Monitor to see how memory and the system swap file are being used. Also, most high-end databases (like Oracle's) will provide memory-use information to help you determine the amount of RAM that will help the database to perform best.

RAM comes in three varieties: nonparity, parity, and error checking and correcting (ECC). Parity RAM uses an extra bit for every byte to store a checksum of the byte's contents. If the checksum doesn't match when the memory is read, the system stops and reports a memory error. Nonparity memory eliminates the parity bit and therefore can't detect any memory errors. Inexpensive desktop computers sometimes use nonparity RAM as a cost-cutting technique, although you should avoid its use whenever possible, even on desktop computers.

Parity-based memory has two problems. First, the system can only detect memory errors; it can't correct them. Second, because only one bit is used to store the parity, it is possible to "fool" the parity mechanism with a more severe error. For instance, if two bits were to simultaneously change polarities, the parity system wouldn't detect the problem. ECC memory is designed to address these problems. Systems using ECC memory can detect up to two bits of errors and can automatically correct one bit of error. Most current servers use ECC memory because of the added protection that it offers.

Disk Subsystems

The third crucial performance subsystem for a server is its disk drives. Hard disk drives are usually the slowest components of any system, and because most of the server's work involves the hard disks, they are the components most likely to bottleneck the system. Also, the data stored on a server is usually critically important to the company, so it's important to have the most reliable disk configuration you can afford.

Disk Interfaces: SCSI vs. SATA

Two types of disk interfaces are in widespread use today: Serial Advanced Technology Attachment (SATA) and Small Computer Systems Interface (SCSI). (A newer form of SCSI is called SAS, which stands for Serial-Attached-SCSI. SAS is popular on mid-range servers.) For a workstation using Windows 7, SATA performs on par with a SCSI-based disk system. For a server running Windows or Linux, however, SCSI offers clear performance advantages. SCSI systems perform much better when they have simultaneous access to more than one hard disk and when they are used on an operating system that can take proper advantage of SCSI's features, such as the Windows server family or UNIX/Linux.

NOTE   SCSI is pronounced "scuzzy." For a while, Macintosh users tried to adopt the pronunciation "sexy," but it never took hold. (SCSI first saw widespread use on the Macintosh, at least in the personal computing world.)

Many varieties of SCSI-based disk systems are available, as follows:

- **SCSI-1**   The basic SCSI specification can transfer data to and from the disks at approximately 5 MBps using an 8-bit transfer width. Advances in SCSI technology have made SCSI-1 obsolete, and it is not used on current systems. (This is good because most SCSI-1 implementations weren't compatible with one another.)

- **SCSI-2**   This is the basic SCSI interface in use today. It extends the SCSI specification and adds many features to SCSI, and it also allows for much faster SCSI connections. In addition, SCSI-2 greatly improved the SCSI compatibility between different SCSI device manufacturers.

- **Fast SCSI**   With Fast SCSI, the basic SCSI-2 specification is enhanced to increase the SCSI bus speed from 5 MHz to 10 MHz and the throughput from 5 MBps to 10 MBps. Fast SCSI is also called Fast Narrow SCSI.

- **Wide SCSI**   Also based on SCSI-2, Wide SCSI increases the SCSI-2 data path from 8 bits to either 16 or 32 bits. Using 16 bits, Wide SCSI can handle up to 20 MBps.

- **Ultra SCSI**   Also called SCSI-3, this specification increases the SCSI bus speed even higher—to 20 MHz. Using a narrow, 8-bit bus, Ultra SCSI can handle 20 MBps. It can also run with a 16-bit bus, increasing the speed further to 40 MBps.

- **Ultra2 SCSI**   Yet another enhancement of the SCSI standard, Ultra2 SCSI doubles (yet again) the performance of Ultra SCSI. Ultra2 SCSI subsystems can scale up to 80 MBps using a 16-bit bus.

- **Ultra160 SCSI**   By now you should know the story: Ultra160 SCSI again doubles the performance available from Ultra2 SCSI. Ultra160 SCSI (previously called Ultra3 SCSI) is named for its throughput of 160 MBps.

- **Ultra320 SCSI** Ultra320 SCSI can move data at a rate of 320 MBps.

- **Ultra640 SCSI** Another doubling of the SCSI interface speed, Ultra640 SCSI was promulgated as a new standard in early 2003.

> **NOTE** A storage connection technology called Fibre Channel can use either fiber-optic or copper cable, is a much more flexible connection scheme than SCSI, and promises throughput many times faster than even that of Ultra640 SCSI. Based loosely on a network paradigm, Fibre Channel is initially expensive to implement, but large data centers will benefit greatly from its advances over SCSI.

As you can see from the preceding list, a dizzying array of SCSI choices is available on the market today. Because of all the different standards, it's a good idea to make sure you purchase matched components when building a SCSI disk subsystem or when purchasing one as part of a server. Make sure the controller card you plan to use is compatible with the drives you will use, that the card uses the appropriate cables, and that it is compatible with both the server computer and the NOS you will use. The good news is that once you get a SCSI disk subsystem up and running, it will run reliably and with excellent performance.

Disk Topologies: It's a RAID!

The acronym RAID stands for redundant array of independent disks. RAID is a technique of using many disks to do the work of one disk, and it offers many advantages compared to using fewer, larger disks.

The basic idea behind RAID is to seamlessly spread a server's data across many disks. For example, a single file might have portions of itself spread across four or five disks. The RAID system manages all those parts so you never know they're actually spread across all the disks. You open the file, the RAID system accesses all the appropriate disks and "reassembles" the file, and provides the entire file to you.

The immediate benefit you get is that the multiple disks perform much more quickly than a single disk. This is because all the disks can independently work on finding their own data and sending it to the controller to be assembled. A single disk drive would be limited by a single disk head and would take much longer to gather the same amount of data. The performance of a RAID system *increases* as you add more disks because of the benefit of having all those disk heads independently working toward retrieving the needed data.

If you think about a simple RAID array with data spread across many disks, you'll probably notice that, while it improves performance, it also increases the chance of a disk failure. Using five disks to do the work of one means that five times more chances exist for a disk failure. Because the data is spread among all the disks, if one fails, you might as well throw away all the data on all the remaining disks because it's useless if a big chunk is missing. Fortunately, different RAID schemes address this problem.

There are many different ways to use multiple disks together in some sort of RAID scheme and, accordingly, a number of *RAID levels* are defined, each of which describes a different technique, as follows:

- **RAID 0**   This scheme is a configuration whereby data is spread (*striped*) across multiple disks, although *with no redundancy*. Losing one drive in a RAID 0 array results in the loss of data on all the disks. RAID 0 is appropriate only for improving performance and should be used only with nonessential data. RAID 0 arrays can stripe data across two or more disks, as shown in Figure 11-1.

- **RAID 1**   This type of array doesn't stripe data across multiple disks. Instead, it defines a standard whereby data is mirrored between disks. Two disks are used instead of one, and the data is kept synchronized between the two disks. If one of the disks fails, the remaining disk continues working just fine until the failed drive can be replaced. RAID 1 is often simply referred to as *mirroring*. An enhancement to RAID 1 is called *duplexing*; the data is still duplicated between two disks, but each disk has its own disk controller, adding another level of redundancy because you can lose either a disk or a controller and still keep operating. Duplexing can also improve performance somewhat, compared to straight mirroring. Some RAID 1 implementations are also intelligent enough to read data from either disk in such a way that whichever disk has its drive head closest to the data performs the read request, while the other one sits idle. However, all writes must occur simultaneously for both disks. Figure 11-2 shows a typical RAID 1 array layout.

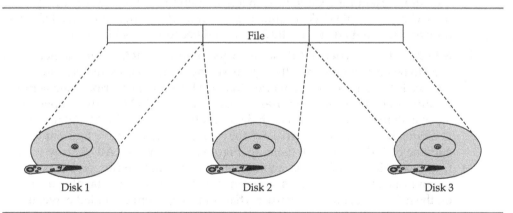

Figure 11-1.   A RAID 0 array stripes data across multiple disks.

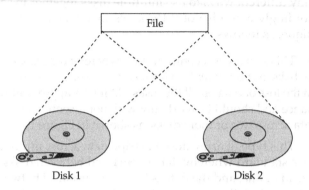

Figure 11-2.   A RAID 1 array mirrors data between two disks.

    TIP   You can combine RAID levels 0 and 1 to achieve the performance benefit of RAID 0 with the high level of redundancy of RAID 1. Imagine a series of RAID 1 arrays with two disks each. Combine each of these RAID 1 arrays so that data is striped across them, and you have what is called a RAID 10 array (with 10 referring to a combination of RAID 1 and RAID 0). This is sometimes also called RAID 0 + 1 or RAID 1 + 0.

- **RAID 2**   You probably won't see RAID 2 implemented in the real world. RAID 2 is a technical specification that stripes data across multiple disks and then uses a Hamming Code ECC that is written to a set of ECC disks. The ratio of ECC disks to data disks is quite high with RAID 2: There are three ECC disks for every four data disks. RAID 2 isn't used because of its inefficiency.

- **RAID 3**   This is where RAID starts to get interesting. RAID 3 implementations used to be fairly common, although these days RAID 3 is extremely rare; you see RAID 5 used far more often than RAID 3. RAID 3 stripes data across multiple data disks and then uses an "exclusive or" (XOR) bit-wise operation against all the stored data on each data disk to come up with ECC data, which is written to a single ECC drive. So, for example, you can have four data drives and one ECC drive to back them up. Figure 11-3 shows a RAID 3 array with five disks. The XOR data has an interesting mathematical property. If you remove one of the data drives, you can take the remaining data, plus the data on the ECC drive, and reconstruct what is missing from the failed drive. It doesn't matter which disk in a RAID 3 array is lost; you always can reconstruct the data provided all the rest of the disks are still functioning. RAID disk controllers do this automatically if a drive fails, although the drives operate at a slower rate than normal because of the overhead of having to reconstruct the data on-the-fly. A more useful technique is to replace the failed drive and then use the ECC data to rebuild the lost data.

Figure 11-3.   A RAID-3 array stripes data across multiple disks, with an ECC disk to protect the data.

 NOTE   If more than one drive is lost from a RAID 3 or a RAID 5 array, all the array's data will be lost. Still, these arrays provide good protection at relatively low incremental cost.

■ **RAID 4**   This is another of the RAID standards that isn't used very much in most servers, although sometimes is used in dedicated storage appliances. RAID 4 is similar to RAID 3, except data is striped between the different data drives in much larger blocks than with RAID 3. RAID 4 still uses a single ECC disk for all the data drives.

■ **RAID 5**   RAID 5, depicted in Figure 11-4, is the current standard for RAID systems. (RAID 1 also remains a current standard, but it has different applications.) Recall how RAID 3 worked, with data striped to a set of data disks and the ECC code written to a single ECC disk. RAID 5 improves on this scheme

Figure 11-4.   A RAID 5 array stripes data across multiple disks and alternately uses all disks for ECC

by interleaving the data and ECC information across all the disks. The big advantage of this approach over RAID 3 is that it doesn't rely on a single ECC drive for all write operations, which becomes a bottleneck on RAID 3 systems. Because all the drives share the ECC work, performance with RAID 5 is somewhat better than with RAID 3. There is a small drawback to this, though, that some commentators miss. In RAID 3, if you lost a data drive, the system slowed down (usually dramatically) as the data was reconstructed on-the-fly. If you lost the ECC drive, however, the system would still run just as fast as if no drive were lost. With RAID 5, if you lose a drive, you're always losing part of your ECC drive because its job is spread among all the disks, so you get a slowdown no matter what.

- **RAID 6**   RAID 6 works the same as RAID 5, but stores parity data on two interleaving drives rather than the one of RAID 5. Also called *dual data guarding*, RAID 6 keeps your data safe while you are recovering from a single drive failure. (In RAID 5, if a drive failed while you were recovering from another drive's failure, you would lose the array's data.)

- **Nested RAID Combinations**   For added performance and data protection, it can be common on highly critical, high-performance disk storage systems (such as Storage Area Network disk systems) to combine RAID levels together. The most common combinations are RAID 1 and 0 (RAID 10), RAID 5 and 0 (RAID 50), and RAID 6 and 0 (RAID 60). So, for example, a RAID 50 array would be made up of three or more RAID 0 striped sets of drives, each of which looks like one drive within an overall RAID 5 array. In this example, the RAID 0 arrays are said to be *nested* within the overall RAID 5 array.

Which level of RAID should you use on your network server? Most network administrators favor RAID 5 because it requires only 20 to 25 percent of the total disk capacity for the redundancy function (depending on how many disks are in the array), yet it performs well and offers a measure of safety. However, RAID 3 and RAID 5 arrays do occasionally fail to recover data properly (although they very rarely lose data). For this reason, you usually should opt for either RAID 1 or a RAID 10 array for network servers that store vital data.

In general, the different RAID configurations offer different levels of reliability. Ranked from best to worst purely in terms of the system's likelihood of losing data would be RAID 1, RAID 10, RAID 6, RAID 5, and RAID 3. There are always trade-offs, though. A system with 20 disks using just RAID 1 would be unwieldy to manage because you would have 10 logical drives to manage and use efficiently. However, if you configured those same 20 disks as two RAID 5 arrays, you would be able to manage more efficiently the two logical disks that would result. However, with 20 disks, you have four times the overall failure rate as an array built using 5 disks.

You must make your own decision based on the importance of the data, the required levels of performance, the capabilities of the server, and the budget available to you. One thing you should *never* do, though, is trust that any RAID level replaces regular, tested, reliable tape backups of network data!

Server-State Monitoring

An important feature of most servers is the capability to monitor their internal components and to notify you if any problems develop or appear to be developing. Higher-end servers can typically monitor the following:

- Proper fan operation
- System voltage
- Memory errors, even if corrected by ECC memory
- Disk errors, even if corrected automatically
- In-case temperature
- Operating system hangs
- Computer case opening

Any of these errors might indicate a current or impending problem with the server. For example, a 1-bit memory error that is corrected by the system's ECC memory might not cause a problem for the server because it was corrected, but it might indicate that a RAM chip or bank of RAM is starting to experience trouble. Similarly, climbing temperatures in a case might not cause an immediate problem, but may indicate that a fan isn't operating properly, has a blocked intake, or is facing another problem, and ultimately temperatures higher than those allowed for in the server design will cause a failure.

Server-state monitoring solutions can alert you to problems either via e-mail or through a pager or Short Message Service (SMS) message. Some even operate if power is lost to the server or the server room (this is called "lights-out" capability). Many high-end servers also offer "prefailure" warranties that state that the manufacturer will replace any components reporting even minor errors so you can replace them before serious trouble actually strikes. For those servers you depend on to be the most reliable possible, such monitoring and warranty features can be a real lifesaver.

Hot-Swap Components

Most modern servers include hot-swap components that you can replace while the system continues to operate. Usually, hot-swap components are limited to disks, power supplies, and fans, all of which are running in a redundant configuration. For example, a system might have two power supplies; if one fails, the system still operates normally and you can replace the failed power supply without needing to turn off the server. Similarly, most RAID disk configurations enable you to replace a failed drive without shutting down the server, provided the disks are installed in a hot-swap configuration.

 TIP   Many RAID disk systems enable you to install a standby disk, and the system itself uses that standby disk to replace any failed drive automatically. Of course, you would then replace the actual failed disk as soon as possible, and the replacement becomes the new standby disk for the disk array.

Choosing Servers for Windows

In this section, you learn about the basics of defining server needs, selecting a server, and purchasing a server.

Defining Server Needs

Before looking at different server models, you need to understand clearly the needs that the server has to meet. Otherwise, you risk either under- or over-purchasing hardware, both of which can cause problems and might lead you to spend more than you needed to. Under-purchasing leads to additional, unplanned purchases, which might include adding more disks or more memory, or even needing to replace the server much too soon. Over-purchasing means you spent more for a server than necessary, which might lead your company to deny your request for a particular server. Instead, you need to find the "sweet spot" for specifying just the right server for your needs; then you can defend your required configuration and its cost. You can't do any of this unless you have clearly defined your needs.

To specify the needs for a server clearly, you must be able to answer all of the following questions:

- What is the useful life of the server? How long do you expect to use the server? Will you replace it in two, three, or four years? (Most servers are used for around three years before being replaced.) Everyone should agree on this timeframe because if you plan to replace the server in two years, you can get by with a smaller server than if you need one to last three or four years. If you specified a server capable of meeting two years' needs, however, you don't want to get to the end of two years and then find out that your company won't approve a replacement.

- What job will the server perform? Will it be a file and print server, a web server, a database server, or some other kind of server?

- How many users will the server support and what are the needs of those users? For example, with a file and print server, you must estimate the storage and bandwidth requirements needed to satisfy all the planned users' requests. For a database server, you must know how quickly the server needs to respond to various database operations.

- How reliable must the server be? What are the consequences (costs and impacts) if the server crashes for one or more hours, or for a day or two?

- Will you use clustering for the server? Clustering is a technique whereby multiple servers share the same essential job. If one fails, everything keeps working, albeit at a slower rate. Once the failed server is repaired, it can then be added back to the cluster.

- How safe must the data on the server be from loss? This is different from the preceding question because you might have cases in which a server must never lose data, even if it isn't a big deal if the server goes down for a few hours. In such a situation, you would use a RAID 1 or RAID 10 configuration, but you might not care too much about, say, redundant power supplies. You might also explore some kind of hierarchical storage scheme, where data is automatically copied to tape or optical disk in real time, or where you make several live incremental backups of files each day.

- If the server fails, what are your recovery plans? Do you plan to keep a hot-spare server (one that's ready to be swapped in at a moment's notice for a failed server) available, or do you plan simply to rely on the server manufacturer's service capabilities? Also, sometimes if a server fails, other existing servers might temporarily meet some of its needs. For example, in a Windows network, if a domain controller fails, you can have other domain controllers to provide this necessary functionality for the network as a whole. Or you might have redundant printer queues defined on another server, ready to be made available if the primary print server fails.

- How do you plan to back up the server? Do you plan to have a tape drive on the server itself, or do you plan to back it up over the network to some other server's backup device? Do you plan to make backups while the server is being used, or overnight when it's not being used? These are important questions to answer because if you host the backup device on the server, you also need to have backup software on the server. If you plan to back up a server while it's being used, you need a fast backup system connected to a fast server bus to minimize the impact to the users during the day. If you plan to back up a server over a network connection, you need a network connection fast enough to handle the amount of data on the server. Think carefully about your backup plans when specifying a server.

- How could the demands placed on the server change over time? Is the company aggressively hiring more employees, so that the server might need to support twice as many users a year from now and four times as many users two years from now? Make sure you understand the company's overall plans and factor them into your assessment of server needs. Also, even in companies where the number of users is relatively static, the amount of storage required by each user will still grow rapidly. A rule of thumb is to estimate that current storage requirements double every 18 months, all else being equal. If you have historical data for how much storage users consume, this data can help you estimate your system's requirements even more accurately. (And don't forget to anticipate any new network services that could more rapidly increase your storage needs!)

- Does the new server need to work with any existing hardware? If you need to reuse a network backup device, for instance, you should make sure that the new server can properly support it (and vice versa).

- How much physical room do you have available to house the server? Are you compelled by space requirements to go with the smallest server possible?

Once you answer these questions and any others that might crop up, you're ready to start looking at different servers that can meet the needs you defined.

Selecting the Server

Aside from choosing the types of equipment you need for a server, you must remember three basic prerequisites that all your server purchases should meet: compatibility, compatibility, and compatibility. If your NOS starts displaying error messages on a particular server, you'll need fast responses to these types of problems. If you built a server yourself by buying a motherboard, a disk controller, a video card, and so forth, you're not going to get effective support, either for the hardware or for any compatibility problems that crop up with the software. For Microsoft NOSs, make sure that each part of the server—as well as the entire system collectively—is certified by Microsoft for the selected version of Windows Server you plan to run.

For Microsoft operating systems, go to the following URL to look at Microsoft's Hardware Compatibility List (HCL) for its Server products and make certain that the hardware you like is certified:

```
http://www.windowsservercatalog.com/
```

When selecting servers, you often select a manufacturer first and then select the actual model you need. This is because, everything being equal, you're slightly better off if all your servers are from the same maker. Managing servers from one manufacturer is much easier than managing servers from many manufacturers. You can do a better job of stocking spare parts that might fit into all of your servers, and you can build a better relationship with the manufacturer or a particular dealer, which might hold additional benefits. For example, Dell lets companies certify their in-house technicians on Dell hardware (including servers), and then allows them to order parts more directly, bypassing the first level of support (the first support people's job being mainly to intercept the easy questions that beginners ask), and also provides other benefits.

Be conservative in selecting servers and server brands. You should stick with the top names in the industry for many reasons, including these:

- They have much more established service organizations and practices.

- They are likely to offer higher-quality support.

- Because so many other networks are based on their equipment, their technical support databases probably already contain any problems you may encounter, and they probably have fixes available.

- The NOS vendor is also more likely to have data on any problems concerning one of the top servers.

- They have much better in-house engineering, and their servers are likely to perform better and to be more reliable.

These are just the biggest reasons. You might remember a time when the mantra in management information systems (MIS) departments was, "Nobody ever got fired for buying IBM." A similar type of mindset makes sense when buying servers, not only because the purchase is more defensible, but because buying from major manufacturers actually makes better business sense, for the reasons cited in the preceding list.

Remember these general differences when you select a server for Windows networks: First, while any server is RAM-hungry, Windows servers generally work better with more RAM. Also, database servers are RAM-hungry for databases of any appreciable size (100GB or larger), so plan on using at *least* 16GB of RAM. (32GB to 64GB of RAM isn't out of the question for the best possible performance.)

Windows server systems can implement certain RAID levels themselves in the operating system itself. For the best performance, however, you should select a disk controller that can take this burden off the NOS. High-throughput disk controllers also often have a significant amount of RAM on them for caching disk data, and they usually have their own processor to help handle their chores. Moreover, I recommend you use a SCSI-based disk subsystem on a server. A workstation running Windows performs equally well with either SATA or SCSI, but a server can take advantage of SCSI's features to improve performance significantly over SATA disk interfaces. SCSI drives also have a tendency to be more reliable than SATA drives. Choosing your actual disk configuration is relatively straightforward. You start by determining your current and planned space requirements, and then you consider your performance and reliability needs to choose a particular RAID level that makes sense. (See the "Disk Topologies: It's a RAID!" section earlier in this chapter for more information.) Once you know these requirements, you can choose the amount of disk space you need and ensure that the server you want can handle your current and planned disk space needs.

Remember this tip: You're better off knowing what your disk requirements will be over time and planning to purchase additional disk space as the need arises. This is because the capacity of disk drives increases at a rapid rate, while prices fall at a rapid rate. Buying a 2TB drive a year from now, for example, will be less expensive than purchasing the same drive today. Just make sure that the server you select can handle all the drives that you plan to purchase, and then install those drives as needed to save your company money.

If you plan to purchase a server for Windows Server, you might also want to consider selecting a system that accepts additional processors. This way, if you find the system is becoming bottlenecked at the processor level, you can install more processors to reduce or remove that bottleneck.

Purchasing the System

Once you decide on the server you want, purchasing it is relatively straightforward. Shop around and get the best price on the system you want. Make sure that the suppliers you approach offer the level of support you need, both for pre-sales selection assistance and for post-sales support.

Depending on your company's financial practices, you might want to consider leasing a server. Doing so brings you several benefits. First, leasing conserves your company's cash. Instead of shelling out $20,000 all at once, you can pay for the use of the server over time. Also, the annual impact of a lease is much lower than with a purchase, and leasing might make it easier to fit a particular server within your budget.

Leases also have a hidden benefit: They force you to consider whether to replace a server at the end of the lease term (usually three years). They also usually make it easy to return the server to the leasing company and then lease a new server with which you can move forward. In the end, you pay about as much for leasing as buying (all things considered), and leases can help discipline a company to keep its computer equipment relatively current. The only drawback to leasing is that you must have enough time to replace the server at the end of the lease, when you might prefer to do it several months before or after the lease is up. Still, in some companies, the benefits of leasing far outweigh the disadvantages. Discuss leasing with your financial department before ordering a server.

Installing Servers

The actual practice of setting up a server is mostly specific to the server itself and the NOS that you plan to use. In subsequent chapters, this book describes basic installations of Windows and Linux.

When you set up a new server, remember to plan on extensively testing its hardware prior to implementing it. While most servers are reliable right out of the box, the fact is that if some part of the server is going to fail, it almost always fails shortly after being set up and used. I prefer to test servers for at least a week, even before installing the NOS onto the server. Most servers come with diagnostic software that you can configure to operate continuously—testing the system's processor, video subsystem, disk surfaces, and RAM—and log any errors that crop up. Right after pulling a server from its box and installing any components that you need to install, plan on putting the server into a diagnostic loop using its diagnostic software and letting it run those tests for as long as possible. In no case should you test the server for less than several days (try to shoot for a week of testing).

TIP   It's important to start testing a server immediately after it arrives. Most vendors have different replacement versus repair policies depending on how long you've had a piece of hardware. For instance, many vendors will simply replace a server with an entirely new one if a failure is discovered in the first 30 days, but after that, they'll go through the normal repair process. If an error does appear during testing, you'll probably be more confident with a new server than going through a repair process. (Plus, the repair process will take more of your time for troubleshooting and such.)

After finishing the testing, you can install the NOS. During this phase, pay careful attention to any peculiarities of the server and to any error messages reported by the NOS or the server during the installation process.

You must resolve these errors fully prior to going live with the server. In particular, watch out for any intermittent messages, such as a message that there was a parity error in the system's RAM or an unexpected lockup of the server during installation. Even if those problems don't recur, consult with the maker of the server. (Be sure you carefully write down any messages or other things that you notice if this happens.) Servers have a tendency to fail at the most inopportune times, so make sure that you have complete confidence in the server before making it available to users. It might make sense also to let the server run its production software configuration for several days as an added test before putting it into use.

In particular, make sure to have all potential Windows services and processes, or UNIX/Linux daemons, running together as part of the testing. When you combine third-party software for these platforms, there are numerous opportunities for bugs or incompatibilities that the vendors did not anticipate (despite a NOS vendor's stamp of approval).

Most server manufacturers have made it easy to install their server and to install the NOS onto the server. Companies such as HP and Dell even ship their servers with special CD-ROMs that mostly automate the process of installing various NOSs onto the server and also install any support files that the NOS needs to work optimally with the server hardware. Prior to installing a NOS onto a server, make sure to read the server's documentation carefully and take advantage of any automated tools provided by the server manufacturer.

 TIP   The top-tier server makers (HP and Dell, for example) maintain e-mail notification systems that let you know about any new patches they release or any serious problems they have with a particular model. These e-mail services are extremely useful, so you should plan on signing up for them immediately on receipt of any new server.

Here's something else to think about: Sometimes servers are built and then sit around in inventory for several months before being sold. Consequently, the server might not come with the most current software. Before installing the server, check the maker's web site for any updates that aren't in your package and consider whether to install those updates during your implementation process.

Maintaining and Troubleshooting Servers

To do the best job of maintaining and troubleshooting servers, you need to take steps to do two things: decrease the chance of failure and improve your chance of rapidly resolving any failures that do occur. Problems are inevitable, but you can greatly decrease your odds of having them, and you can also greatly improve your chances of resolving them quickly, by taking steps *before* you actually have any problems.

To decrease the chance of failure, make sure to follow all the advice previously given: Use reliable, tested servers and components. You should also take these additional steps:

- Whenever possible, try to reduce the number of jobs that a server must do. Although building a single server that will be a file and print server, a database server, an e-mail server, and a web server is certainly possible, you're much better off (from an overall reliability standpoint) segregating these duties onto smaller, separate servers.

- Set up a practice of frequently viewing the server's error logs. If the server NOS supports notification of errors (such as to a pager or SMS message), consider implementing this feature. Many failures start with error messages that might precede the actual failure by a few hours, so getting an early heads-up might help you keep the server running or at least enable you to resolve the problem at the best possible time.

- If a server supports management software that monitors the server's condition, make sure to install the software.

- Most RAID arrays that support hot-swap of failed drives also require that the NOS have special software installed to support this feature fully. Make sure that you install this software before any failures occur.

- NOS software is among the most bug-free available, but it's still true that there is no such thing as completely bug-free software. Over time, any NOS will eventually fail. While many servers run for up to a year without requiring a restart, you're better off establishing a practice of periodically shutting down the server and bringing it back up again. This practice eliminates small transient errors that might be accumulating and could eventually lead to a server crash, such as memory leaks in the NOS. The best frequency for such restarts is monthly.

 CAUTION   Make sure that you do a backup before shutting down the server and restarting it. The greatest chance of hardware failure occurs when the system is powered back up again.

When implementing a server to replace an existing server, it's a good idea to make three good backups and test restorations prior to putting the new server into use. It might seem redundant, but you never know when you might need to restore your data, and it's important to know that your backup and restoration practices will function properly.

You can also do some general things to improve your ability to resolve any server failures rapidly. The most important is to maintain for each server an extensive binder (or file box), which I call a "rebuild kit." This binder should contain the following:

- All purchase data for the server, including your purchase order and a copy of the supplier's invoice.

- A printout of the server's configuration. Most servers' setup programs can generate a detailed list with all components and their versions. HP's Insight Manager is great for this.

■   All software needed to rebuild the server completely from scratch. This includes the setup software for the server, the NOS software, device driver disks, and any patch disks you need or have applied. Remember to add to the box any new drivers or patches that you get during the life of the server so that they will be available.

■   Contact information for service on the server, including any extended warranty contract numbers or other information that you need to get service.

■   Notepaper for documenting all changes to the server's configuration and any error messages that appear. Write all the information clearly, noting the date, the time, and any other details that you (or someone else) might need to fix the server if it fails.

■   A printout or document noting anything special about the server or how you configured the disk drives, including NOS settings. You need these settings if you have to rebuild from scratch. Knowing these settings might enable you to recover the data on the server's disks so that you don't need to restore the data from backup tape.

 CAUTION   You need a strong backup plan for any server, with appropriate tape rotations and regular tests of your ability to restore data from the tapes you make. The goal is to never need to use these tapes, but they give you an absolutely critical safety net if the server's disks crash and lose their stored data.

Even if you're the best computer troubleshooter in the world, you should plan on working with the service department of your server's manufacturer to troubleshoot any problems. Doing so can save you because the people in this department have extensive databases available to them of the problems others have experienced. They also are familiar with the steps needed to help prevent data loss as you work to troubleshoot the problem. Troubleshooting a server on your own, no matter how experienced and knowledgeable you are, is usually a mistake, because the consequences of even a small mistake can be quite large.

Chapter Summary

When building a network, the one component you should pay the most attention to is the server. While other parts of the network, like the wiring, network architecture, or workstations, are also significant, the server is the most likely component to experience trouble over time. The server is the single component you must spend the most time managing. Because of this, take extra care when selecting, implementing, and maintaining your servers. If you take care of your server, your servers will take care of you.

The following chapter concerns network workstation computers and discusses the different requirements desktop computers have, how you should buy and manage them, and how to support them.

CHAPTER 12 | Purchasing and Managing Client Computers

Desktop computers are really where the "rubber meets the road" when it comes to networks. These machines are the users' primary interface to the network and the resource on which users most rely to get their jobs done. In fact, the network is designed to support the desktop computers' work rather than the other way around. Maintaining desktop computers is also the task on which you often spend the most time in managing a network, so their purchase, implementation, and management are important. You can have the best network in the world, but if your desktop computers aren't up to the task, the network's users won't be productive.

This chapter focuses on the management of desktop computers. Chances are that if you're reading this book, you already know about the bits and bytes that make up desktop computers and desktop operating systems. You're probably already a wizard with Windows or the Mac, and you're comfortable installing new computer hardware and repairing problems on desktop computers. If you don't know about these things yet, you can find many good books that cover the technologies in desktop computers in detail. In this chapter, the major concern is how desktop computers integrate with the network and how you can get the most out of them when you're managing or setting up a network.

Choosing Desktop Computers

Choosing desktop computers involves many considerations. Making good choices here will pay big dividends over time. When purchasing new desktop computers, you have the opportunity to select machines to reduce your support burden, improve end-user productivity, and—overall—conserve your company's cash. The following sections explore the different factors that go into selecting desktop computers.

Desktop Platforms

You need to know which desktop computer platform you will use. Generally, companies tend to gravitate toward either PC- or Mac-based desktop computers. (These days, it is rare to find companies that depend much on Macs as a main staple of their desktop computer diet.) In a few rare cases, companies might alternatively gravitate toward Linux- or UNIX-based desktop computers, but you'll usually choose between PCs and Macs.

Advantages and disadvantages exist for each platform. Regardless of the specific pros and cons, you're *much* better off if you can keep the company standardized on a single desktop computer platform. Companies that have purchased their desktop computers in accordance with individual user preferences (users are free to choose a PC, a Mac, or something else) end up with real support headaches, which arise from many different sources. Supporting two desktop platforms is *more* than twice as difficult as supporting one platform. Why? Consider the following:

- You need to maintain expertise in two platforms, as well as expertise in their applications and platform-specific peculiarities. In a small company, you need more people to keep the requisite levels of expertise on both platforms than you would need if you had to support only one platform.

- You need to stock more spare parts and expansion hardware. Generally, components that work in a PC won't work in a Mac, and vice versa.

- You need to license and inventory more software titles (on average, twice as many).

- Problems that would never occur with one platform or another occur when you must support both, even in the network itself. Supporting two platforms is more complex than supporting one, so the servers must run additional software, must allow for the different ways that each platform works, and so forth. All this increases the complexity of the network, and increased complexity means less reliability for everyone.

- Interplatform incompatibilities cause problems for users who must work together. Even if they use the same application (such as Microsoft Word) on both PCs and Macs, platform differences still exist. For example, Adobe fonts with the same name may look and paginate differently on Macs and PCs. Users might painstakingly format a document in Word, Excel, InDesign, or another application available on both platforms, only to find that the other platform doesn't present their work in exactly the same way. When users who frequently interact with one another have their files formatted for a variety of platforms, the incompatibilities become a real problem.

- In some cases, you might be unable to find software titles with matching versions available for both platforms. This usually means users who are using a particular application won't be able to interact with users who are using the other platform's functionally equivalent application. For example, Microsoft Access is available only for Windows.

- You will be limited in the programs you can develop for widespread use. For example, try developing a Microsoft Access–based application and then having Mac users use it. They can't because Microsoft Access doesn't exist on the Mac, and there's no way to use the same database application on both platforms in such cases. You can probably exchange data, but not the program written in Access. The same situation exists for virtually all programming languages: They are almost universally platform-specific, despite the efforts of their makers to make them platform-neutral. Examples of this kind of problem are much more common than not. (One exception to this rule is a more advanced SQL-based application that makes use of something like an Oracle database server.)

These examples should convince you that you're better off running the *wrong* desktop platform than running *two* desktop platforms. If you're in a company where two desktop platforms are in use, you should work toward implementing a standard platform. This process can be difficult and time-consuming, but is important both for increasing overall company productivity and keeping IT costs at a reasonable level.

After deciding whether or not to standardize on a single platform, your next decision is which one to choose. Most often, a company has a history with a particular platform, so sticking with that platform is usually the easiest solution, unless a good reason exists for a change.

If you're lucky enough to be setting up a company network for the first time, then you get to help choose a platform. This choice should always be driven by what the users need to accomplish, which applications they need to run, and the platform that best supports those applications. You need to consider the full range of applications that the company is likely to need, but the users' needs should be the primary driver. For most companies, this means you'll strongly lean toward PCs as the standard. However, for some companies, Macs are still a good idea. Generally, Macs make sense in companies that have a strong artistic or graphic bent to their makeup, such as a web design firm, a graphic design house, and so forth.

NOTE   As you have probably already noticed, many people want to make a platform decision based on the platform they like the best. Many people happily call themselves "PC fanatics" or "Mac fanatics." For some of these people, the issue rises almost to the same level of importance to them as a religion. Such fervent brand loyalty should never influence you in making a smart business decision. However, the presence of such strong opinions also means that you must tread carefully when discussing platform issues with the system's users!

If no need exists that strongly suggests a particular platform, then, for many reasons, you should lean toward PCs. They are the most price competitive, are in the widest use, attract the largest assortment of software and hardware developers, and have much more infrastructure to support them. Also, for certain important business application software categories, good solutions are available on the PC platform but not on the Mac platform. This is changing as business applications become more and more based on client-server database and web browser–based user interfaces, but there will still be some applications that are not really cross-platform.

NOTE   One helpful development over the past few years involves products that allow one to set up a virtualized environment on a Mac and run Windows and its applications within that environment. Products like Parallels Desktop, VMWare Fusion, or VirtualBox can all let you do this. In addition, you can use a product like Apple Bootcamp to set up a dual-boot installation on your Mac. These products do add complexity to the desktop, but in cases where you really must support both platforms, they can help solve compatibility and application availability issues for your users.

Reliability and Serviceability

The most important features to look for in any desktop computer are its reliability and serviceability. Studies have shown that the actual price of a desktop computer is a small percentage of its lifetime cost, which includes software costs, training costs, and support costs.

When assessing reliability, you need to look at the whole picture. Reliability comes from several sources:

- The computer uses tested, high-quality components.

- Those components are engineered to work well together. You can make a cake with the best ingredients available, but if your recipe isn't good, you still get a bad cake. Computers are no different. Even the best components don't always work well together. Top-tier manufacturers test all the components that go into their systems and ensure that they're compatible with one another.

- A reliable combination of software is used on the unit, and whenever possible, the software has been certified on the computer.

Serviceability is closely related to reliability. *Serviceability* simply means that working on or repairing a particular computer is relatively fast and easy. Features that enhance serviceability include cases that are easy to open (requiring no tools), quickly replaceable internal components (such as hard disks, memory, or video cards that require simple or no tools), and a Basic Input Output Software (BIOS) that is easy to update.

Serviceability is also strongly influenced by the services available from the computer's maker:

- Does the computer manufacturer stay current in offering updates to its computers?

- Does its web site offer a lookup that lets you determine the configuration of a computer based on its serial or service ID numbers?

- Is technical information about its systems readily available, or does the vendor tend to gloss over any discovered problems?

- How quickly can you get replacement parts?

- Does the manufacturer include onsite service for a period of time that reduces your support burden?

- What is the warranty on any given computer?

- Is the vendor sufficiently successful and stable that you can expect the company to be around for the entire useful life of the unit?

- What other value-added services are offered if problems occur?

Other factors that strongly influence serviceability are often overlooked. How many computers does the maker sell, and is the specific model that you are buying widely used?

Author's Note

I once joined a company that had been purchasing "no-name" clones for its desktop computers. In my first week, I set up five brand-new units right out of their boxes, only to find that three of them were dead on arrival (DOA). That same week, the company's chief financial officer (CFO), who was working on an important financing activity, had his computer crash repeatedly, losing unsaved work each time, until I finally swapped his entire computer for one of the new ones that actually worked. Was the money saved on those computers (about $400 per unit) worth it? What was the cost to the company for all these mishaps? The answer is simple: far more than the company saved. I immediately changed the company's brand to a more reliable one (the CFO was sympathetic!) and got rid of the existing machines as quickly as possible. The lesson is that you shouldn't be penny-wise and pound-foolish when you purchase computers.

These factors are important because a widely used computer is more likely to be supported when new software or hardware comes out. Companies that make software and hardware know they must ensure that their products work properly with popular computer brands and models.

Suppose that you use computers from a small, local company (or, even worse, build the computers yourself), and some software package or operating system that comes out in a year or two fails to work properly on your machines. The maker of the software or hardware might say something like, "Well, we haven't tested on that computer, so we don't know why our product isn't working right." While the maker might act in good faith to resolve the issue, the problem might take much longer to fix than for a widely used system, and it might never be resolved. On the other hand, if you're using a top-tier computer, such as one from Dell, Lenovo, or HP (or other top-tier brands), the vendor of the new product probably knows how to resolve any problems that arise and has already done so before the product was shipped.

TIP   If your company runs an application that is vital to its business but that is not widely used, it sometimes pays to find out which computers the application maker uses. If you know that the application maker has built the application using a particular make, you can reduce your risk of having trouble with that application by considering using the same brand in your organization.

You can also improve serviceability if you standardize on a particular manufacturer because then you can focus your resources on supporting that line of computers. The people who support the desktop computers in the company will find it easier to stay up-to-date with the peculiarities of that manufacturer and will become more comfortable working with those computers. Also, your company's support staff will be able to solve a problem once and then apply the solution to many computers, rather than having to troubleshoot many different types of problems on many different types of computers. Finally, there might be service-quality benefits when you establish a strong, ongoing relationship with a computer manufacturer.

> **NOTE** If you support many computers, make sure that they are as consistent as possible. Not only do you want to ensure (as much as possible) that they are the same model and the same configuration, you also want to make sure the manufacturer uses the same components for all computers of a particular model. Some manufacturers are not careful about this; they will slip in different motherboards or network interface cards (NICs) without any notice. For someone buying a single computer, this isn't a problem. When you need to support 500 or 5,000 computers that are all supposed to be exactly the same but aren't, it becomes a huge problem, because then you also must keep track of different drivers and configuration information. Also, if you install and maintain computers through the use of disk images (such as those made by Norton Ghost), you will need to maintain different images for all of the different submodels of the computer.

Price and Performance

Once the preceding priorities are satisfied, you can then strike the appropriate balance between performance and price. You need to take into account the useful life that you plan for new computers and make certain to purchase systems that will be productive over that useful life. In determining this balance, don't look at how well a particular configuration can handle today's needs; look at how well it can handle tomorrow's needs.

Some people might disagree, but I firmly believe that price should not be your first priority when you purchase computers. Although purchase price is important, you first need to determine your needs and then find the most reasonably priced computers that best fulfill those needs.

Different strategies exist for getting the best price. These strategies range from straightforward bargaining and competitive bids, to slightly under-purchasing on the performance side but planning to upgrade the existing computers when needed (at least in terms of RAM and hard disk space, both of which decrease pretty rapidly in price over time).

> **NOTE** Don't forget to estimate the cost involved to replace a computer or to upgrade a computer when you choose a system. It might be less expensive overall to purchase a more capable computer that you won't need to upgrade or replace as quickly when you factor in the labor costs and user productivity impact from installing a replacement.

As a rule of thumb, you can estimate that the demands placed on a desktop computer will double every 24 months or so, taking into account your planned useful life. Set your performance levels to meet that need. (People used to assume performance requirements doubled every 18 months, but this seems to be slowing a bit in recent years.)

DEFINE-IT! Useful Life

The term *useful life* refers to the length of time a particular asset, such as a computer, will be able to perform useful work. The useful life of a computer will change depending on the computer, the software it needs to run, the user who uses it, and the budget available to upgrade or replace it. A programmer who needs the latest and greatest hardware and software all the time will get a relatively short useful life out of a computer, while a person who uses a computer only for word processing or e-mail and doesn't care about running the latest software will get a much longer useful life out of a computer. For most desktop computers, the useful life is around three to four years, although exceptions to this rule of thumb are easy to find.

For example, suppose that you've determined that today's user requires 200GB of disk space, 4GB of RAM, and a dual-core processor. In 24 months, your users are likely to be clamoring for 400GB of disk space, 8GB of RAM, and a quad-core processor. In another 24 months (about four years from purchase), these demands will double again, to 800GB of disk space, 16GB of RAM, and the equivalent of an eight-core processor. These projected demands might seem unlikely today, but when you look back at the needs of four years ago, such projections seem reasonable.

Using this way of estimating performance needs, you should be able to find a "sweet spot" between price, performance, and useful life that minimizes your costs and maximizes the benefits that your users will receive.

Chapter Summary

Managing network workstation computers can be a daunting task. Many of them must be managed frequently, each user may have different needs, and because of how they are used, network workstation computers are the most likely to experience trouble. In this chapter, you learned general information about network client computers, along with how to select appropriate client computers for your network.

In the next chapter, you learn about the basics of how you can design a network from the ground up. Generally, the process of network design is to first thoroughly understand the needs that the network must meet, factor in anticipated growth for the network, and then start to lay out how the network will be structured and which technologies will be needed.

CHAPTER 13 | Designing a Network

etworking professionals rarely have the opportunity to walk into a company and design a new network from the ground up, but those who do are certainly lucky. It's true that such an effort involves long hours, stress, deadlines, and the nagging worry that maybe you're forgetting something. But in return, you get to shape the computing environment of a large number of users, and—in many companies—set the tone for how efficiently the company itself can function in coming years. In some companies that rely heavily on information technology, a smoothly running network might even determine whether or not the company will be successful. It's an enormous responsibility, but also a very rewarding job.

In practice, you usually start with some sort of network already in place. Networks start small and simply grow over time. Networks are almost like skin, where you're sure to replace each and every cell every few years, but only a few at a time. The process is usually evolutionary rather than revolutionary. Exceptions exist to this rule, though. For example, a company might move to a new building, decide to scrap the old network during the process, and install an entirely new one. Likewise, a well-funded startup company that goes from 5 to 500 employees in six months is likely to see the need for a new network.

Regardless of whether you're building a brand-new network from scratch or renovating an existing network, the tools you use are much the same, and the process of designing the network is also much the same. The concept is actually simple: You assess the needs that the network must meet and then you design to meet those needs. In practice, this process is much more involved, but the idea is straightforward. Even in an evolving network, using network planning to formulate a long-term plan to renovate the network makes sense.

This chapter describes how to design a network. It relies on all the information you learned in the preceding chapters. Think of this chapter as the one that brings together into a coherent whole all the information that you have already learned. Preceding chapters have focused on the bits and bytes of networks, while this chapter is the view from 30,000 feet where you start to see how everything works together.

The Network Design Process

Network design is not an exact science. Getting it *exactly* right the first time is nearly impossible, even with the best design tools and resources available. This is because every network has different demands placed on it, and these demands often interact in surprising ways. Moreover, predicting what new demands will be placed on the network over time, how users will use the network resources, and what other changes you might need to make is almost impossible. The entire situation is both fluid and chaotic. The trick is to do a good job of estimating needs, and then do the best job possible to create a design to meet those needs.

Having fallback plans is also important in case some part of the network doesn't perform the way you intended. For instance, once the network is up and running, you might find that the distribution of bandwidth across segments is poor. You want to know in advance how you can measure and address these types of problems. You might also find storage requirements are much higher or lower than you expected. You need to know what to do if this happens. The point is that network design is a process, often an iterative one. Your job as a network designer is to get as close as possible to the needed design, and then fine-tune the design as needed.

A lot of the network design process is what you decide to make of it. There are simple network design processes, and there are horrendously complicated processes that involve dozens of people, complex statistical modeling, and even network simulation software to test a planned design and see if it holds together under load. In this chapter, you learn a relatively comprehensive process that is straightforward and simple. Using the information in this chapter, along with a good dose of experience, will yield a flexible network that should easily meet the needs of hundreds of users.

TIP   You can't design a network of any size without plenty of experience running similar networks. You can manage the overall process by understanding the methodology, but you can't create a good design without hands-on experience. If you're new to networking and you are asked to design a network, make sure you get experienced people on the team—either as consultants or as part of a supplier-led team—and listen carefully to their advice.

Assessing Network Needs

"Measure twice and cut once" is a common adage that conveys the importance of planning. "Ready, fire, aim," is one that pokes fun at people who don't properly set goals. Assessing the needs that a network must meet corresponds to taking those measurements and aiming as carefully as possible before you shoot.

Before you even think about any specifics—network topology; network operating system (NOS) platform; a structure for hubs, bridges, and routers; or the grade of wiring—you must first know what the network needs to accomplish. Assessing needs is where you should place the most emphasis during a design process. Failing to do so almost certainly will result in a network that isn't productive for its users.

NOTE   Many IT professionals are, at heart, technologists who love to play with the latest technologies. It's very tempting to design the network around the "hot" technologies, and then try to figure out how the needs fit into those technologies. However, this is not the way to go about designing a network. Instead, start with the needs, and then find out what technologies support those needs.

When assessing needs, you are trying to come up with detailed answers to the following questions:

- How much storage space is required?
- How much bandwidth is required?

- What network services are required?
- What is the budget for the project?

These basic questions are fairly easy to answer as a whole, but you need to break them down further to make sure no holes in the network design could lead to problems. For example, it might be easy to determine that the network must be able to support up to 100 Mbps of bandwidth, but you need to know how, when, and where that bandwidth is used. If the accounting department is using 90 percent of the bandwidth when communicating to the accounting server, for example, then naturally you want to put the accounting system's server and its users on their own subnet. You won't recognize such issues and how to address them unless your assessment leads you to determine with some degree of detail how the network resources will be used.

The following sections discuss what you should examine as you learn what a given network must be able to do. No particular order exists in which you should examine these issues, and you might find that you need to cycle through the list several times to get a complete picture. You also might find a particular company's needs require more or less analysis in each category. Common sense is required when you design a network. The following suggestions are guidelines to start you on the right path.

Applications

A good place to start with a network design is to list and understand the applications that will run on the network. Ultimately, a network is only as good as the work it helps people accomplish, and people do their work most directly through the application software they use. If the applications don't work right, then the users won't work right.

Most networks have both common applications and department- and user-specific applications. Most companies usually meet the common application needs through a suite of desktop applications, such as Microsoft Office. The following is a list of applications that most companies install for all users, whether or not each user needs each one:

- Word processor
- Spreadsheet
- End-user database
- Presentation graphics
- E-mail
- Personal information manager (calendar, contact list, and so forth)
- Virus-scanning software

Your first order of business is to determine just how the common applications will be used. Determine whether all users need to have the entire suite installed, how often different users plan to use the different applications, how many files they will create and store, how large those files might be, and how those files will be shared among users.

For example, in a 1,000-user population, you might determine that 90 percent will use word processing to generate an average of ten documents a month, with each document averaging 100KB, and the users probably will want to keep two years' worth of documents on hand at any given time. Yes, these will be educated guesses, but it's important to come up with reasonable estimates. Experience with similar user populations and companies can pay off handsomely in determining these estimates. With this information alone, you know immediately that you need about 24MB of storage per user, or 21.6GB for the word processing population of 900 users, just for word processing documents. For applications where users frequently will share files, you might need to factor in that most users keep personal copies of some files that they also share with others.

TIP You can help reduce overall network storage requirements by establishing shared directories in which different groups of people can store and access shared files.

Then you come up with the same estimates for the other applications, taking into account their expected size, frequency of creation, and long-term storage requirements.

After determining the common applications, move on to department-specific applications. This step gets trickier for new networks in new companies because you might not know which applications will be used. For existing companies, you have the advantage of already knowing which departmental applications you must support.

Different departmental applications can have wildly different impacts on the network. For example, an accounting system designed around shared database files needs a different network design than one using a client/server database design. The former relies more on file server performance and is more likely to be bandwidth-sensitive than an efficient client/server application that runs on a dedicated server. If a departmental application is not yet selected, talk with the managers of that department to get their best estimates and then proceed.

Following are common departmental applications you should consider:

- Accounting
- Distribution and inventory control
- Manufacturing/material requirements planning (MRP)
- Information technology
- Electronic commerce
- Human resources
- Payroll and stock administration
- Publishing
- Marketing support
- Legal
- Other line-of-business applications specific to the company's industry

For each of the departmental applications you identify, you need to ask several questions: How much storage will they consume? From where will the applications be run (from local computers with data on a server or completely centralized, where both the data and the application run on a central computer)? Will they have their own dedicated servers? How much network bandwidth will the application need? How will all these factors change as the company grows?

Finally, while you might not formally include them in your plan, consider user-specific applications that might be run. For example, you might estimate that the people in the company's research and development group are likely to run two or three unknown applications as part of their job. If you decide that user-specific applications will have a significant impact on the network, then you should estimate their needs, just as you have for the other types of applications. If you believe they will have minimal impact, then you might decide either to include a small allowance for them or none at all.

TIP   Don't get bogged down in "analysis paralysis," worrying about whether you can scientifically prove that your estimates are accurate. Instead, make sure the estimates are reasonable to other network professionals. At a certain point, you need to justify the network design and cost and having reasonable estimates is necessary to do this. Just avoid overdoing it.

Users

Once you know the applications that the network must support, you can estimate how many users need to be supported and which applications each user will use. Estimating total users will likely be easier because the company should already have a business plan or long-range budget from which you can derive these estimates. Your user estimates should be reasonably granular: Know the number of users in each department in the company as well as the company's total number of users.

You should estimate how many users will need to be supported immediately, in one year, in three years, and in five years. Even though five years is a distant horizon to use for an estimate, this information is important to know during the design process. Different growth rates suggest different network designs, even at the inception of the network. A company estimating that it will have 100 users immediately, 115 users in one year, 130 users in three years, and 150 users in five years needs a different network design than a company estimating 100 users immediately, 115 users in one year, 300 users in three years, and 1,000 users in five years. In the latter case, you must invest more in a design that is more quickly scalable, and you are likely to spend much more at inception to build the network, even though the network will have the same number of users in the first two years.

Knowing the number of users isn't enough, though. You need to know more about the users. At a minimum, consider the following questions to determine if any of the following will be important factors for the users generally or for subgroups of users:

- **Bandwidth requirements**   Aside from the bandwidth required to save and retrieve files, send and receive e-mail, and perform an average amount of browsing on the Internet, do any users need significant amounts of bandwidth?

For example, will scientists download a fresh copy of the human genome from the Internet once a week? Will groups of users need to exchange large quantities of data among different sites? Will any users be running videoconferencing software over your network connection? How much web browsing do you expect the network's users to do? Will people be sending large e-mail attachments frequently?

■ **Storage requirements**   Will any group of users need significantly more storage capacity than the overall average? For instance, will an electronic imaging group catalog millions of documents into image files on a server? If so, how many people need access to that data? Will the accounting group need to keep the previous ten years of financial information online? Will the company use or install an executive information system where all the managers have query capability into the company's accounting, distribution, and manufacturing systems, and, if so, how much additional bandwidth or server performance could that capability require?

■ **Service requirements**   Will any groups of users require additional network services not needed by most users? For example, does part of the company do work of such sensitivity that it should be separated from the rest of the local area network (LAN) by a network firewall? Will a subset of users need direct inward fax capability?

When examining user bandwidth requirements, remember to look at the timeliness of the bandwidth needs. If certain known activities require a lot of bandwidth and must be carried out during the normal workday, that high-bandwidth use might interfere with the performance of the rest of the network. Therefore, make sure to estimate both average and peak bandwidth needs.

Network Services

Next, you should look at the services that the network must provide. These can vary widely in different companies. A very basic network might need only file and print services, plus perhaps Internet connectivity. A more complex network will need many additional services. Consider which of the following types of services the network you are designing will need to provide, as well as any others that are specific to the company:

■ File and print services

■ Backup and restore services

■ Internet web browsing

■ E-mail

■ Network security services

■ Remote access to the LAN through a Virtual Private Network (VPN)

■ Fax into and out of the LAN (manually distributed or automatically distributed)

- Dynamic Host Configuration Protocol (DHCP) services
- Centralized virus-protection services
- Wide area network (WAN) services to other locations
- Videoconferencing
- Voice over IP (VoIP)

For each service, you must answer a number of questions. First, you need to know the storage and bandwidth requirements for each service and any other impacts they might have. For instance, a fax-in service might itself require a small amount of storage space, but all the fax bitmaps that users will end up storing could have a large impact on total storage needs.

Second, you need to know how the service is to be provided. Usually, this means that you need to know which server will host the service. Some services require such little overhead that you can easily host them on a server that does other jobs. A DHCP server, which requires minimal resources, is a good example of such a service. On the other hand, an e-mail system might require such high resources that you must plan to host it on its own dedicated server, or even on multiple servers.

Third, you need to know what users or groups of users need which services. This is because to minimize backbone traffic, you might need to break down the network into smaller subnets and locate frequently used services for a particular user population on the same segment as the users of those services.

Security and Safety

The preceding considerations are all related to the bits and bytes required by different parts of the network. Security and safety concern the company's need to keep information secure—both inside and outside an organization—and to keep the company's data safe from loss. You need to know how important these two issues are before attempting to set down a network design on paper.

For both these considerations, a trade-off exists between cost and effectiveness. As mentioned in earlier chapters, no network is ever totally secure and no data is ever totally safe from loss. However, different companies and departments have different sensitivities to these issues, indicating that more or less money should be spent on these areas.

Some applications might be perfectly well suited to keeping their data on a striped RAID 0 array of disks, where the risk of loss is high (relative to other RAID levels), because the data might be static and easy to restore from tape if the disk array is lost. Other applications might require the highest level of data-loss safety possible, with failover servers each having mirrored RAID 1 or RAID 10 arrays and online tape backup systems updating a backup tape every hour or for every transaction, or replicated in real-time to a hot colocation site. Similarly, some companies might work with data that is so sensitive that they must install the best firewalls, perhaps even two levels of firewalls, and hire full-time professionals dedicated to keeping the data secure. Other companies might be satisfied if they are only reasonably secure.

The point is that you must determine how important these issues are to the company for which you are designing the network. Then you can propose different solutions to address these needs and factor them into the rest of your design.

Growth and Capacity Planning

The final area to consider is the expected growth of the network, particularly if the company expects this growth to be substantial. As mentioned earlier in this chapter, a network designed for a rapidly growing company looks different from one for a slowly growing company, even if both companies start out at the same size. In the former case, you want a design that you can quickly and easily expand without needing to replace much of the existing hardware and software. In the latter case, you can get by with a simpler network design.

Consider the impact of growth on the different parts of the network that you've already examined (applications, users, and services), because linear growth does not always mean a matching linear impact to the network. Assuming linear growth, the impact to the network might be much lower or much higher than the curve.

For example, you saw in Chapter 3 how Ethernet uses a collision detection mechanism to manage network traffic. In that chapter, you also learned that Ethernet scales linearly, but only up to a point. Once the network starts to become saturated, performance begins to drop rapidly because of the chaotic nature of Ethernet's collision detection scheme. Consider a 100 Mbps Ethernet network transmitting 30 Mbps of traffic. This traffic probably flows smoothly, with few collisions and few retransmissions required. Push the network demand up to 50 or 60 Mbps, however, and its performance grinds to a halt as the network becomes saturated, and you end up with as many collisions and retransmissions as real data. In fact, the total amount of good data flowing over a saturated Ethernet network will be less than the amount flowing over a less saturated network, all else being equal.

You can also find examples where an increase in demand doesn't cause a corresponding increase in network or server load. For example, the server load for a complex e-mail system might increase only by a small amount if you doubled the number of users, because the system's overhead generates most of the load. The storage requirements for an accounting system might not double just because you keep twice as much data in it to accommodate the overhead that might consume most of the existing space. Alternatively, that same accounting system might consume four times as much storage space if you double the data storage because it might have a relatively inefficient indexing scheme. The point is that you need to know how different applications scale with increased use. The vendors of the main applications you will use should be able to provide useful data in this regard.

TIP   Be careful not only to consider how applications behave as they scale, but how they behave as they are scaled in your planned network environment. Different NOSs, network topologies, and client and server computers will all affect how well a particular application can support growth.

Meeting Network Needs

Once you complete your assessment (by this point, you're probably sick of the assessment process!), you can then start working on finding ways to meet all the needs you've identified. This process is largely holistic and is not worked through by following a series of steps and ending up with a single answer, like an equation. Instead, you should start by mapping out the various parts of the network, considering the three main topics discussed in this section, and "build a picture" of the network design. The design that you create will incorporate all you learned during the assessment process, taking into account your experience and the advice you have received to devise a concrete design that results in an equipment list, specifications, and a configuration.

Seeking criticism of your design from other network professionals, who might have valuable experience that you can then factor into your design, is important. No single networking professional has seen and had to cope with all possible design needs, so you want to combine the advice of as many seasoned people as you can.

Choosing a Network Type

You probably want to start the design by choosing a network type. This should be a relatively straightforward decision, based on the overall bandwidth requirements for the network. For most new networks, you almost certainly will decide to use one of the flavors of Ethernet. Ethernet is by far the most common type of network installed today, and it's an easy default choice.

You also need to decide what level of Ethernet you need. For wiring to the desktop, you should choose, these days, 1000Base-T over Cat5E cable. It's reliable and provides plenty of capacity for most needs.

Structuring the Network

Next, decide how you plan to structure the network. In other words, how will you arrange and wire the various hubs, switches, and routers that the network needs? This is probably the trickiest part to determine, because it's hard to predict how much data must flow from any given set of nodes to any other set of nodes. The estimates you have based on your assessment work will help. If you can identify expected heavy traffic patterns, you should also draw a network schematic with these patterns indicated to help you sort it out. Remember the following tips:

- Ethernet's CDMA/CD collision handling means that an Ethernet network will handle only about one-third of its rated speed. In other words, a 100Base-T segment, which is rated at 100 Mbps, will handle about 33 Mbps of actual data before starting to degrade.

- Whenever possible, use "home-run" wiring (in which each network cable runs from each workstation to a single location) for all nodes to a single wiring closet or server room. Doing so enables you to change the network structure more easily (for example, to break segments into smaller segments) as needs change.

■ Except in the smallest networks, plan on installing a network backbone to which the switches connect. You still must plan to keep each segment's traffic below the Ethernet saturation point, but this structure will give you plenty of flexibility to meet this goal.

■ The physical building might dictate how you structure your network. For example, a building larger than 200 meters (about 600 feet) in any dimension probably means you won't be able to employ a home-run wiring scheme for all your nodes. This is because twisted-pair Ethernet usually reaches only 100 meters (about 300 feet), which includes routing around building obstructions, patch cables, and other things that make the actual cable distance longer than you might measure on a map of the building.

■ For multifloor buildings that are too big for a home-run wiring scheme, consider running the backbone vertically from floor to floor, and then have a wiring closet on each floor that contains the switches to service that floor's nodes. The wiring from the closet on each floor then fans out to each of the nodes on that floor.

■ Most of the time, most nodes do the majority of their communication to one or two servers on the network. If you are planning department-specific servers or if you can identify similar patterns, make sure that each server is on the same subnet as the nodes that it primarily serves.

■ If your servers tend not to be assigned to support departments and instead support the entire company, make sure that the servers are directly connected to the backbone's switch.

■ If you have any high-bandwidth users, consider keeping them on a segment separate from the rest of the network (if appropriate) and also consider upgrading the speed of that segment.

■ As you start to implement the network, carefully watch the ratio of collision packets to data packets. If the number of collisions on any segment climbs to 5 to 7 percent of the total number of packets, performance is starting to suffer, so you need to investigate the cause and find a way to decrease this ratio. You can usually do so by breaking the segment into smaller pieces (subnets) or by configuring capable switches into what is called a virtual LAN (VLAN).

Selecting Servers

As discussed in Chapter 12, list the various network services that your servers must provide. You need to look for efficient ways to host these various services on your servers, balancing a number of factors:

■ All else being equal, using more small servers to host fewer services each is more reliable—from a software standpoint—than using fewer large servers to each host many services.

- Conversely, having more small servers makes hardware failures more likely (although it can also limit the scope of disruption from a particular server being down).

- Using more small servers is more expensive and requires more maintenance than using fewer large servers.

- Consider which services should be redundant on another server or how you plan to deal with the failure of any server.

Using your assessment information, you can determine how much storage capacity your servers will need. However, it's much harder to know how capable each server should be in terms of processor power, installed RAM, and other features, such as bus configuration. For these specifications, you need to rely on the advice of the NOS vendor and the manufacturer of the servers that you are considering.

Chapter Summary

Designing an entire network can be extremely complex. If you are in the enviable position of designing a network, your best bet is to start with the framework described in this chapter and to use other resources to answer specific questions. Many resources are available to help you do this, ranging from books devoted to aspects of network design, server management, network performance tuning, and specific NOS management, to consultants and network engineers experienced with similar networks and the various vendors you are working with on any planned purchases.

Always remember to leave some headroom in any network design so you can respond quickly to new or changed requirements, many of which will occur while you're finalizing the design. The good news is that if you follow the advice in this chapter and the rest of the book, along with the other resources mentioned, it's a safe bet you'll end up with a solid, expandable, maintainable network design that meets the needs of the company and of which you can be proud.

PART II | Hands-On Knowledge

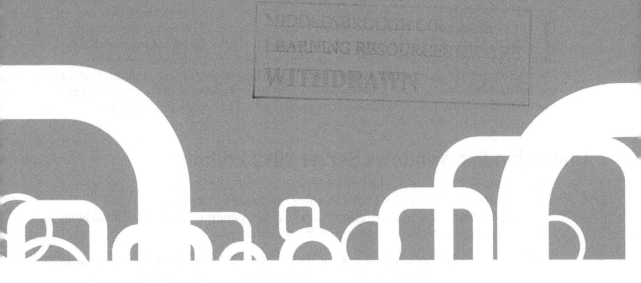

CHAPTER 14 | Installing and Setting Up Windows Server 2012

In this chapter, you learn how to install Windows Server 2012. Before you install Windows Server 2012, however, you first must conduct a variety of pre-installation checks that prepare the system for the process. Next, you perform the actual installation, providing information that the installation program needs. Finally, you test the installation by having a client computer log in to the server properly and perform some basic network duties. All these steps are described in detail in this chapter.

Understanding Windows Server 2012 Editions

Windows Server 2012 is an entire family of products, all built on essentially the same programming code, but with significant feature and tuning differences.

Standard Edition is the mainstream server version of Windows Server 2012. It includes all the power of Active Directory, as well as the following features:

- New management tools; a graphical user interface (GUI)–based Server Manager, and an extensive array of PowerShell-based scripts (called *cmdlets*)

- Remote Desktop Services (which used to be called Terminal Services), which allows Windows Server 2012 to provide virtualized remote desktop computers

- Internet and web services, including Dynamic Host Configuration Protocol (DHCP), Domain Name System (DNS), Internet Information Services (IIS), and Index Server

- Remote access and Virtual Private Network (VPN) services

- Transaction and messaging services

- Support for up to 640 processors

- Support for up to 4TB of RAM

- Support for the latest versions of the standard network protocols

- Hyper-V virtual computing, with support for up to two running virtual machines per Standard Edition license (you can install multiple licenses to increase this value)

Datacenter Edition is essentially the same as Standard Edition, except that it includes unlimited license rights for virtual machines, and it can run an unlimited number of virtual machines (limited only by the hardware capabilities).

Microsoft has dramatically changed how it approaches Windows Server editions and licensing. For both Standard Edition and Datacenter Edition, you require an additional server license for every two physical processors installed into the server. So, for example, if you are installing either Standard Edition or Datacenter Edition onto a server with six physical processors, you will need three licenses.

For Standard Edition, you also may need additional licenses if you want to run more virtual machines. Two virtual machines are included per each license. So, if you want to run eight virtual machines on a server that only has two physical processors, you will need four Standard Edition licenses. For various combinations of physical processors and virtual machines, you will need a quantity of Standard Edition licenses that is adequate to cover the higher of the two values.

For smaller businesses, there are two new Windows Server editions:

- *Essentials Edition* is limited to no more than 25 users and 50 computers. It can run on a server with up to two processors, and use of the server does not require a Client Access License. Essentials Edition is designed for businesses with very little or no in-house IT resources, and includes features for simplified administration.

- *Foundation Edition* is limited to no more than 15 users, and is only available from server manufacturers as part of a server purchase.

Both Essentials and Foundation Editions can be upgraded to Standard Edition.

Preparing for Installation

Before installing Windows Server 2012, you first must prepare the server computer that you will use and make important decisions about the installation. This preparation stage consists of a number of tasks, including the following:

- Make sure the server hardware is certified for use with Windows Server 2012.
- Make sure the server is properly configured to support Windows Server 2012.
- Carry out any needed pre-installation testing on the server hardware.
- Survey the hardware prior to performing the installation.
- Decide how you will install Windows Server 2012 after gathering all the configuration information you will need during the installation.
- Back up the system prior to an upgrade.

These tasks are discussed in the following sections.

Checking Hardware Compatibility

Microsoft maintains an extensive Hardware Compatibility List (HCL) that lists different hardware components and their testing status on various Microsoft products, such as Windows Server 2012. To avoid problems with your server, make sure that the server itself and any installed peripherals have been tested with Windows Server 2012 and work properly. The latest version of the HCL can be found at www.windowsservercatalog.com. You can also find a text-based copy on the Windows Server 2012 CD-ROM. Using the web-based HCL is preferred, however, because it might have more current data than the file included on the installation CD-ROM.

If a particular hardware component in your planned server isn't listed on the HCL, all is not lost. For one thing, the HCL might not have the most current data, and the hardware that you wish to use might be certified but not yet listed. It's best to check with the hardware's maker, because that company will know the current status of the hardware's certification.

> **NOTE**   Products not listed in the HCL might work fine with Windows Server 2012. If you are deploying a server for testing purposes or to support limited services, and you are comfortable doing so, you can still proceed to install Windows Server 2012 and begin working with it. You should not do this for production servers that many people will depend on, however. Not only might an undiscovered incompatibility cause serious problems with an uncertified server, but you will be unable to get the highest level of support from Microsoft for hardware that is not yet certified. For this reason, you should avoid deploying important servers that are not yet certified by Microsoft.

Checking the Hardware Configuration

Purchasing a computer for use as a server can be a complex task. You must contend with the myriad details of installed RAM, processor configuration, disk configuration, and so forth, as well as factor in your anticipated needs to come up with a reasonable server configuration. (Chapter 11 contains information about different server technologies and about specifying a server for general use.)

Windows Server 2012 requires the following *minimum* hardware configuration:

- One 1.4 GHz (x64 processor) or greater
- 512MB of RAM
- At least 32GB of free disk space
- A DVD-ROM or network connection from which to install Windows Server 2012

For any kind of server (even one that will support only a few users), you should consider using more capable hardware than that specified as the minimum by Microsoft. Here is some advice for configuring a server for Windows Server 2012:

- **Processor**   Start with at least an Intel Core i5 processor running at 2.4 GHz or greater. Intel Xeon processors are a benefit in a server, and you should carefully consider the price of such systems relative to the expected performance improvement. Also, if you are considering a system with two or more processors, only the Xeon family of processors supports more than one processor.

- **RAM**   Windows Server 2012 runs best on systems that have plenty of RAM. For a server, make sure you have at least 1GB of RAM. If you plan on supporting all the different services available with Windows Server 2012 (such as Remote Desktop Services, Routing and Remote Access Service, DHCP, DNS, and so forth), then 2GB to 4GB of RAM might be a better choice than 1GB of RAM.

- **Disk**   A fast Small Computer System Interface (SCSI)–based disk subsystem is important, particularly for servers that will store a lot of data. (See Chapter 11 for more information about choosing SCSI systems, using different redundant array of inexpensive disks [RAID] levels, and other important disk information.)

Use the information in Chapter 11 to help you size your server, but remember this rule of thumb: Get the most capable server you can afford, and make sure it is expandable to meet your future needs through the addition of more RAM, more processors, and more disk space. Even with all of that, it is common for servers to be replaced three to four years from the date they were placed into service.

Testing the Server Hardware

You found all your server hardware in the Windows Server 2012 HCL, you made sure your server is adequately sized, you purchased it, and you have your shiny new Windows Server 2012 DVD-ROMs sitting there, all ready to be installed. Is it time to start the installation yet? Well, not quite. Before installing any network operating system (NOS), particularly on a server that will be used for production, make sure you carry out hardware testing (also called *burn-in*) on the server before installing Windows Server 2012.

Computer hardware tends to be most reliable after it has been running for a while. In other words, failures tend to happen when equipment is new, and the chance of hardware failure decreases rapidly after the hardware has been up and running for 30 to 90 days. Because of this, it's a good idea to test new servers for at least a week (testing for two weeks is even better) before proceeding to install the NOS. Doing this can help provoke any early failures in the equipment during a time when they're easy to fix and they won't affect any users or the network. Moreover, many servers have a 30-day return or exchange policy from their manufacturer, so if you discover problems, you'll have a chance to return the system and perhaps start over with a different model.

You test the hardware using diagnostic software that came with the server computer or that is available from the maker of the server. Most such diagnostic software lets you to choose which components of the system are tested and enables you to test them in an endless loop, logging any discovered errors to a floppy disk, USB key, or the screen. You should focus the tests on the following components:

- Processor(s)
- System board components, such as interrupt controllers, direct memory access (DMA) controllers, and other motherboard support circuitry
- RAM
- Disk surfaces

 TIP Server-testing software often enables you to choose between nondestructive and destructive testing of the disks. (Destructive means any data on the disks is erased during the testing.) Destructive testing is best to discover any errors on the disks. This is one reason that you want to carry out this testing before you install your NOS.

If the diagnostic software allows you to do so, you can usually safely skip testing components such as the keyboard or the display. Your primary concern is that the unit continues running properly when it is under load for an extended period of time. You also want to make sure that the RAM is working properly and that no bad sectors show up on the disks during testing. It's also a good idea during testing to power the unit on and shut it down a number of times, since the impact to the unit of initially powering on often can provoke a failure in any marginal components, especially if the unit is allowed to cool down first.

Making Pre-installation Decisions

After configuring, checking, preparing, and testing your hardware, you can actually begin installing Windows Server 2012. During this process, you first spend time making a number of important pre-installation decisions that you must be prepared to specify during the installation. The following sections discuss these choices.

 NOTE This chapter and the following chapter provide an overall introduction to Windows Server 2012. Certain advanced installation scenarios and techniques are not described here. To learn about other features and choices available when installing, administering, or using Windows Server 2012, consult a book devoted to Windows Server 2012.

Upgrade or Install?

You can upgrade a server running Windows Server 2008 to Windows Server 2012, or you can perform a full installation, where you wipe out any existing NOS on the server. The main benefit to upgrading is that all your existing settings under Windows Server 2008 will be maintained and automatically carried forward into your Windows Server 2012 installation. These include networking details, such as TCP/IP configuration information, as well as security settings that you might have tediously set up over time. In fact, if the server can be upgraded, you should plan on doing so, unless you need to change something fundamental in the server.

Domain Controller, Member Server, or Stand-alone Server?

Another choice you need to make is in which mode you will configure your server. To make this decision, you need to understand two important concepts: Windows Server 2012 domains and workgroups. A *domain* is a sophisticated administrative grouping of computers on a Windows network that makes it possible to administer the network's resources from a single point and to implement strong security. Domains enable you to manage multiple Windows Servers more easily. A *workgroup* is a simple collection of computers on a network and is suited only for pure peer-to-peer networks.

You can configure Windows Server 2012 in one of three modes to support either domains or workgroups, as follows:

- *Domain controllers* hold the domain's Active Directory information and authenticate users and access to resources. Most Windows Server 2012 networks have at least one domain and, therefore, need at least one domain controller.

- *Member servers* are part of a domain but do not hold a copy of the Active Directory information.

- *Stand-alone servers* do not participate in a domain, but instead participate in a workgroup.

Earlier versions of Windows servers (NT and 2000) needed to be designated as either primary domain controllers (PDCs) or backup domain controllers (BDCs). The PDC performed all administrative tasks, and the BDCs simply kept read-only copies of the domain information to continue authenticating security on the network in case the PDC failed.

Newer Windows servers, such as those running Windows Server 2008 or 2012, simplify matters so that all Windows Server 2012 domain controllers are just that—domain controllers. Each domain controller holds a copy of the Active Directory data and can perform all the functions of the other domain controllers. Windows Server 2012 uses the concept of *multimaster domain controllers*, which all seamlessly operate the same way as the other domain controllers.

 TIP   Except in the smallest of networks, it's a very good idea to have two domain controllers. This way, all of your domain information is preserved and available to the network should one of the domain controllers crash. Domain information is automatically synchronized between the available domain controllers.

Per Seat or Per Server?

Yet another important choice to make when installing Windows Server 2012 is how the server will manage its Client Access Licenses (CALs). Windows Server 2012 supports two different ways of managing CALs:

- *Per-server licensing* assigns the CALs to the server, which will license only as many connections from computers as there are installed CALs on that server.

- *Per-user and per-device licensing* requires purchasing a CAL for each of your users or client computers (including a combination of users and devices), which gives them the right to access as many Windows servers as they wish; the servers will not monitor the number of connections.

Generally, Microsoft recommends that you use per-server licensing when running a single server and per-seat licensing when running multiple servers. If you are unsure of which mode to use, Microsoft recommends that you choose per server, because Microsoft lets you change to per-device or per-user mode to per-server mode once at no cost (changing from per seat to per server has a price). Carefully review licensing options with your Windows Server 2012 reseller to determine the most economical way to license your network servers properly.

Wait! Back Up Before Upgrading!

If you are installing Windows Server 2012 as an upgrade to another NOS, such as Windows Server 2008, it's vital that you fully back up the server prior to installing Windows Server 2012. (It's a good idea to make two identical backups, just in case.) You should use whatever backup software you normally use for your existing NOS, making sure the software can properly restore the previous NOS in case you need to "unwind" the upgrade process and revert to your starting point.

Even when you are performing an upgrade and will not be reformatting any of the disks, making a pre-installation backup is good insurance in case of trouble.

Installing Windows Server 2012

To begin the installation of Windows Server 2012, you can either configure the server computer to boot from the Windows Server 2012 DVD-ROM or insert the Windows Server 2012 DVD-ROM while running Windows Server 2008. Most servers can boot from their DVD-ROM drives, which is the best way to start the installation.

Running the Windows Server 2012 Setup Program

The following steps outline the process of running the installation program for Windows Server 2012 and installing it onto a server. If you are learning about Windows Server 2012 and have a suitable computer to use, you should take the time to install Windows Server 2012 so that you understand how the process works. Or, if you like, you can read along through the following steps to familiarize yourself with the installation process. (I recommend actually performing an installation such as the one described here and then playing with the resulting server as a way of more quickly and completely learning about Windows Server 2012.)

- When you boot from the Windows Server 2012 DVD-ROM, the program first presents a screen that lets you choose the language to install, the formatting to use for time and currency displays, and the keyboard or input method (see Figure 14-1). Make the appropriate choices, and then click Next to continue.

- You see the screen shown in Figure 14-2. If you booted your Windows Server 2012 DVD-ROM in order to try to repair an existing installation, you can choose Repair Your Computer. To start the installation, click Install Now to continue.

- You are next prompted to choose whether you want to install Standard Edition or Datacenter Edition, and whether you want a GUI installed (see Figure 14-3). Generally, you will want to install with the GUI. Use the Server Core (no GUI) installation option only when you will be installing a production server *and* will be administering the server entirely with remote tools.

- After selecting which edition to install, you will be prompted to accept the license terms. If you accept the license terms, click the I Accept The License Terms checkbox, and click Next to continue.

- Next, select whether you are performing the installation as an upgrade of an existing system or as a brand-new installation, as shown in Figure 14-4. See the discussion earlier in this chapter for more information on making this decision.

- You now are prompted to choose the location to which you want to install Windows Server. From the available choices, choose the appropriate target disk and click Next to continue.

- The installation now proceeds, and you will see an installation screen similar to the one shown in Figure 14-5.

Figure 14-1. Choosing the language and other preferences

- You are next prompted to assign a password for the built-in Administrator account in the system, as shown in Figure 14-6. It's important to choose a strong password, and also to ensure that it is not lost.

- After setting the Administrator password and clicking Finish, you will be prompted to press CTRL-ALT-DELETE to sign in as Administrator.

Figure 14-2. Choosing to install the software

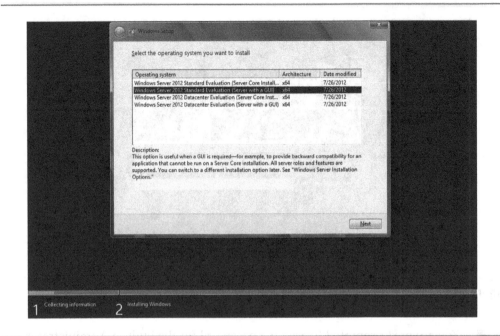

Figure 14-3. Choosing which edition to install and whether or not to install the GUI administration tools

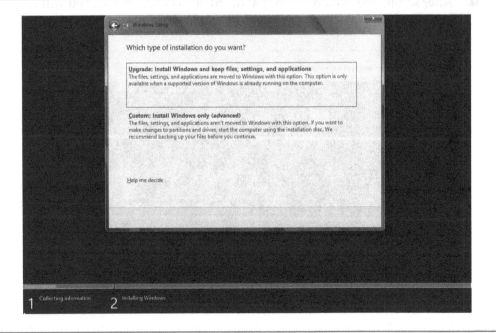

Figure 14-4. Choosing the type of installation

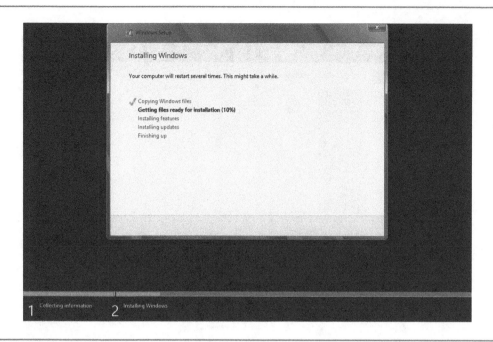

Figure 14-5.   Installation progress dialog box

Figure 14-6.   Setting the Administrator password

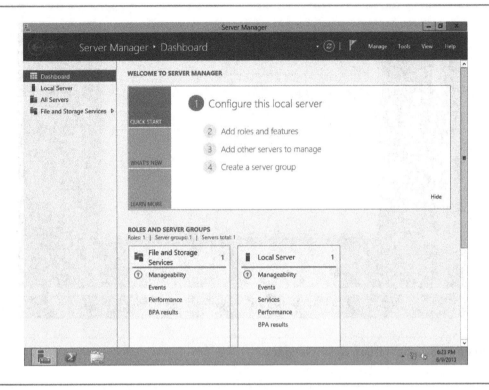

Figure 14-7.   After the main installation, you then proceed to configuration with Server Manager.

At this point, you are now logged in to your new server installation. By default, the graphical Server Manager will start in configuration mode, as shown in Figure 14-7.

Performing the Initial Configuration

To complete the setup of Windows Server 2012, you can use the links that make up the Configure This Local Server window shown in Figure 14-7. However, before doing that, you should run Windows Update so you can ensure that all of the server software is current.

In the Server Manager, first click Local Server in the left pane. Then, in the Properties pane, in the column on the right, you will see a row marked Windows Update, as shown in Figure 14-8. Click the hyperlink to the right, labeled Never Check For Updates, which

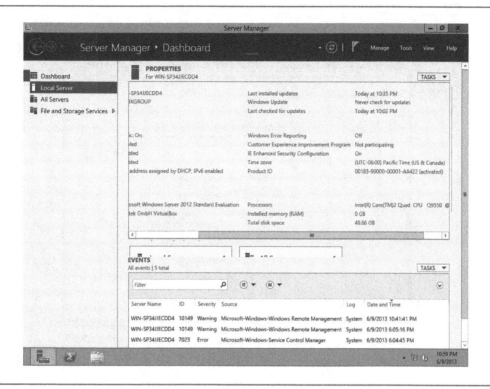

Figure 14-8.   The Properties pane of the Local Server window

will bring up the Windows Update dialog box shown in Figure 14-9. Click the Check For Updates button, and then follow the prompts to download and install any available updates.

If you are installing Windows Server 2012 simply to learn more about it and the network it's connected to already has a DHCP server, Windows will automatically obtain an IP address and access the network, so you do not need to change the network settings. However, in a production environment, most servers are assigned static IP addresses to use.

To assign a static IP address, click Local Server in the left pane of Server Manager. In the main pane, find the entry titled Ethernet, and click the hyperlink to the right of it. This will open the Network Connections window shown in Figure 14-10.

Figure 14-9. The Windows Update dialog box

Right-click the Ethernet object in the Network Connections window, and choose Properties. This activates the Ethernet Properties dialog box shown in Figure 14-11.

Now, click the entry in the list called Internet Protocol Version 4 (TCP/IPv4), and then click the Properties button. You will see the Internet Protocol Version 4 (TCP/IPv4) Properties dialog box shown in Figure 14-12.

You can now click the Use The Following IP Address option, and then fill in the values you want to use for IP address, subnet mask, and default gateway. Click OK to save your changes and close the dialog box.

CAUTION   When assigning static IP addresses, it is important not to assign an address already in use on the network and not in the pool of available addresses managed by the DHCP server.

After configuring networking, you will also want to assign a computer name and, if there is an existing domain, connect this server to the domain. Back at the main screen

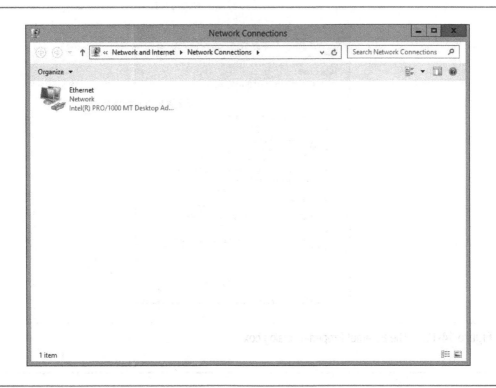

Figure 14-10.   The Network Connections window

for Server Manager, select Local Server in the left pane, and then click the hyperlink to the right of the Computer Name entry to display the System Properties dialog box shown in Figure 14-13.

Next, click the Change button in the dialog box, which will bring up the Computer Name/Domain Changes dialog box shown in Figure 14-14.

In this dialog box, enter an appropriate name for the new server. I usually recommend something relatively short and easy to remember and to type. If you want to connect this server to an existing Active Directory domain, click the Domain option and enter the correct domain name. (You will need an administrative account and password on a target domain in order to join this computer to it.) If you are just learning about Windows Server 2012, or if you are going to create an Active Directory domain, you can leave the server in workgroup mode at this time. Click OK to save the new server name, which will require a restart of the server.

Figure 14-11. The Ethernet Properties dialog box

Figure 14-12. The Internet Protocol Version 4 (TCP/IPv4) Properties dialog box

Figure 14-13.   The System Properties dialog box

Figure 14-14.   Setting the server name and workgroup or domain

Add Roles and Features

Windows Server 2012 makes setting up the server to perform different roles a snap. In Server Manager, make sure you're on the Dashboard section in the left pane, and then click Add Roles And Features, which activates the Add Roles And Features Wizard shown in Figure 14-15.

When you first click Next to move through the wizard, you will see the Installation Type section of the wizard, in which you choose whether to perform a role-based or feature-based installation, or to perform a Remote Desktop Services installation. In this example, choose role-based or feature-based installation and click Next to continue.

You are then prompted to choose a server onto which you want to install roles and features. Since this example is for a single server, there should only be the server you're working on listed. Choose the Select A Server From The Server Pool option, ensure the server you're setting up is selected, and click Next to continue.

Next you will see a list of roles that you can choose to install, shown in Figure 14-16. You select the roles that you want to install by checking the box next to each one. You can click each of the roles to read a brief description of what the role does.

If you are configuring the server as a file server, just ensure that File And Storage Services is installed, as indicated in Figure 14-16. To configure it as a web server using

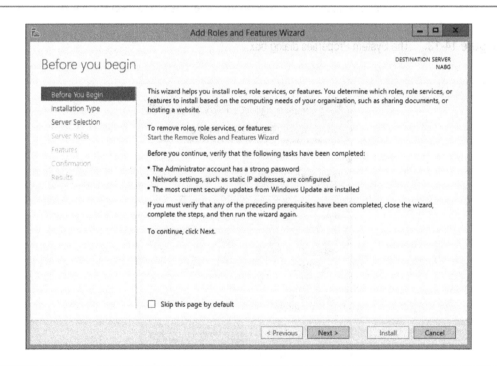

Figure 14-15. The Add Roles And Features Wizard

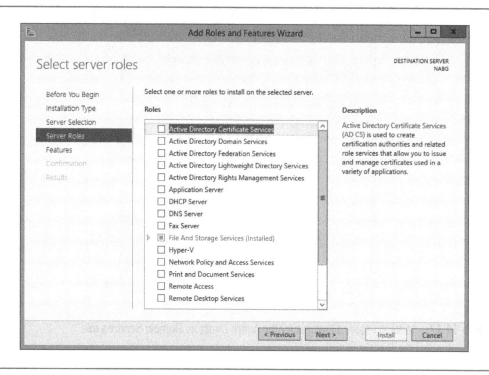

Figure 14-16.   The Server Roles section of the Add Roles And Features Wizard

IIS, click the Web Server (IIS) checkbox. You can choose any combination of roles that you need, and the wizard will walk you through any necessary additional setup with a minimum of hassle. In this example, we are installing Windows Server 2012 as a stand-alone domain controller, so click the checkbox next to Active Directory Domain Services, which will immediately activate a dialog box that informs you that additional features are required to be installed, and that offers to install them for you, as shown in Figure 14-17. Click Add Features to install them and continue, which will return you to the Select Server Roles screen. From there, click Next to continue in the main wizard.

Next, you will see the Select Features section of the wizard, shown in Figure 14-18. Features are various additional capabilities that you can choose to install on the server. It makes sense to familiarize yourself with this list as you learn about Windows Server 2012. For this example, Group Policy Management should already be a selected feature to be installed, so click Next to continue.

The next step in the wizard, for this example, is a screen that describes additional information relating to the installation of Active Directory Domain Services, and notes that any dependent features will be automatically installed during the main installation process. Click Next to continue, which will bring you to the final confirmation screen, in which you can click the Install button to begin the actual installation.

Figure 14-17. Adding required features for the Active Directory Domain Services role

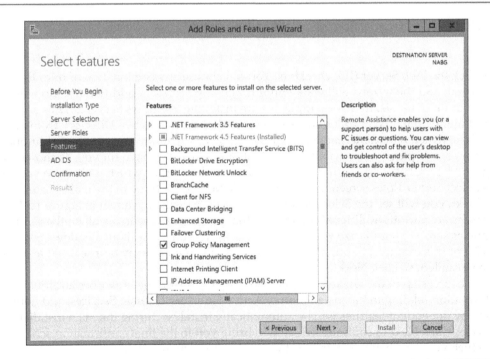

Figure 14-18. The Select Features section of the wizard

After the installation is complete, you should restart the server. After the restart, some additional steps are required. If you look at the top of the Server Manager dashboard, you will see a flag icon with a yellow warning sign. Clicking the flag icon will display the alert, which in this case is letting you know that you need to promote the server to be a domain controller (see Figure 14-19).

To perform the promotion, click the Promote This Server To A Domain Controller hyperlink in the alert window, which will activate the Active Directory Domain Services Configuration Wizard, shown in Figure 14-20. Since this is a stand-alone server and domain, choose Add A New Forest, enter the name you would like to use for the root domain, and click Next to continue.

You now choose the functional level of the Active Directory forest and the domain. (A forest is a grouping of domains. Even a single domain in Active Directory needs to belong to a forest.) Since this is a demo system, leave both the forest and domain functional levels set to Windows Server 2012. The checkboxes for both Domain Name System (DNS) Server and Global Catalog (GC) should also be checked, as Active Directory domains need both resources installed to function. Finally, enter a password that can be

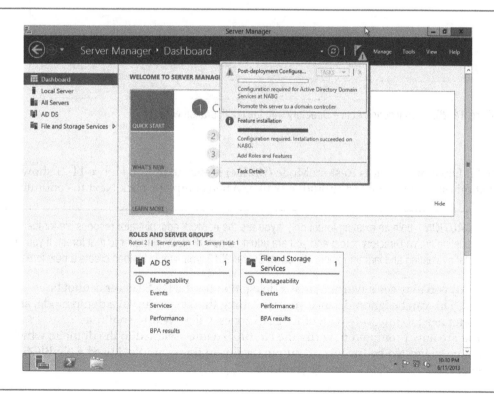

Figure 14-19.   A warning letting you know that you need to promote the server

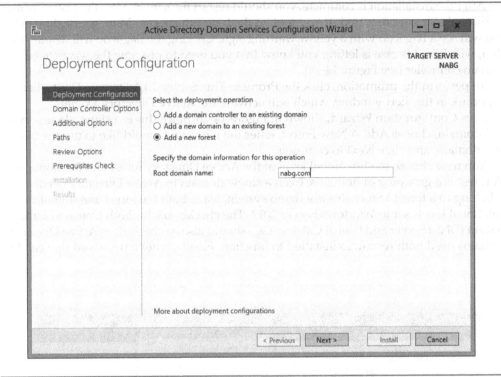

Figure 14-20.   Configuring Active Directory with the configuration wizard

used if Directory Services Restore Mode (DSRM) is ever required. Figure 14-21 shows what this step of the wizard should look like. When complete, click Next to continue.

CAUTION   Join an existing forest only if you are the network administrator responsible for the existing Active Directory forest and you are adding a new domain controller to that forest. If you are just evaluating and learning about Windows Server 2012, you should instead create a new forest.

Next, you may see a warning that a delegation for the DNS server cannot be created. This can be ignored, since you are setting this system up in a demo mode, and it will not need to integrate with other DNS zones. Click Next to continue.

You are now prompted to verify the NetBIOS name assigned to the domain, which should be suggested by the wizard automatically. In this example, I used a NetBIOS name of NABG-AD. Click Next to continue.

Figure 14-21.   Setting domain controller options

The final settings will prompt you for directory locations where three resources will be stored on the system. By default, the Active Directory database files and the log files will be stored in C:\Windows\NTDS, while a folder called SYSVOL will be created at C:\Windows\SYSVOL. Accept these defaults by clicking Next to continue.

Finally, the wizard will confirm all of the selections you have made. After you click Next, the wizard will verify that all prerequisites for a domain controller are met by the system, after which you will be able to click Install to perform the installation, which should complete within a few minutes. After it's complete, the system will automatically restart.

Congratulations! With the preceding steps, you have finished the installation and configuration of Windows Server 2012 acting as a domain controller. You now have a server capable of meeting the needs of many users and of performing a number of useful tasks.

Chapter Summary

In this chapter, you learned how Windows Server 2012 is installed and set up, using basic installation choices that will be appropriate for many servers in small businesses. As you saw, installing Windows Server 2012 is really not much more difficult than installing Windows 8.

This chapter did not cover all the myriad choices available to you during the installation of Windows Server 2012 or discuss more complex installation topics appropriate for larger networks. Instead, this chapter was intended to help beginners to networking understand the basic steps to install Windows Server 2012 and to provide enough information to get a basic server up and running with minimal problems.

If you will be installing Windows Server 2012 into a production environment—no matter how small—it's vital for you to learn much more about Windows Server 2012 than presented in this book. Fortunately, many fine training classes and books are available to teach you all you must do to set up and administer a Windows Server 2012–based network.

Installing the NOS is only a small part of the battle. Even more important is that you know how to administer the server and perform various administrative tasks for the NOS. These include managing user accounts, groups, printers, and other required maintenance tasks. Chapter 15 discusses the basics of Windows Server 2012 administration.

CHAPTER 15 | Administering Windows Server 2012: The Basics

Installing and setting up Windows Server 2012 is only the tip of the iceberg. Far more important and time-consuming is the process of administering the server. This process includes regular and common duties, such as adding new users, deleting old users, assigning permissions to users, performing backups, and so forth. These topics are covered in this chapter. Good administration habits will ensure that the network and the server remain productive and secure.

Thinking About Network Security

Before delving into the administrative activities discussed in this chapter, you should spend some time thinking about network security and how it relates to your specific company. Administering a server must be predicated on maintaining appropriate security for your network.

The key here is to remember that every network has an *appropriate* level of security. The security requirements for a Department of Defense (DoD) contractor that designs military equipment will be different from the security requirements for a company that operates restaurants.

Many beginning network administrators think they need to set up their networks to follow the strongest security measures available. The problem with this approach is that these measures almost always reduce the productivity of people using the network. You need to strike a balance between productivity and security in accordance with the needs of your company.

For example, Windows Server 2012 enables you to set various security policies that apply to users. These include forcing password changes at specified intervals, requiring that passwords be a certain minimum length, disallowing reuse of old passwords, and so on. For example, you could set up policies to require passwords that are at least 20 characters long and that must be changed weekly. In theory, these settings should be more secure than shorter, less frequently changed passwords. A 20-character password is virtually impossible to crack using standard methods, and weekly password changes reduce the chance that someone else will discover a user's password and be free to use it for an extended period of time.

One problem with such strict policies is that users may resort to writing down their passwords so they can remember them from week to week. A written password is far less secure than one that is remembered, because someone else can find the written password and bypass security easily after doing so. Another problem is that users might frequently forget their passwords, which will lead to them being locked out of the system for periods of time. This means they will require help from the network administrator (you!) to clear up these problems each time they occur. For a DoD contractor, these trade-offs might be worthwhile. For the restaurant operator, however, they would be inappropriate and would probably end up hurting the company more than they help.

The primary reason you should pay attention to this subject before learning about administration is that you should determine the appropriate network security early, so that you can allow for it as you administer the network on a daily basis. Network security doesn't need to take up much of your time, provided you set up your administrative procedures so they presuppose the level of security you require. For example, if you know what your password policies will be on the network, it takes only a few seconds to ensure that new users have those policies set for their account. If you know that you maintain a paper-based log of changes to security groups in the network, then it takes only a second to follow this procedure as you change group membership occasionally. Failing to determine these security practices and policies early on will result in needing to undertake much larger projects as part of a security review or audit. Security is an area where you're much better off doing things right the first time!

Working with User Accounts

For anyone—including the administrator—to gain access to a server running Windows Server 2012, the user must have an account established on the server or in the domain. (A *domain* is essentially a collection of security information shared among Windows servers.) The account defines the *user name* (the name by which the user is known to the system) and the user's password, along with a host of other information specific to each user. Creating, maintaining, and deleting user accounts is easy with Windows Server 2012.

NOTE Every account created for a Windows Server 2012 domain is assigned a special number, called a security ID (SID). The server actually recognizes the user by this number. SIDs are said to be "unique across space and time." This means that no two users will ever have the same SID, even if they have the same user name and even the same password. This is because the SID is made up of a unique number assigned to the domain and then a sequential number assigned to each created account (with billions of unique user-specific numbers available). If you have a user called Frank, delete that account, and then create another account called Frank, the accounts will have different SIDs. This ensures that no user account will accidentally receive permissions originally assigned to another user of the same name.

To maintain user accounts, you use the Active Directory Users And Computers console. You can open this console by going to the Start screen and then clicking Active Directory Users And Computers. Alternatively, from Server Manager, you can open the Tools menu, and select Active Directory Users And Computers from the menu. To accomplish activities in the console, you first select either a container in the left pane or an object in the right pane, and then either right-click the container or object or open the Action pull-down menu and choose from the available options. Because the available options change based on the selected container or object, first selecting an object with which to work is important.

Adding a User

To add a user with the Active Directory Users And Computers console, start by selecting the Users container in the left pane (with the tree open to the domain you are administering), as shown in Figure 15-1. Then right-click the Users container, choose New from the pop-up menu, and choose User from the submenu. You see the New Object – User dialog box, as shown in Figure 15-2. Fill in the First Name, Last Name, and User Logon Name fields. Then click the Next button to move to the next dialog box.

TIP   You should establish standards by which you assign logon names on your network. Small networks (those with fewer than 50 users) often just use people's first names, followed by the first initial of their last names when conflicts arise. For somewhat larger companies, a common convention is to use the user's last name followed by the first initial of their first name. For still larger companies, it is common to see a person's full first and last name used, with a period separating the names. This latter standard allows far more combinations before conflicts arise, and you can then resolve any conflicts that arise by adding the person's middle initial, a number, or some other change so that all user names at any given time on the system are unique.

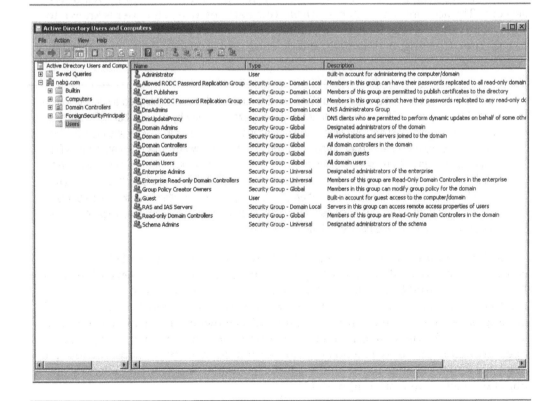

Figure 15-1.   The Active Directory Users And Computers console allows you to manage user accounts.

Figure 15-2.   Use the New Object – User dialog box to add a new user.

In the second dialog box, shown in Figure 15-3, you enter the initial password that the account will use. You also select several options that apply to the account, as follows:

- **User Must Change Password at Next Logon**   Selecting this checkbox forces users to choose their own password when they first log in to the system.

- **User Cannot Change Password**   You might select this option for resource accounts if you do not want to allow users to change their passwords. (For instance, you might have a specific user account established for a particular computer that performs a particular function that many people employ.) Generally, however, you should not select this option; most sites allow users to change their own passwords, and you want to permit them to do so if you've also set passwords to automatically expire.

- **Password Never Expires**   Choose this option to allow the password to remain viable for as long as the user chooses to use it. Activating this option for most users is generally considered a poor security practice.

- **Account Is Disabled**   Selecting this option disables the new account. The administrator can enable the account when needed by clearing the checkbox.

After entering the password and selecting the options you want, click Next to continue. You will then see a confirmation screen. Click Next a final time to create the account, or click Back to return to either dialog box to make changes.

Figure 15-3. Setting the user's password

Modifying a User Account

The dialog box in which you modify the information about a user account contains many other fields than the ones to create the account. You can use these to document the account and to set some other security options.

To modify an existing user account, right-click the user object you wish to modify and choose Properties from the pop-up menu. You then see the tabbed dialog box shown in Figure 15-4.

In the first two tabs, General and Address, you can enter some additional information about the user, such as job title, mailing address, telephone number, e-mail account, and so forth. Because Active Directory also integrates with Exchange Server, this information might be important to enter for your network.

In the Account tab, shown in Figure 15-5, you can set some important user account options. At the top of the tab, you can see the user's logon name, as well as the Windows domain in which the user has primary membership. Below that is the user's Windows NT logon name (called the pre–Windows 2000 logon name), which the user can optionally use to log in to the domain from a Windows NT computer or to use an application that doesn't yet support Active Directory logins. (Although you can set these two logon names to be different, doing so rarely is a good idea.)

Clicking the Logon Hours button displays the dialog box shown in Figure 15-6. In this dialog box, you select different blocks of time within a standard week, and then click the appropriate option button to permit or deny access to the network for that

Figure 15-4.   Setting properties for a user's account

time period. In Figure 15-6, the settings permit logon times for a normal workday, with some cushion before and after those times to allow for slightly different work hours. By default, users are permitted to log on to the network at any time, any day of the week. For most networks, particularly smaller networks, permitting users to log on at any time is generally acceptable.

Clicking the Log On To button on the Account tab opens the Logon Workstations dialog box, as shown in Figure 15-7. By default, users can log on to any workstation in the domain, and the domain authenticates them. In some cases, a system might require stricter security, where you specify the computers to which a user account can log on. For example, you might set up a network backup account that you use to back up the network, and then leave this account logged on all the time in your locked computer room. Because the backup account has access to all files on the network (necessary to do its job), a good idea is to limit that account to log on only to the computer designated for this purpose in the computer room. You use the Log On To feature to set up this type of restriction. (Note that the Log On To feature works only if the network

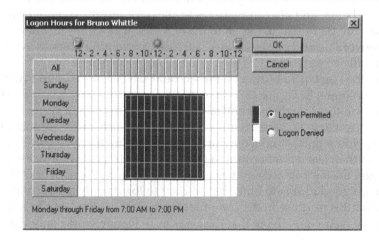

Figure 15-5. The Account tab of a user's Properties dialog box lets you set some important user account options.

Figure 15-6. Setting logon time restrictions for a user

Figure 15-7.   Restricting the computers to which a user can log on

uses the NetBIOS or NetBEUI protocols; it will not work with TCP/IP-only networks unless the Windows Internet Naming Service is set up on the network.)

NOTE   Allowing a user to log on to another user's computer does not mean that user can log on with the other user's permissions or access anything that only the other user can access. This simply means the user can use the listed physical computer to log on to his own account from that computer.

The Account Options section of the Account tab enables you to select various binary (on/off) account options. You set some of the options, such as requiring a user to change the password at the next logon, as you add the account. Some options listed are unique to the user's Properties dialog box. The two most important of these additional options are Account Is Disabled and Account Is Trusted for Delegation.

Account Is Disabled, if selected, disables the user account while leaving it set up within Active Directory. This option is useful if you need to deny this user account access to the network, but might need to re-enable the account in the future. (Account Is Disabled is handled as a high-priority change within the domain, and it takes effect immediately, even across large numbers of domain controllers.) Because deleting an account also deletes any permissions the user might have, you should always disable an account if instead you might need to grant access to the network again to that user.

For example, if someone is on vacation, you could disable the user's account while they are gone, and then clear the Account Is Disabled checkbox when they return.

You must select the Account Is Trusted For Delegation option if you want to designate the user account to administer some part of the domain. Windows Server 2012 enables you to grant administrative rights to portions of the Active Directory tree without needing to give administrative rights to the entire domain.

The last option on the Account tab of the user's Properties dialog box is the expiration date setting, Account Expires. By default, it is set to Never. If you wish to define an expiration date, you may do so in the End Of field. When the date indicated is reached, the account is automatically disabled (but not deleted, so you can re-enable it if you wish).

Another tab that you will use often in the user's Properties dialog box is the Member Of tab, in which you define the security groups for a user, as shown in Figure 15-8. Security groups are discussed after the description of deleting or disabling a user account.

Figure 15-8.   Controlling a user's membership in groups

Deleting or Disabling a User Account

Deleting a user account is easy using the Active Directory Users And Groups console. In the left pane, select the Users folder, and then select the user in the right pane. Either right-click the user and choose Delete, or open the Action pull-down menu and choose Delete.

Disabling an account is just as easy. Select the user account, right-click it, and choose Disable Account (or open the Action pull-down menu and choose Disable Account).

TIP   If you need to delete a large number of accounts, you can save time by selecting them all before choosing the Delete or Disable Account command. Just be sure you haven't selected accounts that you don't want to delete or disable!

Working with Active Directory Security Groups

On any network, you usually need to administer permissions to many different folders and files. If you were able to grant access only by user account, you would quickly go crazy trying to keep track of all the necessary information.

For example, suppose that a group of people, such as an accounting department, has specific permissions to access 20 different folders on the server. When a new accountant is hired, do you need to remember or look up all those 20 folders so you can give the accountant the same permissions as the rest of the department? Or suppose that a user who has many different permissions changes departments. Do you need to find each permission so you can make sure he has only the appropriate permissions for his new department?

To address such problems, network operating systems support the concept of *security groups* (or just *groups*). You first create the group, and then assign all the appropriate users to it so you can administer their permissions more easily. When you grant permission to a folder on the server, you do so by giving the group the network permission. All the members of the group automatically *inherit* those permissions. This inheritance makes maintaining network permissions over time much easier. In fact, you shouldn't try to manage network permissions without using groups. Otherwise, you might quickly become overwhelmed trying to keep track of everything, and you're almost certain to make mistakes over time.

Not only can users be members of groups, but groups can be members of other groups. For instance, suppose that you define a group for each department in your company. Half of those departments are part of a larger division called Research and Development (R&D) and half are part of Sales, General, and Administration (SG&A). On your network, some folders are specific to each department, some are specific to all of R&D or SG&A, and some can be accessed by every user on the network. In such a situation, you would first create the departmental groups and then create the R&D and SG&A groups. Each departmental group would then become a member in either R&D or SG&A. Finally, you would use the built-in Domain Users group, or another one you created that represents everyone, and then assign R&D and SG&A to that top-level group for every user.

Once you've set up your groups, you can grant permissions in the most logical way. If a resource is just for a specific department, you assign that departmental group to the resource. If a resource is for R&D or SG&A, you assign those divisions to the resource; then all the individual departmental groups within that division will inherit permission to access the resource. If a resource is for everyone, you assign the master, top-level group to the resource.

Using such hierarchical group levels makes administering permissions even easier, and this approach is practically necessary for larger networks with hundreds or thousands of users.

Creating Groups

You create groups using the Active Directory Users And Computers console. Groups appear in two of the domain's containers: Builtin and Users.

The built-in groups, shown in Figure 15-9, are fixed. They cannot be deleted or made members of other groups. The built-in groups have certain important permissions already assigned to them, and other groups you create can be given

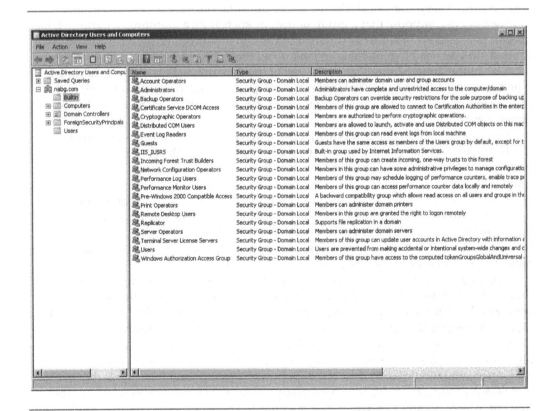

Figure 15-9. Viewing the list of built-in groups

membership in the built-in groups. Similarly, if you want to disable a particular built-in group, you would do so simply by removing all its member groups.

> **CAUTION**   Be careful changing the membership of the built-in groups. For most networks, while it's important to understand what these groups are and how they work, you generally want to leave them alone.

Generally, you work only with groups defined in the Users container. Figure 15-10 shows the default groups in the Users container, which you can distinguish from user accounts by both the two-person icon and the type designation.

To add a new group, select the Users container in the left pane. Then open the Action pull-down menu, choose New, and choose Group. You see the New Object – Group dialog box, as shown in Figure 15-11. Enter the name of the group in the first field. You'll see the name you enter echoed in the second field. This field enables you to specify a different group name for Windows NT (pre–Windows 2000) computers. However, using different group names is usually not a good idea, because it can quickly make your system confusing.

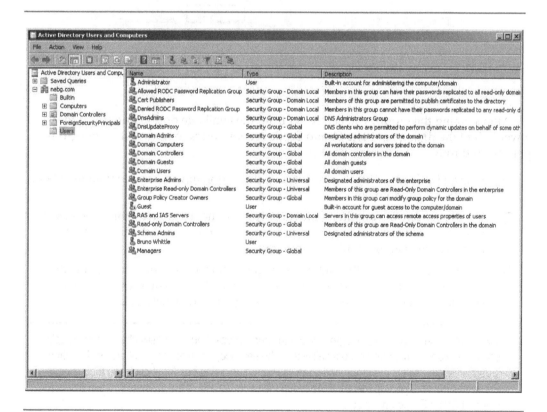

Figure 15-10.   Default groups in the Users container

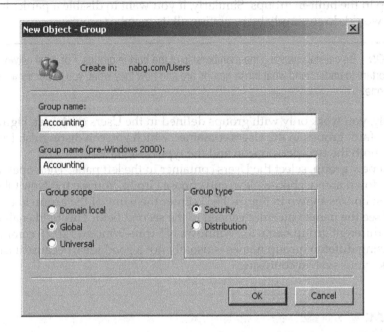

Figure 15-11. Creating a new group

After naming the group, you can select from the available option buttons in the lower half of the dialog box. The Group Scope section refers to how widely the group is populated throughout a domain:

- *Domain local* groups exist only within a single domain and can contain members only from that domain.

- *Global* groups can contain members only from the domain in which they exist. However, you can assign global group permissions to any domain within the network, even across multiple domains.

- *Universal* groups exist throughout an organization, even when the organization's network is made up of many individual domains. Universal groups can also contain members from any domain in an organization's network.

TIP Don't worry if you create a group with the wrong scope. You can easily change the group's scope, provided its membership doesn't violate the new scope's rules for membership. To change a domain scope, select the group and open its Properties dialog box (right-click and then choose Properties from the pop-up menu). If the group membership allows the change, you can select a different Group Scope option button.

After you set the group's scope, you can also select whether it will be a security group or a distribution group. Distribution groups are used only to maintain e-mail distribution lists for e-mail applications such as Microsoft Exchange Server. They have no security impact in Windows Server 2012.

Finally, click OK to create the group. Now you can add members to the group, as described in the next section.

Maintaining Group Membership

A new group starts out without any members. To set the membership for a group, follow these steps:

1. Select the group, right-click it, and choose Properties from the pop-up menu. The Properties dialog box appears. Then click the Members tab, as shown in Figure 15-12.

2. Click the Add button. You see the Select Users, Contacts, Computers, Or Groups dialog box, as shown in Figure 15-13.

Figure 15-12. A brand-new group does not have any members.

Figure 15-13.   Adding a member to a group

3. Type in enough of a user or another group's name to identify it, and then click the Check Names button. If you type in too few characters to uniquely identify the user or group, Windows will show you a list of the possible matches from which you can select the correct one.

4. Choose the member you want to add, and then click OK.

5. Repeat steps 3 and 4 to complete the group membership.

Working with Shares

Drives and folders under Windows Server 2012 are made available to users over the network as shared resources, simply called *shares* in Windows networking parlance. You select a drive or folder, enable it to be shared, and then set the permissions for the share.

Understanding Share Security

You can set both drives and folders as distinct shared resources, whether they are located on a File Allocation Table (FAT)-formatted drive or on an NT File System (NTFS)-formatted drive. In the case of an NTFS-formatted drive (but not a FAT-formatted drive), you can also set permissions on folders and files within the share that are separate from the permissions on the share itself. Understanding how Windows Server 2012 handles security for shares, folders, and files on NTFS drives is important.

Suppose that you created a share called RESEARCH and you gave the R&D security group read-only access to the share. Within the share, you set the permissions on a folder called PROJECTS to allow full read and write access (called *change permission*) for the R&D security group. Will the R&D group have read-only permission to that folder or change permission? The group will have read-only permission. This is because the security permissions for the share define the maximum permissions that will be allowed for everything within the share.

A better way to set up share permissions is to allow everyone change permission to the share and then control the actual permissions by setting them on the folders within the share itself. This way, you can assign any combination of permissions you want; then the users will receive the permissions that you set on those folders, even though the share is set to change permission.

Also, remember that users receive permissions based on the groups of which they are members, and these permissions are cumulative. So, if you are a member of an Everyone group that has read-only permission for a particular file, but you're also a member of the Admins group that has full control permission for that file, you'll have full control permission in practice. This is an important rule: Permissions set on folders and files are always cumulative and take into account permissions set for the user individually, as well as any security groups of which the user is a member.

Another important point is that you can set permissions within a share (sometimes called *NTFS permissions*) on both folders and files, and these permissions are also cumulative. So, for instance, you can set read-only permission on a folder for a user, but change permission for some specific files. The user then has the ability to read, modify, and even delete those files without having that ability with other files in the same folder.

There's a special permission called *no access*, which overrides all other permissions, no matter what. If you set no access permission for a user on a file or folder, then that's it—the user will not be able to access that file or folder. An extremely important corollary to this rule is that no access permission is also cumulative and overriding. So, if the Everyone security group has change permission for a file, but you set a particular user to no access for that file, that user will receive no access permission. If you set no access permission for the Everyone group, however, then all members of that group will also receive the no access permission because it overrides any other permissions they have. Be careful about using no access with security groups!

To summarize, you can resolve most permission problems if you remember the rules discussed here:

- Share permissions define the maximum permissions that can be effective within the share. When files or folders in a share grant more permissions than the share itself, the share's permissions win.

- Aside from the preceding rule, permissions are cumulative, taking into account permissions assigned to users and groups, as well as files and folders.

- When a permission conflict occurs, the no access permission always wins if it is set.

Creating Shares

As a network administrator, you will frequently create and manage the shares on the network. The following steps walk you through creating a new share.

1. Open either My Computer or Windows Explorer on the server.

2. Right-click the folder or drive you want to share, and then choose Share from the pop-up menu. You will see the File Sharing dialog box, as shown in Figure 15-14.

3. In the field provided, enter enough of a user's name to identify that person in the system, and then click Add.

4. Click the down arrow next to the user's name to set that user's permission level. The permission levels available are Owner, for full read and write access, plus the ability to grant permissions to other users; Read/Write, for full read and write access; and Read, for read-only access.

5. Click the Share button to create the share. You will see a confirmatory dialog box. Click OK, and the share will be created. By default, the share uses the folder's name as the share name.

Figure 15-14.   Creating a share

Once a share is created and the share information has propagated through the domain (usually within several minutes), users can browse it through Network Neighborhood (Windows 9*x* and NT), My Network Places (Windows 2000 and XP), or Network (Windows Vista and later). Double-clicking the share will open it (if allowed by the permissions).

Mapping Drives

You can use shares by opening them through Network Neighborhood, My Network Places, or Network, and they function just like the folders in My Computer. However, you might frequently want to simulate a connected hard disk on your computer with a share from the network. For example, many applications that store files on the network require that the network folders be accessible as normal drive letters. The process of simulating a disk drive with a network share is called *mapping*. You create a map (link) between the drive letter you want to use and the actual network share to remain attached to that drive letter.

You can create a drive mapping in many ways. The easiest way is to open Network from the client computer, locate the share you want to map, right-click it, and choose Map Network Drive. In the dialog box that appears, the name of the domain and share will already be filled in for you. Simply select an appropriate drive letter for the mapping and click OK. From then on, the share will appear to your computer as that drive letter, and users will see this share's letter in My Computer.

You can also map drives using a command-line utility called NET. The NET command takes a variety of forms and can fulfill many different needs, depending on the parameters you give it. To map a drive, you use the NET USE command. Typing NET USE by itself and pressing ENTER will list all currently mapped drives. (You can type NET HELP USE for more detailed help on the command.) To add a new drive mapping, you would type the following:

```
NET USE drive_letter: UNC_for_share
```

Most network resources in a Windows network use a naming system called the Universal Naming Convention (UNC). To supply a UNC, you start with two backslashes, then the name of the server, another backslash, and the name of the share. (Additional backslashes and names can refer to folders and files within the share.) For example, to map drive G: to a share called EMPLOYEES located on the server SERVER, use the following command:

```
NET USE G:\\SERVER\EMPLOYEES
```

TIP   You can use the NET command from any Windows client for any Windows network. Type NET by itself to list all of the different forms of the command. Type *NET command HELP* to see detailed help on the different NET commands.

Working with Printers

Before setting up and working with printers on a network, you need to understand the components involved in network printing and how they interact.

Understanding Network Printing

A *print job* is a set of binary data sent from a network workstation to a network printer. A print job is the same data that a computer would send to a locally connected printer—it's just redirected to the network for printing.

The network workstation that sends the print job to the print queue is responsible for formatting the print data properly for the printer. This is done through software installed on the workstation, called a *print driver,* which is specific to each type of printer. Printer drivers are also specific to each operating system that uses them. In other words, an HP LaserJet 5si driver for a Windows XP computer is different from an HP LaserJet 5si driver for a Windows 2000 workstation computer. More troublesome, different versions of the same operating system sometimes use different drivers, so a driver for a Windows XP computer might not work with a Windows Vista computer and vice versa.

Print jobs are often sent to the network through a captured printer port. The network client software redirects to the network one of the printer ports on a networked workstation, such as LPT1. The process of redirecting a printer port to a network printer is called *capturing.* Usually, captured ports are persistent and continue through multiple logins until they are turned off.

Print jobs sent to the network go to a place called a *print queue.* The print job sits in the queue until the network can service the print job and send it to the printer. Print queues can hold many jobs from many different users and typically are managed in a first-in, first-out fashion.

Print jobs are removed from print queues and sent to actual printers by *print servers.* After sending the complete job to the printer, the print server removes the job from the queue. You can accomplish print serving in many different ways. If the printer you are using is connected to a server or workstation on the network, that server or workstation handles the print server duty. If the printer is directly connected to the network (it has its own network port), then the printer usually has a built-in print server as part of its network hardware. This built-in print server has the intelligence to log in to the network and to service a particular printer queue.

Print jobs start at the printing application, which sends its printer output to the local operating system. The local operating system uses the printer driver requested by the application to format the actual print job for the printer in question. The local operating system works with the installed network client software to send the formatted print job to the print queue, where the job sits until the printer is available. Then the print server sends the print job from the queue to the actual printer.

Many steps are involved, but once everything is set up, it works smoothly, as you will see in the next section. Figure 15-15 shows an overview of how network printing works.

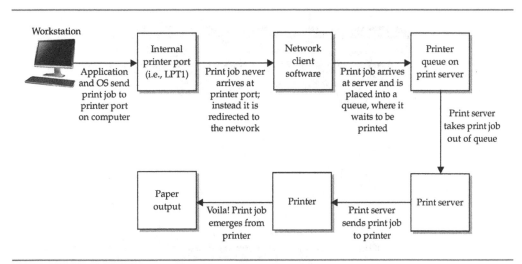

Figure 15-15. Overview of the network printing process

Setting Up a Network Printer

You can easily set up a printer connected to a server (or workstation) so other network users can access it. However, for networks with more than about 20 users, you're better off buying printers with network interfaces and built-in print servers (most laser printers appropriate for business use will have this already).

Also, printers with built-in print servers are far easier to relocate on the network. They can go anywhere a network connection exists and where power is available. Once connected to the network at a new location, the printer logs in to the network and starts doing its work immediately.

If you want to share a printer connected directly to a Windows Server 2012 server, this is easy to do. First, open the server's Devices And Printers folder, which lists all the installed printers. Right-click the one you want to share and choose Printer Properties from the pop-up menu. The Properties dialog box for the printer will appear. Choose the Sharing tab, which displays the dialog box shown in Figure 15-16.

NOTE   In this example, the printer and its driver are already installed properly, as they would normally be during the installation of Windows Server 2012. If they are not properly installed, open the Printers folder and use the Add Printers icon to set up the printer on the server itself.

On the Sharing tab, click the Share This Printer checkbox, and then assign the printer a share name by which the client computers will recognize the printer. At this point, you can click the OK button because the default permissions for a shared printer are for the Everyone group to be able to print to it. Alternatively, if you want to

Figure 15-16.   Enabling printer sharing

set other permissions for a shared printer, use the Security tab of the printer's Printer Properties dialog box.

The groups assigned in the Security tab are the default assignments for a shared printer, with the Administrators permissions shown. Three main permissions are assigned to each entity: Print, Manage Printers, and Manage Documents. The Everyone group has permission to print, but not to manage documents in the queue. However, a special group called Creator Owner has permission to manage documents. This means that the user who sent the print job automatically has permission to modify or delete his own print job, but not others waiting in the queue.

For high-throughput requirements, you might want to use a feature called *printer pooling*, which enables you to set up a number of identical printers, all connected to a single printer queue, that appear to the network as one printer. Users print to the listed printer, and the first available real printer services the job. Using printer pooling, you could have a whole bank of printers appear as one printer to the users and dramatically increase the number of print requests you can handle. Keep in mind that pooled printers must be identical because they will all use the same print driver. Figure 15-17 shows the Ports tab on which printer pooling is enabled.

Figure 15-17.   Enabling printer pooling

As you can see, setting up networked printers with Windows Server 2012 is a relatively straightforward process that gives you considerable flexibility in how you set up and manage your shared printers. Remember, too, that other printing models are also possible, such as network-connected printers. Consult the documentation that comes with such printers for details on setting them up on your network.

Chapter Summary

No single chapter can do justice to all the tools and knowledge needed to administer Windows Server 2012 professionally. This chapter briefly covered how the most common and important tasks are handled. If you are or will be administering a Windows Server 2012 system, you should pursue more detailed knowledge about the topics discussed in this chapter and the many other subjects you will need to master.

In particular, start out by researching and learning about these important tools:

- Reliability And Performance Monitor for troubleshooting, performance tuning, and ongoing monitoring of important server statistics. Reliability And Performance Monitor can be configured to take certain actions when triggers that you set occur, such as sending you an SMS message or sending alert messages to other computers on the network. It is also an extremely useful tool for resolving any performance problems you encounter.

- Event Viewer is key to your ability to find and diagnose Windows Server 2012 problems. You should use Event Viewer on a regular basis (I recommend using it daily) to view new events and decide whether they need your immediate attention. You can use Event Viewer to save the event logs periodically, creating a long-term record of error and informational messages stored in its logs.

- Task Scheduler can be used to schedule recurring tasks you want to run frequently on your server, such as virus scans (with third-party virus software), disk defragmentation, and disk testing.

These are some of the core tools you should learn for basic Windows Server 2012 administration.

CHAPTER 16 | Introducing Exchange Server 2013

Microsoft offers a number of specialized server systems, including the widely used Exchange Server application. Exchange Server is Microsoft's e-mail solution, and it is designed to be able to handle virtually any organization's e-mail needs.

This chapter introduces Exchange Server. You learn how to install it, perform basic configuration tasks, and access a mailbox using Exchange Server's Outlook Web App functionality.

Exchange Server 2013 Features

Exchange Server is a comprehensive e-mail solution for organizations of all sizes, from small companies to large multinational conglomerates. It is highly reliable and scalable, and has been in very wide use for many years. Some of Exchange Server's features include the following:

- Numerous access methods for users to get to their e-mail, including from an e-mail client application such as Microsoft Outlook, a mobile device (such as a smartphone or tablet), a web browser, and even a voice-response system

- Unified Messaging, in which not only e-mail messages are delivered to users' inboxes, but also voicemail messages and faxes

- Support for collaborative features, such as calendaring, shared resource scheduling (such as conference rooms or equipment), meeting scheduling, and out-of-office notifications

- Support for user-defined rules that allow for the automation of routine e-mail tasks

TIP   Automating e-mail tasks can be very useful. For instance, you could set up a human resources department mailbox to which employment applicants send their resumes, and on receipt of each resume, the server responds to the sender with an immediate acknowledgment. It might also forward the resumes to appropriate personnel automatically.

- Close integration with Active Directory, which means that you can maintain user accounts, and their associated mailboxes, in one centralized place

- Some antispam and antivirus technologies, and easy addition of third-party add-on software for these tasks

Whether you need a basic internal e-mail system for a small organization or a sophisticated, powerful system to handle a company of hundreds of thousands of users, Exchange Server can meet those needs.

Installing Exchange Server 2013

If you are just learning about Exchange Server 2013 or evaluating it, you can download a fully functional copy from Microsoft that will operate for 120 days. Before installing it, however, review the following prerequisites:

- Windows Server 2008 R2 or Windows Server 2012 (not set up for Server Cord mode)

- A 64-bit processor compatible with Intel 64 or AMD64 architectures

- An Active Directory domain with the forest set to at least the Windows Server 2003 functional level

- At least 4GB of RAM for the Client Access role, and 8GB of RAM for the Mailbox role, or for both roles combined

- At least 30GB free disk space on the installation partition

- An additional 0.5GB of disk space for each Unified Messaging language pack that will be installed

- At least 200MB free space on the system partition

- All disk partitions formatted with NT File System (NTFS)

There are a number of other detailed requirements, but the Exchange Server installer will survey your system and will notify you of any additional requirements you must meet.

For this example installation, you can use the Windows Server 2012 installation that was discussed in Chapter 14. Before you begin, you should run Windows Update to ensure that you have all current system patches.

When you first start the Exchange Server installation program, you'll be prompted to check for updates to Exchange before running the installation. This is always a good idea, and you should do so before clicking Next to continue.

Next, you're prompted for which roles you wish to install on the server. In Exchange Server 2013, the number of roles has been simplified to two main roles: Mailbox role and Client Access role, as shown in Figure 16-1.

The Mailbox role holds the database that contains user mailboxes and public folders, while the Client Access role acts as the main function to which clients connect to and use Exchange Server. For large installations, you may want to separate these roles in order to balance the load on the servers you are using.

For a smaller installation, and especially for setting up a system for familiarization, you should install both the Mailbox role and Client Access role.

Next, in the installation, you're prompted for the location to which you want to install Exchange Server, as shown in Figure 16-2. If the default is acceptable, click Next to continue. Otherwise, type or browse to the folder in which you want to install Exchange Server before clicking Next to continue.

MICROSOFT EXCHANGE SERVER 2013 SETUP   ? ✕

Server Role Selection

Select the Exchange server roles you want to install on this computer:

☑ Mailbox role

☑ Client Access role

☑ Management tools

☑ Automatically install Windows Server roles and features that are required to install Exchange Server

E Exchange   back   next

Figure 16-1.   Selecting the roles to install on the server

The installation program then requires you to specify the name for the Exchange organization, as shown in Figure 16-3. Usually, this will be your company name, although there are limitations on the characters you are allowed to use, which must be only

- A through Z (both uppercase and lowercase are allowed)
- 0 through 9
- A space, but it cannot be a leading or trailing space
- A dash

MICROSOFT EXCHANGE SERVER 2013 SETUP   ?   ✕

Installation Space and Location

Disk space required: 7869.3 MB

Disk space available: 26954 MB

Specify the path for the Exchange Server installation:

C:\Program Files\Microsoft\Exchange Server\V15   browse

E Exchange   back   next

Figure 16-2.   Choosing the location for the Exchange Server installation

After entering the organization name, click Next to continue.

You are now asked whether or not to disable malware scanning in Exchange Server. By default, Exchange Server includes its own malware protection, but this can be disabled if you will be using another company's antimalware software. Make your selection and click Next to continue.

Figure 16-3.   Specifying the Exchange Organization name

The installation program now scans your system and will indicate if there are any installation prerequisites that are not yet met. If additional software needs to be installed, the installation program provides links to the location of the missing software so that you can install it. The installer will also highlight any warnings of which you should be aware. Figure 16-4 shows an example of the Readiness Checks screen.

MICROSOFT EXCHANGE SERVER 2013 SETUP   ?   ✕

Readiness Checks

The computer will be checked to verify that Exchange is ready to be installed.

Prerequisite Analysis   100%

> **Error:**
> This computer requires the Microsoft Unified Communications Managed API 4.0, Core Runtime 64-bit. Please install the software from http://go.microsoft.com/fwlink/?LinkId=260990.
> For more information, visit: http://technet.microsoft.com/library(EXCHG.150)/ms.exch.setupreadiness.UcmaRedistMsi.aspx
>
> **Warning:**
> Installing Exchange Server on a domain controller will elevate the permissions for Exchange Trusted Subsystem to domain administrators.
> For more information, visit: http://technet.microsoft.com/library (EXCHG.150)/ms.exch.setupreadiness.WarningInstallExchangeRolesOnDomainController.aspx
>
> **Warning:**
> Setup will prepare the organization for Exchange 2013 by using 'Setup /PrepareAD'. No Exchange 2010 server roles have been detected in this topology. After this operation, you will not be able to install any Exchange 2010 servers.
> For more information, visit: http://technet.microsoft.com/library(EXCHG.150)/ms.exch.setupreadiness.NoE14ServerWarning.aspx

🅴▧ Exchange   [retry]

Figure 16-4. Exchange Server Readiness Checks screen

Once any outstanding prerequisites are satisfied, you will be able to click Install to begin the actual installation.

When the installation is complete (which will take around 15 to 30 minutes, depending on the server hardware), you will see the completion screen shown in Figure 16-5.

MICROSOFT EXCHANGE SERVER 2013 SETUP   ?   ✕

Setup Completed

Congratulations! Setup has finished successfully. To complete the installation of Exchange Server 2013, reboot the computer.

You can view additional post-installation tasks online by clicking the link: http://go.microsoft.com/fwlink/p/?LinkId=255372. You can also start the Exchange Administration Center after Setup is finished.

☐ Launch Exchange Administration Center after finishing Exchange setup.

🅴🅱 Exchange   ┌─────────┐
                                                                    │ finish │
                                                                    └─────────┘

Figure 16-5.   Exchange Server is installed.

Setting Up Mailboxes

Exchange Server 2013 makes use of a new web-based management tool called the Exchange Admin Center. You access the tool by navigating to the following address, replacing <exchange_server_name> with either the IP address or server name of your Exchange Server:

```
https://<exchange_server_name>/ecp
```

Once the Exchange Admin Center opens, you will see the screen shown in Figure 16-6.

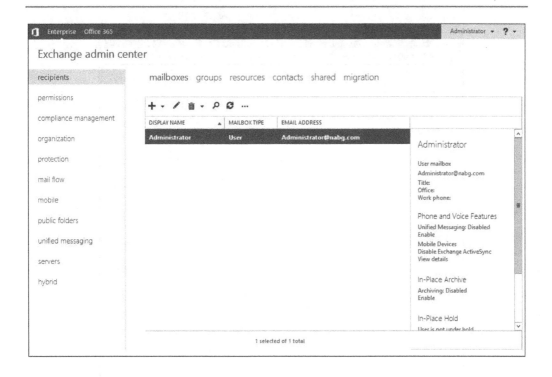

Figure 16-6. Exchange Admin Center

Creating a Mailbox

To create a mailbox in Exchange, follow these steps:

1. In the Exchange Admin Center's left pane, navigate to Recipients. In the central pane, ensure that Mailboxes is selected (your screen should look like Figure 16-6). Then, to create a mailbox, click the plus sign underneath Mailboxes. You will see the screen shown in Figure 16-7.

2. If you are creating a mailbox for an existing domain user, click the Existing User option, and then click Browse to select a user. If you would like to create both a mailbox and a login account, click the New User option. Then, complete the fields as indicated. Figure 16-7 illustrates adding a new user with all fields completed and ready to save.

Figure 16-7. Adding a mailbox in Exchange Admin Center

3. If your organization has multiple mailbox databases and you want to select which database will hold the new user's mailbox, click More Options.

4. Once the user's information is complete, click Save to create the mailbox, and if a new user, the user account.

After the mailbox is created, you can edit it to define additional details about the user and the mailbox. To do so, from the main Recipients screen, click the pencil icon (next to the plus sign you clicked to create the mailbox) to access the User Mailbox screen shown in Figure 16-8.

Figure 16-8.   Editing a mailbox

Along the left are "tabs" that let you choose which element of the user's mailbox you want to edit. These are summarized as follows:

- **General** Allows editing of the user's name, e-mail address, and login name

- **Mailbox Usage** Displays usage information about the user's mailbox, such as when they last accessed it

- **Contact Information** Lets you specify their physical address and telephone numbers

- **Organization** Defines the user's title, the department in which they work, the company name, and their manager

- **Email Address** Each user has a default reply address, which is the address you assigned them. However, you may use this screen to add alias e-mail addresses. For example, your company's CEO may have a normal e-mail address using their name, but also have an alias of "ceo@yourcompany.com." In this screen, you can define alias e-mail addresses for each user.

- **Mailbox Features** This screen lets you set various features for the selected mailbox. For example, you can select from various policies that you have set up that control things like how your users can share calendar and contact information outside your organization. You can also set things like mail retention policy, an address book policy, whether the Outlook Web App is enabled for the mailbox, and so forth. You can also set message size restrictions here.

- **Member Of** This defines the e-mail distribution groups to which the mailbox belongs.

- **MailTip** This lets you display what Microsoft calls a MailTip whenever another user messages this mailbox.

- **Mailbox Delegation** The final screen in the User Mailbox function lets you define which other users have the right to send e-mail on behalf of the owner of the mailbox, or send mail as if they were the actual mailbox owner. These features are frequently used by administrative assistants to manage their supervisor's e-mail.

Once you're done editing the mailbox properties, click Save to store your changes.

Testing Your Mailbox

To enter the test mailbox that you just created, you'll use Outlook Web Access (OWA) on the server itself. Open Internet Explorer, and enter the URL https://*local_host_name*/owa/.

You can use https://localhost/owa/ for testing, but Internet Explorer will likely complain that the certificate for localhost does not match the machine name. However, if you tell Internet Explorer to continue, it will work fine.

When you first log in to OWA, you will be prompted to set your default language and time zone, as shown in Figure 16-9. Make the appropriate selections and click Save to continue.

You are now in OWA, as shown in Figure 16-10. For a web-based e-mail system, you'll find that it's very complete and mimics regular Office Outlook to a large degree.

Spend some time exploring OWA. Although local users will typically use Microsoft Office Outlook to work with Exchange Server, you'll find that OWA is an excellent remote-access solution to allow users to access e-mail, calendar information, and contacts stored on Exchange Server from virtually any web-enabled device.

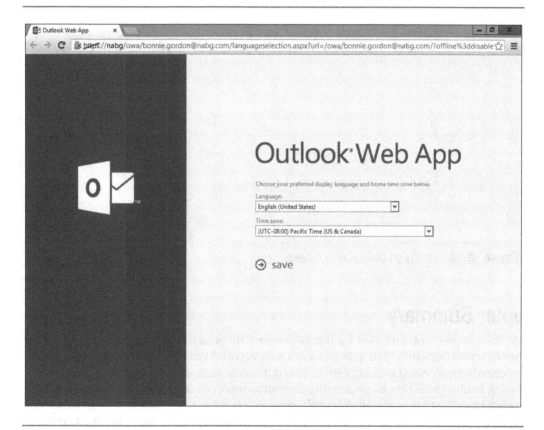

Figure 16-9.   Setting options when first accessing a new mailbox

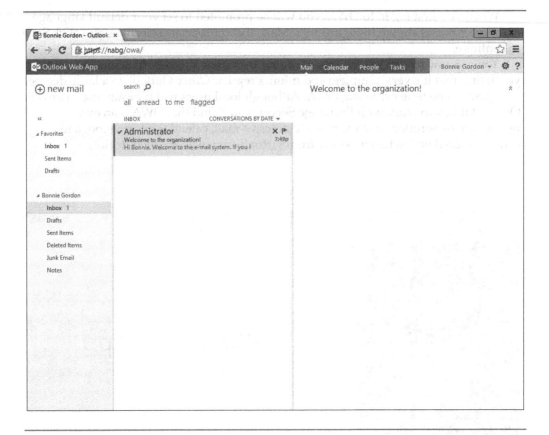

Figure 16-10.   You're in! Outlook Web Access

Chapter Summary

In this chapter, you installed Exchange Server 2013 onto a Windows Server 2012 server with Active Directory. You also created a user account with an attached mailbox and successfully accessed it using OWA. This demonstration showed that installing and using Exchange Server is not terribly difficult. However, if you will be working with a production system, you will definitely need much more information. One place to start is Microsoft's documentation, which you can find at http://technet.microsoft.com/exchange/.

While many applications and services are available for Windows Server 2012, the services described in the next chapter are mainstays that are used in virtually every network. In Chapter 17 you learn about DHCP, DNS, remote access, Internet Information Services, and Remote Desktop Services, all of which are a part of Windows Server 2012.

CHAPTER 17 | Understanding Other Windows Server 2012 Services

O ne of the strengths of Windows Server 2012 is that it can perform many functions and fill many roles. Not only is Windows Server 2012 a powerful and effective file server and print server, but it's also extremely capable of performing many other tasks right out of the box.

Chapters 14 and 15 explained how to set up Windows Server 2012 as a basic file server and print server, and how to administer Windows Server 2012 on a daily basis. To get the most out of Windows Server 2012, you need to know what additional services are available, how they work, and what they do. This chapter introduces some of the other services that come with Windows Server 2012. You can find detailed instructions for implementing these services in a book devoted to Windows Server 2012.

Exploring DHCP

If you've been involved with computers for long, you probably remember what it was like to manage TCP/IP addresses manually. You needed to visit every computer on the network to set its TCP/IP address. You also had to keep track of which computers used which addresses because you had a limited number of addresses with which to work. Plus, as you probably know, when two computers on a network try to use the same TCP/IP address, trouble quickly follows, and you must spend time sorting out these problems.

As discussed in Chapter 6, the Dynamic Host Configuration Protocol (DHCP) saves the day in such situations. A DHCP server is a computer on the network that keeps track of which TCP/IP addresses are available and parcels them out to computers and other devices that boot up and request a TCP/IP address from the server. With a DHCP server, you don't need to worry about address conflicts or renumbering the addresses used on computers if your TCP/IP address range ever changes.

 NOTE Because TCP/IP is the default protocol for Windows Server 2012–based networks, and because Windows Server 2012 is designed to operate correctly over a TCP/IP-only network, DHCP services are installed with Windows Server 2012 by default. However, the DHCP services are not enabled by default because you should not set up conflicting DHCP servers on a network.

To use DHCP, you must define a scope and other associated TCP/IP settings that the servers give to client computers. A *scope* is simply the range (or ranges) of TCP/IP addresses that the server is allowed to parcel out.

Among the associated TCP/IP settings that the server distributes are the addresses for Domain Name System (DNS) or Windows Internet Naming Service (WINS) servers also on the network. When a DHCP server assigns a TCP/IP address to a client computer, the address is said to be *leased*, and it remains assigned to that client computer for a set period of time. Leases are usually configured to last for two to seven days. (The default setting in Windows Server 2012 is eight days.) During this period, the assigned TCP/IP address is not given out to a different computer.

When a client computer boots up and joins the network, if it is configured to seek a DHCP server, the client computer does so while initializing its TCP/IP protocol stack. Any available DHCP servers respond to the client's request for an address with an available address from the DHCP server's address database. The client computer then uses this address for the duration of its lease.

The administrator can cancel and reassign TCP/IP information as necessary (usually, this is done after business hours, when the client computers are turned off). The administrator can then make changes to the DHCP scope information, which is then communicated to the clients when they reconnect to the network. In this way, you can easily make changes to information such as DNS server addresses or even TCP/IP address ranges without needing to visit all the computers.

Although DHCP is a great tool for managing TCP/IP addresses, you should use it only for client computers that do not host any TCP/IP services provided to other computers. For example, you would not want to set up a web server to use DHCP to get a dynamic TCP/IP address, because client computers wishing to connect to the web server would not be able to find the address when it changed. Instead, you should assign fixed addresses to computers that offer TCP/IP-enabled services either to the local network or through the Internet. You can assign these addresses in one of two ways:

- You can simply assign those computers fixed TCP/IP addresses locally and then set up *exclusion ranges* to the scope that the DHCP server manages, which prevents the DHCP server from using or offering those addresses to other computers.

- You can set up a *reservation* on the DHCP server, which forces the server always to assign the reserved address to a specific computer.

 TIP   It's a good idea to use static IP addresses for your network printers. Doing so makes troubleshooting printer connectivity problems easier.

Investigating DNS

As discussed in Chapter 6, DNS is a technology that allows easily remembered names to be mapped to TCP/IP addresses and ports. For instance, when you use a web browser and enter the address www.yahoo.com, you are using a DNS server to resolve the domain name www.yahoo.com to a particular TCP/IP address. Your web browser transparently uses the TCP/IP address to communicate with the server in question. The DNS system makes the Internet much easier to use than it otherwise would be. (Imagine how excited advertisers would be to say, "Visit our web site at http://65.193.55.38!")

Windows Server 2012 includes a full DNS server. In fact, a DNS server is required for Active Directory to function. If you install the first Active Directory server into a Windows Server 2012 domain, DNS services are automatically installed at the same time; otherwise, you must select them manually to add them.

A Windows Server 2012 server running DNS services can manage your own domains and subdomains, and you can also set up multiple DNS servers that each manage a portion of the domain namespace. Of course, on small networks, it is possible—and probably desirable because of cost issues—to use only a single DNS server.

You manage the DNS services with the DNS Microsoft Management Console (MMC) plug-in, which you access by opening the Server Manager, then the Tools menu, and choosing DNS. Figure 17-1 shows the DNS Manager window.

When you set up DNS for an organization, you first establish a root namespace (a virtual location in which domain names are stored), usually using the domain name you have registered for the Internet, such as omh.com. You can then create your own subdomains by prepending organizational or geographic units, such as italy.omh.com or accounting.omh.com.

Each DNS server is responsible for storing all the DNS names used for its managed namespace and for communicating any changes to other DNS servers. When you use multiple DNS servers to manage separate portions of your DNS namespace, each DNS

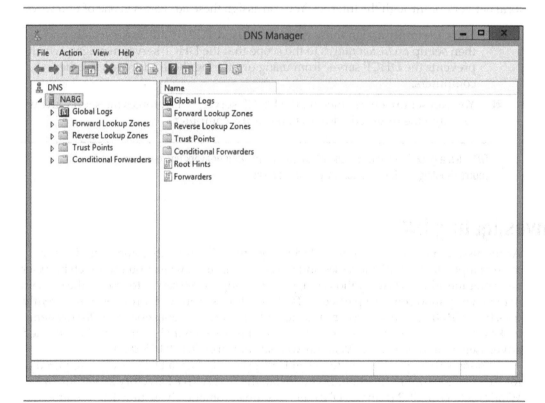

Figure 17-1.   Use the DNS Manager to manage DNS services.

server manages a *zone.* Updates between different zones are called *zone transfers.* Windows Server 2012 DNS Service supports both full and incremental zone transfers. (Incremental zone transfers exchange only updated information, which cuts down on network traffic considerably on networks with large DNS namespaces.)

Because DNS is integral to Active Directory, it's important for you to establish redundancy for your DNS servers. Microsoft recommends that each domain controller also act as a DNS server, and you must have at least one primary and secondary DNS server for each managed zone.

Understanding Remote Access

Prior versions of Windows supported a service called Routing and Remote Access Service (RRAS, pronounced "ar-razz") for remote access. In Windows Server 2012, it is now referred to as Remote Access. It includes routing capabilities that enable connections to the network over a public network, such as the Internet, using Virtual Private Network (VPN) technology (discussed in Chapter 8). A VPN works by setting up a secure "tunnel" between a client and the Remote Access server through which encrypted packets pass. The client computer dials up its normal Internet service provider (ISP), and then forms a secure VPN connection to the Remote Access server over the Internet.

Remote Access services under Windows Server 2012 are secure and offer considerable flexibility, so you can set them up to meet the requirements of your organization.

Before using or administering Remote Access, you must first install the Remote Access role onto the server. You do this, as discussed in Chapter 15, through Server Manager. Then, follow the steps discussed in Chapter 15 to add the role.

To administer Remote Access, open the Server Manager, choose Tools, and then choose Remote Access Management from the menu. After Remote Access Manager starts, you can run the Getting Started Wizard to perform the initial configuration. The wizard guides you through the process and enables you to choose whether to enable only remote access, only routing/remote access, or both. Figure 17-2 shows the Remote Access Management Console once Remote Access has been enabled.

First, you must enable a user to access the network remotely, which you can do by editing the user's Properties dialog box (setting user properties is discussed in Chapter 15). Then you can configure Remote Access to use a number of control features that enable you to keep remote access secure, including the following:

- Set times and days when remote access is operational.
- Set times and days when specific users or groups can use remote access.
- Limit access to only the Remote Access server or to specific services on the network.
- Set access policies based on a remote client computer name or TCP/IP address.

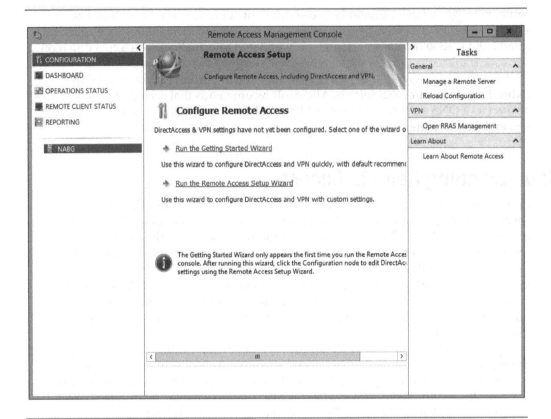

Figure 17-2. Use the Remote Access Management Console to administer remote access.

Through the use of Remote Access, you can easily set up Windows Server 2012 to provide important secure access services to remote users, both over dial-up connections and through the Internet.

Exploring IIS

Windows Server 2012 includes a set of Internet services that run as part of Internet Information Services (IIS). These include the following:

■ **Web** IIS web services provide comprehensive web-hosting software. You can define multiple web sites with IIS, each one administered separately. For each site, you specify the directory in which the site's files can be found, as well as security settings for the site and performance parameters to optimize the performance of the web site.

■ **File Transfer Protocol (FTP)**   IIS FTP services enable you to set up an FTP site on a Windows Server 2012 computer. You define the FTP directory, as well as whether directory listings will be shown in UNIX or MS-DOS style formats. You can also set security settings to allow or disallow different client computers or client networks access to the FTP server, and specify whether you will permit anonymous FTP logins.

■ **Simple Mail Transfer Protocol (SMTP)**   The SMTP server allows SMTP connections to be formed between the system running IIS and remote SMTP mail systems. SMTP is the standard protocol for exchanging e-mail over the Internet.

Each of these services can be started or stopped independently.

IIS is administered through the Internet Services Manager program found in the Server Manager's Tools menu. Figure 17-3 shows the Internet Information Services (IIS) Manager window.

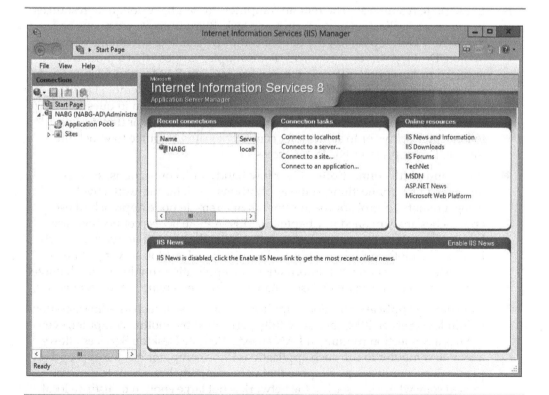

Figure 17-3.   The Internet Information Services Manager provides a single place to administer Internet services.

Understanding Remote Desktop Services

Remote Desktop Services—formerly called Windows Terminal Services—is possibly one of the most powerful services discussed in this chapter. Using Remote Desktop Services, you can set up a Windows Server 2012 server almost as if it were a mainframe—where computers can connect to virtual desktop computers and all the work is performed on the central computer, which in this case would be a Windows Server 2012 computer.

A client computer connects to a Remote Desktop server using a TCP/IP connection—over a local area network (LAN) or wide area network (WAN) connection—and logs in. From then on, the client computer is responsible only for displaying screens and accepting keyboard and mouse input—all of the work is actually being done on the Remote Desktop server through the creation of a virtual Windows machine on the server. A Remote Desktop server can create many virtual Windows machines, each one carrying out its own tasks and running its own programs.

When would you use a Remote Desktop connection to a network instead of a remote node connection, such as the remote node connections offered via RRAS? The answer depends on a number of factors, including the following:

- **Inadequate resources**   The remote computer doesn't have adequate resources to run some application or perform some task. By running its programs on the Remote Desktop server, the remote computer can take advantage of the Remote Desktop server's resources. For example, suppose that a particular application runs optimally only when it has 16GB of RAM with which to work. A Windows 7 client with 4GB of RAM could connect to the Remote Desktop server (which has, say, 64GB of RAM) and run the application in question. Similarly, some applications might require many processors or direct access to large disk arrays or to some other centrally located resource to which the Remote Desktop server has faster access.

- **Low-bandwidth connections**   Over low-bandwidth connections, such as low-speed DSL connections, some applications work far more effectively using a remote control approach rather than a remote node approach (these approaches are explained in Chapter 8). Most remote access connections are low bandwidth, yet some applications need high bandwidth to work properly. Because a remote computer connected to a Remote Desktop server just needs to transfer display and input information, the application running on the Remote Desktop server can run much faster than it could over a remote node connection.

- **Demanding applications**   Some applications and tasks, such as administration of Windows Server 2012, cannot be fully performed by another computer, even if it has a connection running at LAN speeds. Remote Desktop Services allows a remote computer to run such applications if the computer has the appropriate permissions. For instance, suppose that your company has a remote network located somewhere in Asia, but the network is not large enough to justify a local administrator. Using Remote Desktop Services, you could connect to that network over the company WAN and perform the necessary administrative tasks, such as configuring hard disks, shares, additional network protocols, and so forth.

Certain applications might require that you use Remote Desktop Services. However, in any case, you might want to consider Remote Desktop Services as an adjunct to your remote access services. If you have many remote users to support, you might find that some users have needs best served by remote node connections and some have needs best served by remote control connections. Running both services on your network will give you considerable flexibility in supporting remote users and solving any problems that they might encounter.

 CAUTION   If you implement Remote Desktop Services, make sure that you carefully review Microsoft's license agreement and pricing models, which differ when you use Remote Desktop Services.

Chapter Summary

The Windows family of servers, including Windows Server 2012, is perhaps the richest network operating system environment available today. While other products can perform all the tasks described in this chapter, none include all these capabilities out of the box; add-on purchases are required. Because of the richness with which Windows Server 2012 is packaged, you can more easily put together a server to meet nearly any need you may have. And because the various Windows Server 2012 services work so well together, you can easily implement nearly all these advanced services on just a single server!

This out-of-the-box flexibility and ease of administration are two of the reasons the Windows family of network operating systems has gained a leading share of the market, and why it's a safe bet Windows Server 2012 will continue this trend.

Although Windows servers probably run most servers in most companies, another popular choice is servers that run Linux. In the following three chapters, you learn about installing and administering Oracle Linux, as well as installing an Apache web server under an Oracle Linux installation.

CHAPTER 18 | Installing Linux

A key component of Linux's success has been the remarkable improvement in installation tools. What once was a mildly frightening process many years back has now become almost trivial.

Most default configurations in which Linux is installed are already capable of creating a server. This is, unfortunately, due to a slightly naïve design decision: A server serves everything, ranging from disk services to mail. Often, all of these services are turned on from the start (depending on the distribution you are using and whether it was installed as a workstation or a server). As you know, most servers are dedicated to performing one or two tasks, and any other installed services simply take up memory and slow down performance.

This chapter discusses the installation process of Oracle Linux as it pertains to servers. This process has two objectives: to differentiate servers from client workstations and to streamline a server's operation based on its dedicated purpose.

You may be wondering why of all the available Linux distributions, I chose to focus on Oracle's Linux. The answer is simple: Oracle Linux is popular, compatible with Red Hat Linux, and support contracts and other advanced features available for enterprise use. Moreover, it is both popular and technically sound. It is friendly to a lot of different types of users and serves many uses. (That the entire distribution is available free from the Internet is also a plus!) As you become more experienced with Linux, you might find other distributions interesting and should look into them. After all, one of the war cries of Linux users everywhere is that freedom of choice is crucial. You should never feel locked into a proprietary system.

Configuring Computer Hardware for Linux

Before you get into the actual installation phase, you need to consider the hardware on which the system will run and how the server will be configured to provide the services you need from it. Let's start by examining hardware issues.

Hardware Compatibility

As with any operating system, determining which hardware configurations work before starting an installation process is prudent. Each commercial vendor publishes a list of compatible hardware and makes that list available on its web site. Be sure you obtain the latest versions of these lists so you are confident that the vendor fully supports the hardware you are using. In general, most popular Intel-based configurations work without difficulty. For Oracle Linux, you can check for certified hardware at http://linux.oracle.com/hardware-certifications. Red Hat's certified hardware list is at http://bugzilla.redhat.com/hwcert. For Novell's SUSE Linux you can search compatibility at http://developer.novell.com/yessearch/Search.jsp.

> **TIP** Some manufacturers sell computers with Linux preloaded on them. When you purchase a computer like this, you can usually be confident that the manufacturer has ensured that the hardware is fully compatible with the installed Linux version and that the appropriate Linux drivers are loaded and work properly.

A general suggestion that applies to all operating systems is to avoid bleeding-edge hardware and software configurations. Although these appear impressive, they have not undergone the maturing process that some of the slightly older hardware has experienced. For servers, the temptation to use a bleeding-edge configuration usually isn't an issue because a server has no need for the latest and greatest toys, such as fancy video cards. After all, the main goal is to provide a highly available server for the network's users, not to play the latest games.

Server Design

When a system becomes a server, its stability, availability, and performance are significant issues. These three issues are usually addressed through the purchase of more hardware, which is unfortunate. Paying thousands of dollars extra to get a system capable of achieving all three objectives when the desired level of performance could have been attained from existing hardware with a little tuning is a waste. With Linux, achieving these objectives without overspending is not hard. Even better, the gains are outstanding!

The most significant design decision that you must make when managing a server configuration is not technical, but administrative. You should design a server *not* to be friendly to casual users. This means without any cute multimedia tools, sound card support, or fancy web browsers (when possible). In fact, your organization should make a rule that casual use of a server is strictly prohibited. This rule should apply not only to site users, but to site administrators as well.

Another important aspect of designing a server is making sure that it has a good environment. As a systems administrator, you must ensure the physical safety of your servers by keeping them in a separate, physically secure room. The only access to the servers for nonadministrative personnel should be through the network. The server room itself should be well ventilated, cool, and locked. Failing to ensure such a physical environment is an accident waiting to happen. Systems that overheat and helpful users who "think" they know how to fix problems can be as great a danger (arguably an even greater danger) to server stability as bad software. Moreover, Linux is particularly vulnerable to hacking at its command prompt.

Once the system is well secured behind locked doors, installing battery backup is also crucial. This backup serves two key purposes. The first purpose is to keep the system running during a power failure so that it can gracefully shut down, thereby avoiding the loss of any files. The second is to ensure that voltage spikes, drops, and electrical "noise" don't interfere with the health of your system.

To improve your server situation, you can take the following specific actions:

■ Take advantage of the fact that the graphical user interface (GUI) is uncoupled from the core operating system, and avoid starting the GUI unless someone needs to sit on the console and run an application. After all, the system's GUI, like any other application, requires memory and central processing unit (CPU) time to work, both of which are better off going to the server processes instead.

■ Determine which functions you want the server to perform, and disable all other functions. Not only are unused functions a waste of memory and CPU time, but they are also just another security issue that you need to address.

■ Linux, unlike some other operating systems, enables you to choose the features that you want in the kernel. The default kernel you get is already reasonably well tuned, so you shouldn't need to adjust it. If you do need to change a feature or upgrade a kernel, though, be picky about what you add and what you leave out. Make sure that you need a feature before including it.

Server Uptime

All this chatter about taking care of servers and making sure that silly things don't cause them to crash stems from a longstanding UNIX philosophy: *Uptime is good. More uptime is better.*

The **uptime** command tells the user how long the system has been running since its last boot, how many users are currently logged in, and how much load the system is experiencing. The latter two statistics are useful measures necessary for daily system health and long-term planning. For example, if server load has been staying consistently high, you should consider a more capable server.

But the all-important number is how long the server has been running since its last reboot. Long uptimes are a sign of proper care, maintenance, and, from a practical standpoint, system stability. You often find UNIX administrators boasting about their server's uptimes the way you hear car buffs boast about horsepower. This focus on uptime is also why you hear UNIX administrators cursing at Windows installations that require a reboot for every little change. In contrast, you'll be hard-pressed to find any changes to a UNIX system that require a reboot in order to take effect.

Dual-Booting Issues

If you are new to Linux, you might not be ready to commit the use of a complete system for the sake of "test driving." Because the people who built Linux understand that we live in a heterogeneous world, all distributions of Linux have been designed so that they can be installed on separate partitions of your hard disk while leaving other partitions alone. Typically, this means that Microsoft Windows can coexist on a computer that also can run Linux. In addition, many Linux distributions can be run from a bootable "live" CD-ROM, which lets you run a fully functional build of the Linux distribution without affecting your computer's existing installed operating system. If you like the Linux distribution, there is usually a simple procedure you can run from within the live CD environment to install that distribution to the hard disk.

Because the focus of this chapter is server installations, this section will not cover the details of building a dual-boot system. Anyone with a little experience in creating partitions on a disk should be able to figure out how to build such a system. If you are having difficulty, you can refer to the installation guide that came with your distribution or one of the many beginners' guides to Linux.

To repartition a system that has already had Windows installed on it without reformatting the disk and rebuilding from scratch, you can use a partition management software program.

Installing Oracle Linux

This section describes how to install Oracle Linux (version 6.4) on a stand-alone system. The section takes an easy approach to the process, and focuses on installing the system in a desktop configuration so that you will have the benefit of the GUI and user programs available for your Linux exploration. Don't worry, however; specific server programs, such as Apache, can be added to it, and the system will still function as a server in all respects.

Before you begin the actual installation procedure, you need to decide how you will run the installation program.

Choosing an Installation Method

With the improved connectivity and speed of both local area networks and Internet connections, an increasingly popular option is to perform installations over the network rather than using a local DVD-R. Network installations can be a great convenience when installing a large number of hosts.

 TIP In UNIX (or Linux) parlance, a *host* is any computer on a network, regardless of whether the computer is functioning as a server of some kind or as a workstation.

Typically, server installations aren't well suited to being automated because each server usually has a unique task and thus a slightly different configuration. For example, a server dedicated to handling logging information sent to it over the network will have especially large partitions set up for the appropriate logging directories. This is in contrast to a file server that performs no logging of its own.

Because servers are not usually set up using a "one-size-fits-all" approach, the focus in this section is exclusively on the technique for installing a system from a DVD-R. After you have gone through the installation process from a DVD-R once, you will find performing the network-based installations straightforward.

Starting the Installation

Usually, you will start the installation by downloading a copy of Oracle Linux and burning it onto a DVD-R. Here are the steps for installing that copy:

1. To start the installation process, boot off the DVD-R. This will boot Oracle Linux in its installation mode, as shown in Figure 18-1.

2. Using your arrow keys, or by pressing the I key, choose Install or upgrade an existing system from the menu. This launches the Oracle Linux installation program.

3. You are prompted to test your installation media. Since errors can occur during download or during the burning process to the DVD-R disc, you should do this. You test the media by pressing ENTER while the OK button is highlighted.

4. Next, you will see a splash screen for the installation program. Click the Next button to continue.

5. You are prompted for the language to use when installing. By default, English is selected. Click Next to continue.

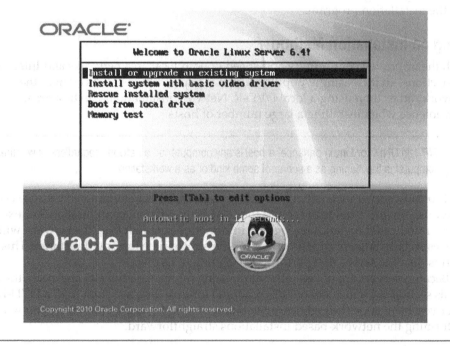

Figure 18-1.   Oracle Linux started in installation mode

6. You now are prompted to choose the appropriate keyboard layout. By default, U.S. English is selected. Click Next to continue.

7. Next, you are prompted for the type of storage devices you will use for the installation, as shown in Figure 18-2. You can choose between Basic Storage Devices, which includes hard disks, and Specialized Storage Devices, which includes redundant array of inexpensive disks (RAID) arrays, Storage Area Networks (SANs), and other enterprise storage devices. Choose Basic Storage Devices and click Next to continue.

8. The installation program will now scan the computer's storage devices. You will see a warning dialog box stating that if you proceed, the storage devices will be overwritten and any data on them will be lost. After you've ensured that there is no data on the system that needs to be kept, click the Yes button to discard any data.

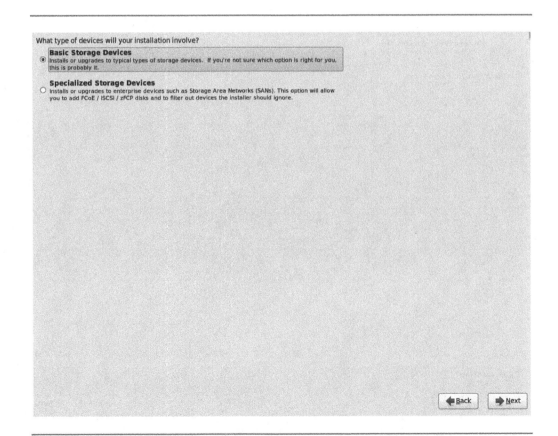

Figure 18-2. Choosing what type of storage devices you will use

9. You are prompted to name the computer in the format *computer_name.domain,* as shown in Figure 18-3. Enter an appropriate name for your computer, and then click Next to continue.

10. Choose the time zone in which you are located, as shown in Figure 18-4. You can click the map until a city in the same time zone as you is located, or you can choose from the available options in the drop-down menu. Once you have selected the time zone, click Next to continue.

11. You are prompted to enter a password for the system's *root account,* which is a user named *root* that has full and complete access to change anything about the system. It is similar to the administrator password on a Windows server. Accordingly, you should choose a good, strong password for the root account. Enter your password where prompted, and also in the confirmation field. Click Next to continue.

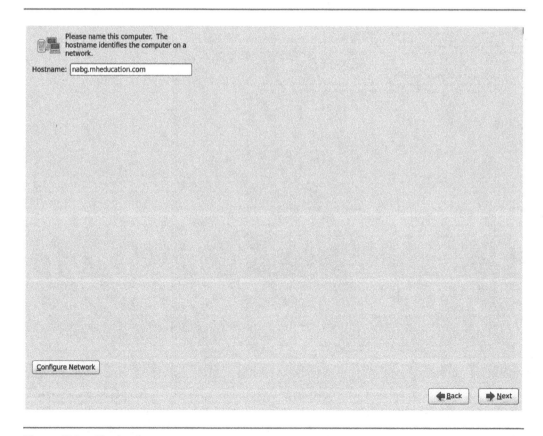

Figure 18-3. Naming the computer

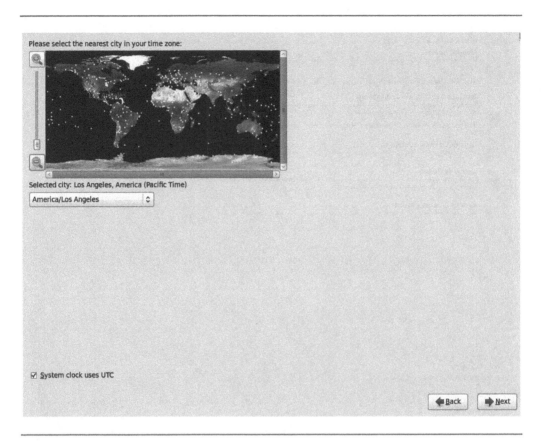

Please select the nearest city in your time zone:

Selected city: Los Angeles, America (Pacific Time)

America/Los Angeles

☑ System clock uses UTC

◀ Back   ➡ Next

Figure 18-4. Choosing a time zone

12. You now need to partition the hard disk for the computer. This example assumes that you are installing Oracle Linux on a system with a blank hard disk. You will see on the overall partitioning menu shown in Figure 18-5 that there are a number of options to choose from. For this example, choose Use All Space, which will erase the hard disk and set it up for Linux.

13. If you would like to see what the default partitioning scheme looks like, select the Review And Modify Partitioning Layout checkbox before clicking Next to continue. Figure 18-6 shows an example of a default partitioning scheme on a 12GB disk.

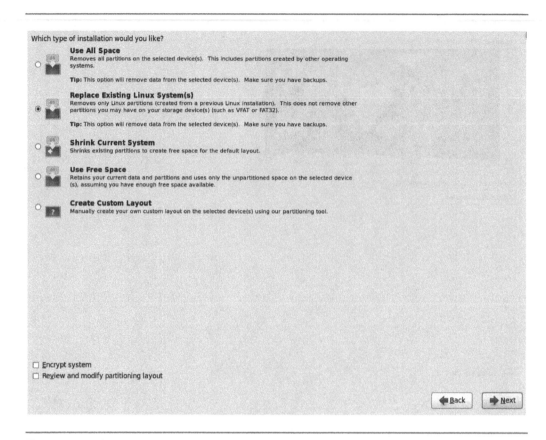

Figure 18-5. Choosing a partitioning method

 NOTE While the Oracle Linux installer lets you customize the partitioning scheme in a variety of ways, for most uses, the default choices will work best. If you decide to install Linux for production use, you will want to explore other options in the partitioning, such as setting up RAID disk arrays.

14. After confirming the creation of the partitioning scheme you have selected, you will see a menu from which you can choose the type of installation you want to perform, shown in Figure 18-7. If you were performing this installation for a production system that did not need a GUI interface, you would choose from the various server types of installations. However, since you're setting up a system that will be able to be used with a GUI and that can also perform server tasks, choose Desktop from the list and then click Next to continue.

Please Select A Device

Device	Size (MB)	Mount Point/ RAID/Volume	Type	Format
▽ LVM Volume Groups				
▽ vg_nabg	11784			
lv_root	7752	/	ext4	✓
lv_swap	4032		swap	✓
▽ Hard Drives				
▽ sda (/dev/sda)				
sda1	500	/boot	ext4	✓
sda2	11787	vg_nabg	physical volume (LVM)	✓

Create   Edit   Delete   Reset

⇐ Back   ⇒ Next

Figure 18-6. Default partitioning scheme for a 12GB disk

At this point, Oracle Linux will be installed onto the hard disk. Typically, the process is fairly quick and should take around five to ten minutes. When it's complete, you are prompted to restart the system. After the system restarts, you will need to do some initial configuring, as described in the next section.

Initially Configuring Oracle Linux

When your new Oracle Linux system boots for the very first time after the main installation, you are walked through various initial configuration options. Initially, you will see the screen shown in Figure 18-8. The left pane lists the basic configuration areas.

The default installation of Oracle Linux Server is a basic server install. You can optionally
select a different set of software now.

○ Basic Server
○ Database Server
○ Web Server
○ Identity Management Server
○ Virtualization Host
○ Desktop
○ Software Development Workstation
○ Minimal

Please select any additional repositories that you want to use for software installation.

☐ High Availability
☐ Load Balancer
☑ Oracle Linux Server

[➕ Add additional software repositories]   [📄 Modify repository]

You can further customize the software selection now, or after install via the software
management application.

◉ Customize later   ○ Customize now

[⬅ Back] [➡ Next]

Figure 18-7.   Choosing a Desktop installation type

Here is the procedure for completing the initial configuration of Oracle Linux:

1. First, you are prompted to accept the software license. As you will read, there
   are no restrictions on using, copying, or modifying the Oracle Linux code.
   However, there are restrictions on redistribution of the code, use of the Oracle
   trademarks, and other matters.

2. Next, you will be prompted to configure software updates. The network
   connection on your installation may not yet be functioning. If so, skip this step
   and click Forward. (You can set this up later).

3. You are prompted to create a user account, as shown in Figure 18-9. It is
   important to avoid using the root account except for when you absolutely need
   it. Instead, create a user account for yourself to use, even if you are the only
   person using the system.

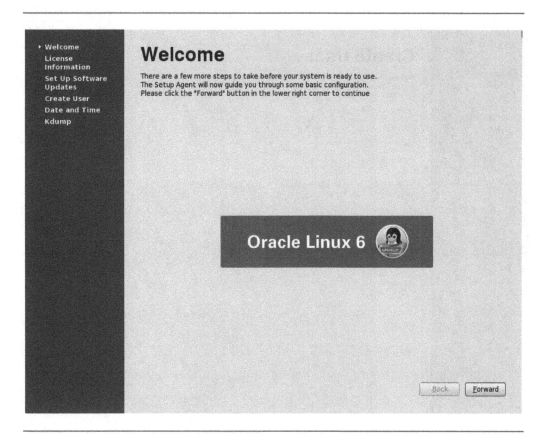

Figure 18-8.   Initially configuring Oracle Linux

4. Check the time and date for the system, as shown in Figure 18-10. If this computer will not be connected to the Internet, update the time and date, if necessary. Otherwise, click the Synchronize Date And Time Over The Network checkbox, and then click Forward.

5. Finally, you are prompted to choose whether or not to enable Kdump, which will gather system state information in the background, and will create a dump file that could be used to diagnose any crashes that might occur. Kdump consumes some of your system's random access memory (RAM) at all times when it is running. For a production server, this option is good to enable. However, if you are setting up a system for your own education, you probably do not need to enable this feature. Make whichever choice you prefer, and then click Finish to complete the configuration.

Figure 18-9. Creating your nonadministrative user account

Logging In to Oracle Linux

After completing the configuration, you will see the normal login screen for Oracle Linux, as shown in Figure 18-11. This screen will display all of the normal user accounts available on the system. If you followed the procedure outlined in this chapter, you will have only one user account (aside from the root account, which is not shown by default).

To choose an account to log in with, double-click the name in the login screen. You will be prompted for your password. After you've successfully logged in, you will see the Oracle Linux desktop.

On your installation, your network connection may not be enabled. If it is not (see Figure 18-12), you can quickly enable it by clicking the network icon in the title bar (which has a red X next to two overlapping computers) and choose System eth0 from

Figure 18-10.   Adjusting the system's date and time

the menu that appears. The red X should disappear after a moment, indicating that the system's network connection is now active.

And You're Finished!

That's it! The installation process is over. I recommend you spend time exploring Oracle Linux's menus and various functions.

Keep in mind that if you make a change that will be system-wide and is considered an administrative change to the system, you will be prompted for the root password you set up during the installation. Prompting you for the root password for important system changes is how most Linux distributions ensure that a valid system administrator is making the change and not some random person who happened to connect to the computer remotely over a network.

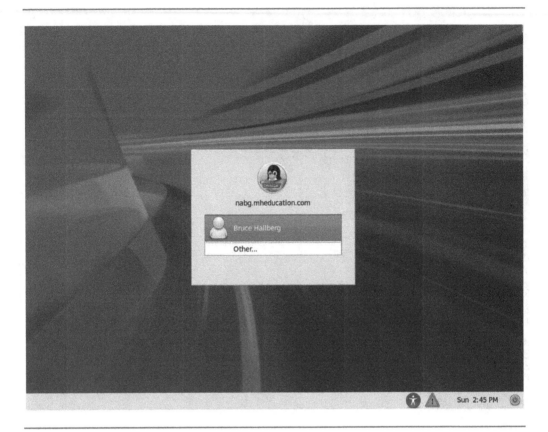

Figure 18-11. Logging in to Oracle Linux

If It Just Won't Work Right

You've gone through the installation procedure, maybe more than once. This book said it should work. The installation manual said it should work. The Linux guru with whom you spoke last week said it should work. But it's just not working.

In the immortal words of Douglas Adams, "Don't panic!" No operating system installs smoothly 100 percent of the time. (Yes, not even Mac OS!) Hardware doesn't always work as advertised, combinations of hardware conflict with each other, or that DVD-ROM that your friend burned for you has errors on it. (Remember that it is legal for your friend to burn you a copy of most Linux distributions!) Or, as much as you might hope that it does not, the software has a bug.

With Linux, you can take several paths to get help. If you have purchased a support contract from Oracle, you can call their tech support lines and talk to a knowledgeable person who is dedicated to working through the problem with you. If you didn't purchase a support contract, most Linux distributions have rich help available online.

Figure 18-12.   Oracle Linux desktop

For Oracle Linux, you can find a lot of helpful documents, including a discussion forum, at www.oracle.com/technetwork/server-storage/linux/overview/index.html.

Chapter Summary

In this chapter, you learned about the process of installing a popular and very capable Linux distribution. The steps to installing Oracle Linux are quite straightforward. If you ever witnessed the procedure for prior versions, you will be aware of how much easier the process has become, with fewer configuration choices to make to begin working with the operating system. What makes Linux wonderful is that even though those options are no longer part of the installation process, you can still change them and tweak them to your heart's delight once you complete the installation and start the system.

The next chapter continues with the system as it was installed here and shows you how to perform basic administrative tasks within Oracle Linux.

CHAPTER 19 | Introduction to Linux Systems Administration

When Linux first came out in 1991, you had to be either a systems administrator with a lot of time or a good hacker to be able to use the system effectively. While this was fine for folks who were willing to expend the effort, it wasn't great for the vast majority who saw potential for using Linux but shied away from the learning curve. Thankfully, many Linux distribution developers have realized this shortcoming and have gone to great lengths to make Linux not only easy to install, but relatively painless to administer.

This chapter provides an overview of some of the basic administrative chores necessary to keep a Linux server running smoothly. Although it is by no means a complete guide to systems administration, this chapter will get you started in the right direction.

This chapter assumes that you have Oracle Linux already installed and the graphical user interface configured. The chapter also assumes that you are logging in to the system and running all programs as the user root.

CAUTION   The root user is almighty under Linux. If you are familiar with Windows server, you can think of root as being somewhat equivalent to the administrator account. With root access, you have full control of the system, including the ability to break it. If you are new to Linux, you should definitely take some time to practice on a nonproduction system before trying things out on your system's users.

This chapter is divided into two main sections. The first section deals with configuring Oracle Linux with graphical tools for systems administration functions. The second part of the chapter deals with the command-line interface. While this section isn't about systems administration per se, the commands it covers are the foundation for basic systems administration tasks.

Managing Oracle Linux with Graphical Tools

The graphical tools are the basis for most of the administrative tasks you will need to do. They handle user administration, network administration, disk administration, and so on. What makes these tools especially helpful is that they provide a very consistent interface for Linux administrative tasks. The only downside is that, like other graphical user interfaces (GUIs), these tools have limitations. You might find that for more advanced tasks, you will need to use the command-line interface, as described later in this chapter.

Managing Users

To take advantage of the multiuser nature of Linux, you need to be able to add, edit, and remove users from the system. You can perform all of these actions through the User Manager program, as follows:

1. Open the System menu and choose Administration and then Users And Groups. After being prompted for the system's root password, you see the User Manager program window shown in Figure 19-1.

Figure 19-1. User Manager handles user administration.

2. Click the Add User button in the toolbar at the top of the window to open the Create New User dialog box, as shown in Figure 19-2.

3. In the Create New User dialog box, you must, at a minimum, fill in the login name and a password for the user. The user's home directory and type of shell will be filled in automatically, and you can accept those default options. Click OK to create the user account.

TIP As discussed in Chapter 9, picking a good password means not using a dictionary word (including foreign language words). One technique is to take the first letter of each word in a phrase. For example, "Snacking on Oatmeal Squares is good for you" translates into SoOSigfy. The phrase is easy to remember, and the resulting password is cryptic. Another strategy is to take a word of six letters or more and substitute two or more letters with numbers. For example, the password le11ers (with 1's in the middle instead of the letter *l*) is not a bad password. But be warned that sophisticated password-cracking programs often will try these sorts of number substitutions within dictionary words.

Figure 19-2.   Creating a new user

Once the account is created, you can double-click it in the list of user accounts in order to set some additional properties for the account through the User Properties dialog box, as shown in Figure 19-3:

- The User Data tab lets you change the user's name, password, home directory, and login shell.

- The Account Info tab lets you set an account expiration date for the user, if you desire, and also to lock the user account if that becomes necessary for any reason.

- The Password Info tab lets you set password expiration settings for the selected user account.

- The Groups tab lets you assign security group membership to the selected user account.

To remove a user, from the main User Manager window, select the user account to be deleted, and then click the Delete button in the toolbar.

Figure 19-3. Setting user properties

Changing Root's Password

As mentioned in the previous chapters, the root user is a special user who has a lot of power on the system. Obviously, an account with this much power needs to be protected with a good password. If you think that someone might have gotten the root password, or that someone who had the root password should no longer have it (for example, a former employee), you should immediately change it.

To change the root password on a system, first make sure you are logged in to the system as root. Then, from the Applications menu, choose System Tools, and then Terminal. This will open a terminal window on the desktop. Type the command **passwd** and press ENTER, and then follow the prompts to change the root password. Figure 19-4 illustrates this change. The program will not let you change the root password if both entries do not match exactly. (Remember that Oracle Linux, like all UNIX operating systems, uses case-sensitive passwords.) Click OK to complete the change.

Configuring Common Network Settings

Linux is very much at home in a networked environment. In fact, its design from the onset supports its use on a network. Networks are dynamic, and Linux makes it easy to change the network configuration to accommodate any changes.

You manage network settings through the Network Connections dialog box, as shown in Figure 19-5. To access this dialog, open the System menu, choose Preferences, and then choose Network Connections.

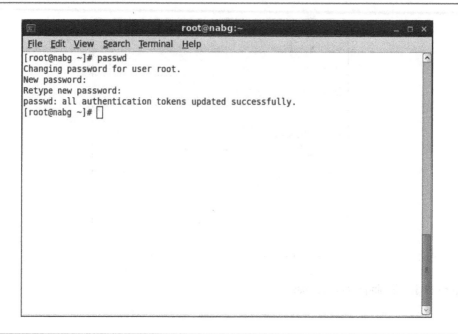

Figure 19-4.   Changing the root password

Figure 19-5.   Use the Network Connections dialog box to change the network configuration.

Changing Your IP Address

In most cases, if a system is configured to use Dynamic Host Configuration Protocol (DHCP) to acquire its IP address, you should not change the IP address setting. However, at times you will need to set a static IP address on a system. To change the IP address of your system, select the Ethernet interface you are using in the Network Connections dialog box, and click the Edit button. In the resulting dialog box, choose the IPv4 Settings tab, which brings up the Ethernet Device dialog box, as shown in Figure 19-6.

Click the Method button, and choose Manual. Then, click the Add button, and enter the appropriate IP address information in the Addresses area of the dialog box. Once you have made all of your selections, click OK to accept the changes.

Figure 19-6. Changing Ethernet device settings

Mastering Linux Command-Line Basics

Historically, the aspect of UNIX that makes it so powerful and flexible has been the options available through the command line. Casual observers of UNIX gurus are often astounded at how a few carefully entered commands can result in powerful actions. Unfortunately, this power comes at the expense of ease of use. For this reason, GUIs have proliferated and have become the de facto standard for so many tools.

As you become more experienced, however, you will find that it is difficult for GUIs to present all of the available options to a user because doing so would make the interface just as complicated as the command-line equivalent. Thus, the GUIs have remained overly simplified, and experienced users have needed to resort to the command line.

TIP   Before you get into a "which interface is better" holy war with someone, remember that both types of interfaces serve a purpose, with each having weaknesses as well as benefits. In the end, the person who chooses to master both will come out ahead.

This section covers some of the Linux command-line tools that are most crucial for day-to-day work. All of the commands discussed in this section are to be performed in a terminal window. You can open a terminal window by opening the Applications menu and choosing System Tools and then Terminal. This window displays a prompt that looks something like [root@*hostname* /root]#, where *hostname* is the name of your machine.

Working from the Command Line

One of the difficulties in moving to the Linux command-line interface, especially if you are used to using Windows command-line tools such as cmd.exe, is dealing with a shell that has a great number of shortcuts that might surprise you if you're not careful. This section reviews the most common of these shortcuts.

Filename Expansion

Under UNIX-based shells such as bash, you expand wildcards seen on the command line *before* passing them as a parameter to the application. This is in sharp contrast to the default mode of operation for DOS-based tools, which often need to perform their own wildcard expansion. This also means that you must be careful where you use the wildcard characters.

The wildcard characters themselves are identical to those in cmd.exe. The asterisk (*) matches against all filenames, and the question mark (?) matches against single characters. If you need to use these characters as part of another parameter, you can "escape" them by placing a backslash (\) in front of them. This character will cause the shell to interpret a wildcard as just another character.

Environment Variables as Parameters

You can use environment variables as parameters on the command line. This means that issuing the parameter $FOO will result in passing the value of the FOO environment variable instead of the string "$FOO."

Multiple Commands

Under the bash shell, it is possible to execute multiple commands on the same line by separating them with a semicolon (;). For example, suppose that you want to execute the following sequence of commands on a single line:

```
[root@system /root]# ls -l
[root@system /root]# cat /etc/hosts
```

You could instead type the following:

```
[root@system /root]# ls -l ;cat /etc/hosts
```

Backticks

How's *this* for wild: You can make the output of one program the parameter of another program. Sound bizarre? Well, it's time to get used to it—this is one of the most creatively used features available in all UNIX shells.

A backtick (`) enables you to embed commands as parameters to other commands. A common instance of the use of this character is to pass a number sitting in a file as a parameter to the **kill** command. A typical instance of this occurs with the DNS server *named*. When this server starts, it writes its process identification number into the file /var/run/named.pid. Thus, the generic way of killing the *named* process is to look at the number in /var/run/named.pid using the **cat** command, and then issue the **kill** command with that value, as in the following example:

```
[root@system /root]# cat /var/run/named.pid
253
[root@system /root]# kill 253
```

One problem with killing the *named* process this way is that you cannot automate the killing, so you are counting on the fact that a human will read the value in /var/ run/ named.pid and then kill the number. The second problem isn't so much a problem as it is a nuisance—it takes two steps to stop the Domain Name System (DNS) server.

Using backticks, however, you can combine the steps into one and do so in a way that you can automate. Here's the backticks version:

```
[root@system # kill`cat /var/run/named.pid`
```

When the bash shell sees this command, it will first run **cat /var/run/named.pid** and store the result. It will then run the **kill** command and pass the stored result to it—all in one graceful step.

Environment Variables

The concept of environment variables is almost the same under Linux as it is under Windows. The only difference is in how you set, view, and remove the variables.

Printing Environment Variables

To list all of your environment variables, use the **printenv** command, as in the following example:

```
[root@system /root]# printenv
```

To show a specific environment variable, specify the variable as a parameter to **printenv**. For example, to see the environment variable USER, type the following:

```
[root@system /root]# printenv USER
```

Setting Environment Variables

To set an environment variable, use the following format:

```
[root@system /root]# variable=value
```

where *variable* is the variable name, and *value* is the value that you want to assign the variable. For example, to set the environment variable FOO with the value BAR, type the following:

```
[root@system /root]# FOO=BAR
```

After setting the value, use the **export** command to finalize it. The format of the **export** command is as follows:

```
[root@system /root]# export variable
```

where *variable* is the name of the variable. In the example of setting FOO, type the following:

```
[root@system /root]# export FOO
```

You can combine the steps of setting the environment variable with the **export** command, as follows:

```
[root@system /root]# export FOO=BAR
```

If the value of the environment variable you want to set has spaces in it, you need to surround the variable with quotation marks. For example, to set FOO to "Welcome to the BAR of FOO," type the following:

```
[root@system /root]# export FOO="Welcome to the BAR of FOO."
```

Clearing Environment Variables

To remove an environment variable, use the **unset** command:

```
[root@system /root]# unset variable
```

where *variable* is the name of the variable you want to remove. For example, to remove the environment variable FOO, type the following:

```
[root@system]# unset FOO
```

Documentation Tools

Linux comes with two tremendously useful tools for making documentation accessible: man and info. Currently, the two documentation systems have a great deal of overlap between them, as many applications are moving their documentation to the info format. Info is considered superior to man because it allows the documentation to be hyperlinked together in a web-like way, without actually being written in HTML format. The man format, on the other hand, has been around for decades. Thousands of utilities have only man pages as their source of documentation. Furthermore, many applications continue to release their documentation in man format since many other UNIX-like operating systems such as Sun Solaris default to the man format for their documentation. As a result, both of these documentation systems will be around for a long while to come. Becoming comfortable with both of them is highly advisable.

man: View Man Pages

Man (short for *manual*) pages are documents found online covering the usage of tools and their corresponding configuration files. The format of the **man** command is as follows:

```
[root@system /root]# man program_name
```

where *program_name* is the name of the program for which you want to read the manual page. Here's an example:

```
[root@system /root]# man ls
```

While reading about UNIX and UNIX-related sources for information (such as newsgroups), you might find references to commands followed by numbers in parentheses, as in ls(1). The number represents the *section* of the manual pages; each section covers various subject areas. The section numbers are handy for some tools, such as **printf**, that are commands in the C programming language as well as command-line commands. Thus, two entries would exist for such a command under two different sections.

To refer to a specific section, simply specify the section number as the first parameter and the command as the second parameter. For example, to get the C programmers' information on **printf** (assuming that the C programming man files are installed), enter the following:

```
[root@system /root]# man 3 printf
```

To get the command-line information, enter the following:

```
[root@system /root]# man 1 printf
```

By default, the manual page for the lowest section number is printed first. The section numbers' meanings are shown in Table 19-1.

A handy option to the **man** command is **-k**. With this option, **man** will search the summary information of all the man pages and list which pages have a match along with their section number. For example, the following command will find pages matching the search criteria "printf":

```
[root@system /root]# man -k printf
```

info: View Info Pages

In addition to man pages, info pages are another common form of documentation. Established as the GNU standard, info is a documentation system that more closely resembles the Web in the sense that documents can be hyperlinked together, whereas man pages are single, static documents. Thus, info pages tend to be easier to read and understand.

To read the info documents on a specific tool or application, simply invoke **info** with the parameter specifying the tool's name. For example, to read about emacs, simply type the following:

```
[root@system /root]# info emacs
```

Section Number	Meaning
1	User tools
2	System calls
3	C library calls
4	Device driver-related information
5	Configuration files
6	Games
7	Packages
8	System tools

Table 19-1. Manual Page Section Numbers

Usually, you will first want to check if there is a man page. This is because a great deal more information is still available in the man format than in info format. However, some man pages will explicitly state that the info pages are more authoritative and should be read instead.

File Listings, Ownerships, and Permissions

Managing files under Linux is different from managing files under Windows. This section discusses the tools necessary to perform basic file management.

ls: List Files

The **ls** command is used to list all of the files in a directory. The command has more than 26 options. The most common of these options are shown in Table 19-2. See the man page for the complete list of options.

You can use these options in any combination with one another. For example, to list all files in a directory with a long listing, type the following:

```
[root@system /root]# ls -la
```

To list nonhidden files in a directory that starts with *A*, type the following:

```
[root@system /root]# ls A*
```

About Files and Directories

Under Linux (and UNIX in general), you will find that almost everything is abstracted to a file. Linux's developers originally did this to simplify the programmer's job. Thus, instead of having to communicate directly with device drivers, you use special files (which to the application appear as ordinary files) as a bridge instead. To accommodate all of these uses of files, different types of files exist:

- **Normal files**   Normal files are just that—normal. They contain data or executables, and the operating system makes no assumptions about their contents.

Option	Description
-l	Long listing. In addition to the filename, show the file size, date/time, permissions, ownership, and group information.
-a	All files. Show all files in the directory, including those that are hidden. Hidden files begin with a period.
-1	Single column listing. List all files in a single column.
-R	Recursive. Recursively list all files and subdirectories.

Table 19-2.   Common ls Command Options

■ **Directories** Directory files are a special instance of normal files in that their contents list the location of other files. Among the files to which directories point might be other directories. In your day-to-day work, it won't matter to you much that directories in Linux (and UNIX) are actually files, unless you happen to try to open and read the directory file yourself rather than use existing applications to navigate directories.

■ **Hard links** Each file in the Linux file system gets its own *i-node*. An i-node keeps track of a file's attributes and location on the disk. If you need to be able to refer to a single file using two separate filenames, you can create a *hard link*. The hard link will have the same i-node as the original file, so it will look and behave just like the original file. With every hard link that is created, a *reference count* is incremented. When a hard link is removed, the reference count is decremented. Until the reference count reaches zero, the file will remain on disk.

NOTE A hard link cannot exist between two files that are on separate partitions. This is because the hard link refers to the original file by i-node. A file that is referred to by one i-node on one file system will refer to another file on another file system.

■ **Symbolic links** Unlike a hard link, which points to a file by its i-node, a symbolic link points to another file by its name. Thus, *symbolic links* (often abbreviated as *symlinks*) can point to files located on other partitions or even on other network drives.

■ **Block devices** Since all device drivers are accessed through the file system, files of type *block device* are used to interface with devices such as disks.

■ **Character devices** Similar to block devices, character devices are special files that allow you to access devices through the file system. The obvious difference between block and character devices is that block devices communicate with the actual devices in large blocks, whereas character devices work one character at a time. A hard disk is a block device; a modem is a character device.

■ **Named pipes** A named pipe is a special type of file that allows for interprocess communication. Using the **mknod** command (discussed later in the "File Management and Manipulation" section), you can create this special kind of file that one process can open for reading and another process can open for writing, thus allowing the two processes to communicate with one another. Named pipes work especially well when a package refuses to take input from a command-line pipe, you have another program that you need to feed data, and you don't have the disk space for a temporary file.

Block devices, character devices, and named pipes have certain characteristics that identify their file type.

The three identifying traits of a block device are that it has a major number, has a minor number, and when viewed using the **ls -l** command, shows the first character of the permissions to be a *b*. Here's an example:

```
[root@system /root]# ls -l /dev/sda1
brw-rw----   1 root      disk      8,   1 2013-04-10  /dev/sda1
```

In this case, the *b* is at the beginning of the file's permissions, the 8 is the major number, and the 1 is the minor number. The significance of the major number is that it identifies which device driver the file represents. When the system accesses this file, the minor number is passed to the device driver as a parameter to tell the driver which device it is accessing. (For example, if there are two serial ports, they will share the same device driver and thus the same major number, but each serial port will have a unique minor number.)

The distinguishing characteristics of a character device are that its permissions start with a *c*, and the device has a major and minor number. Here's an example:

```
[root@system /root]# ls -l /dev/ttyS0
crw-------   1 root      tty       4,  64 May   5   2013  /dev/ttySo
```

You can tell that a file is a named pipe by the fact that the first character of its file permissions is a *p*, as in the following example:

```
[root@system /root]# ls- l mypipe
prw-r--r--   1 root      root          0 June  16  10:47  mypipe
```

chown: Change Ownership

The **chown** command allows you to change the ownership of a file to someone else. Only the root user can change this ownership. (Normal users may not "give away" or "steal" ownership of a file from another user.) The format of the command is as follows:

```
[root@system /root]# chown [-R] username filename
```

where *username* is the user's login to which you want to change the ownership and *filename* is the name of the file that will have its ownership changed. The filename may be a directory as well.

The **-R** option applies when the specified filename is a directory name. It tells the command to descend recursively through the directory tree and apply the new ownership not only to the directory itself, but to all of the files and subdirectories within it.

chgrp: Change Group

chgrp is another command-line utility that allows you to change the group settings of a file. The command works in much the same way as **chown** does. The format of the command is as follows:

```
[root@system /root]# chgrp [-R] groupname filename
```

where *groupname* is the name of the group to which you want to change *filename*. The filename may be a directory as well.

The **-R** option applies when the specified filename is a directory name. As with **chown**, the option tells the **chgrp** command to descend recursively through the directory tree and apply the new ownership not only to the directory itself, but to all of the files and subdirectories within it.

chmod: Change Mode

Permissions are broken into four parts. The first part is the first character of the permissions. If the file is a normal file, then it will have no value and be represented with a hyphen (-). If the file has a special attribute, it will be represented with a letter. The two special files that you are most interested in are directories that are represented with a *d* and symbolic links that are represented with an *l*.

The second, third, and fourth parts are represented in three-character chunks. The first part is the permissions for the owner of the file. The second part is the permissions for the group. Finally, the last part is the permissions for the world. In the context of UNIX, the world is simply all the users in the system, regardless of their group settings.

The letters used to represent permissions are *R* for read, *W* for write, and *X* for execute. Each permission has a corresponding value. The read attribute is equal to 4, the write attribute is equal to 2, and the execute attribute is equal to 1. When you combine attributes, you add their values. The reason that these attributes need values is to ensure that you can use the **chmod** command to set them. Although the **chmod** command does have more readable ways to set permissions, it is important that you understand the numbering scheme since it is used for programming. Plus, not everyone uses the naming scheme, and Linux users often assume that if you understand file permissions, you understand the numeric meanings as well.

The most common groups of three and their meanings are listed in Table 19-3.

Permission	Values	Meaning
---	0	No permissions
r--	4	Read only
rw-	6	Read and write
rwx	7	Read, write, and execute
r-x	5	Read and execute
--x	1	Execute only

Table 19-3.   Common Permission Combinations

Each of these three-letter chunks is then grouped together three at a time. The first chunk represents the permissions for the owner of the file, the second chunk represents the permissions for the group of the file, and the last chunk represents the permissions for all of the users on the system. Table 19-4 lists some common permissions.

Permission	Numeric Equivalent	Meaning
-rw-------	600	The owner has read and write permissions. You want this setting for most of your files.
-rw-r--r--	644	The owner has read and write permissions. The group and world have read-only permissions. Be sure that you want to let other people read this file.
-rw-rw-rw-	666	Everyone has read and write permissions on a file. Be careful with this one, as you don't usually want other people to be able to change your files.
-rwx------	700	The owner has read, write, and execute permissions. You want this setting for programs that you wish to run (such as the file that results from compiling a C or C++ program).
-rwxr-xr-x	755	The owner has read, write, and execute permissions. The rest of the world has read and execute permissions.
-rwxrwxrwx	777	Everyone has read, write, and execute privileges. Like the 666 setting, this can be an insecure setting.
-rwx--x--x	711	The owner has read, write, and execute permissions. The rest of the world has execute-only permissions. This setting is useful for programs that you want to let others run but not copy.
drwx------	700	This is a directory created with the **mkdir** command. Only the owner can read and write to this directory. Note that all directories must have the executable bit set.
drwxr-xr-x	755	Only the owner can change this directory, but everyone else can view its contents.
drwx--x--x	711	A handy trick is to use this setting when you need to keep a directory world-readable, but you don't want people to be able to list the files by running the **ls** command. The setting enables users to read a directory only if they know the filename that they want to retrieve.

Table 19-4.   Common File Permissions

File Management and Manipulation

This section provides an overview of the basic command-line tools for managing files and directories. Most of this overview should be familiar if you have used a command-line interface before. Basically, you use the same old functions, just with new commands.

cp: Copy Files

The **cp** command is used to copy files. By default, this command works silently, displaying status information only if there is an error condition. For example, to copy index.html to index-orig.html, type the following:

```
[root@system /root]# cp index.html index-orig.html
```

The **cp** command has a large number of options, which are detailed on its man page. The most common options are **-f** to force copy (do not ask for verification) and **-i** for an interactive copy (ask for verification before copying). For example, to copy interactively all files ending in .html to the /tmp directory, type the following:

```
[root@system /root]# cp -i *.html /tmp
```

mv: Move Files

Use the **mv** command to move files from one location to another. The command can move files across partitions as well; however, realize that when moving a file between partitions you are actually copying the file to the other partition and then erasing the original, so it can take longer than moving a file within a partition. Moving a file within a single partition just tells the system that the file is in a different directory; the file isn't copied or physically moved on the disk.

For example, to move a file from /usr/src/myprog/bin/* to /usr/bin, type the following:

```
[root@system /root]# mv /usr/src/myprog/bin/* /usr/bin
```

The most common options are **-f** to force a move and **-i** to move interactively.

Although Linux has no explicit rename tool, you can use **mv** to accomplish this task. To rename /tmp/blah to /tmp/bleck, type the following:

```
[root@system /root]# mv /tmp/bleck /tmp/blah
```

ln: Link Files

The **ln** command allows you to establish a hard link or a soft link. (See the "About Files and Directories" section earlier in this chapter for additional information.) The general format of this command is as follows:

```
[root@system /root]# ln original_file new_file
```

The **ln** command has many options, most of which you'll never need to use. The most common option is **-s**, which creates a symbolic link instead of a hard link. For example, to create a symbolic link so that /usr/bin/myadduser points to /usr/ local/ bin/myadduser, type the following:

```
[root@system /root]# ln -s /usr/local/bin/myadduser /usr/bin/myadduser
```

find: Find a File

The **find** command enables you to find files based on a number of criteria. The following is the command's general format:

```
[root@system /root]# find start_dir [options]
```

where *start_dir* is the directory from which the search should start.

find, like the other commands that we have already discussed, has a large number of options that you can read about on its man page. Table 19-5 list the most common options used with **find**.

For example, to find all files in /tmp that have not been accessed in at least seven days, type the following:

```
[root@system /root]# find /tmp -atime 7 -print
```

To find all files in /usr/src whose names are *core* and then remove them, type the following:

```
[root@system /root]# find /usr/src -name core -exec rm {} \;
```

To find all files in /home with the extension .jpg that are bigger than 100KB, type the following:

```
[root@system /root]# find /home -name "*.jpg" -size 100k
```

dd: Convert and Copy a File

The **dd** command reads the contents of a file and sends them to another file. What makes **dd** different from **cp** is that **dd** can perform on-the-fly conversions on the file and can accept data from a device (such as a tape or floppy drive). When **dd** accesses a device, it does not assume anything about the file system and instead pulls the data in a raw format. Thus, you can use the data to generate images of disks, even if the disk is a foreign format. Table 19-6 lists the most common parameters for **dd**.

For example, to generate an image of a floppy disk (which is especially useful for foreign file formats), type the following:

```
[root@system /root]# dd if=/dev/fd0 of=/tmp/floppy_image
```

Option	Description
-mount	Do not search file systems other than the file system from which you started.
-atime *n*	Specify that the file was accessed at least *n**24 hours ago.
-ctime *n*	Look only for files changed at least *n**24 hours ago.
-inum *n*	Find a file that has i-node *n*.
-amin *n*	Specify that the file was accessed *n* minutes ago.
-cmin *n*	Look only for files that were changed *n* minutes ago.
-empty	Find empty files.
-mmin *n*	Specify that the file was modified *n* minutes ago.
-mtime *n*	Search only for files modified *n**24 hours ago.
-nouser	Find files whose UID does not correspond to a real user in /etc/passwd.
-nogroup	Look only for files whose GID does not correspond to a real group in /etc/group.
-perm *mode*	Specify that the file's permissions are exactly set to *mode*.
-size *n[bck]*	Search only for files at least *n* blocks/characters/kilobytes big. One block equals 512 bytes.
-print	Print the filenames found.
-exec *cmd*\;	On every file found, execute *cmd*. If you are using the bash shell, be sure to follow every *cmd* with a \; otherwise, the shell will become very confused.
-name *name*	Specify that the filename should be *name*. You can use regular expressions here.

Table 19-5.   Common find Command Options

gzip: Compress a File

In the original distributions of UNIX, a tool to compress a file was appropriately called **compress**. Unfortunately, an entrepreneur patented the algorithm, hoping to make a great deal of money. Instead of paying out, most sites sought and found **gzip**, a different compression tool with a patent-free algorithm. Even better, **gzip** consistently achieves better compression ratios than **compress** does. Note that **gzip** compresses the file "in place," meaning that after the compression takes place, the original file is removed, leaving only the compressed file.

Option	Description
if=*infile*	Specify the input file as *infile*.
of=*outfile*	Specify the output file as *outfile*.
count=*blocks*	Specify *blocks* as the number of blocks on which **dd** should operate before quitting.
ibs=*size*	Set the block size of the input device to be *size*.
obs=*size*	Set the block size of the output device to be *size*.
seek=*blocks*	Skip *blocks* number of blocks on the output.
skip=*blocks*	Skip *blocks* number of blocks on the input.
swab	Convert big endian input to little endian, or vice versa.

Table 19-6.   Common dd Command Options

 TIP   You can usually distinguish files compressed with **gzip** from those compressed by **compress** by checking their extensions. Files compressed with **gzip** typically end in .gz, whereas files compressed with **compress** end in .Z.

Table 19-7 lists the most-used optional parameters to **gzip**. See the man page for a complete list.

For example, to compress a file and then decompress it, type the following:

```
[root@system /root]# gzip myfile
[root@system /root]# gzip -d myfile.gz
```

Option	Description
-c	Write compressed file to the standard output device (thereby allowing the output to be piped to another program).
-d	Decompress.
-r	Recursively find all files that should be compressed.
-9	Provide the best compression.
-1	Achieve the fastest compression.

Table 19-7.   Common gzip Command Options

To compress all files ending in .html using the best compression possible, enter the following command:

```
[root@system /root]# gzip -9 *.html
```

> **NOTE** The **gzip** tool does not share file formats with either PkZip or WinZip. However, WinZip can decompress gzip files.

mknod: Make Special Files

As discussed earlier, Linux accesses all of its devices through files. To create a file that the system understands as an interface to a device, you must specify that the file is of type block or character and has a major and minor number. To create this kind of file with the necessary values, you use the **mknod** command. In addition to creating interfaces to devices, you can use **mknod** to create named pipes.

The command's format is as follows:

```
[root@system /root]# mknod name type [major] [minor]
```

where *name* is the name of the file and *type* is the character *b* for block device, *c* for character device, or *p* for named pipe. If you choose to create a block or character device, you need to specify the *major* and *minor* number.

The only time you will need to create a block or character device is when installing some kind of device driver that requires it. The documentation that comes with your driver should tell you which values to use for the major and minor numbers.

For example, to create a named pipe called /tmp/mypipe, type the following:

```
[root@system /root]# mknod /tmp/mypipe p
```

mkdir: Create a Home Directory

The **mkdir** command in Linux is identical to the one in other flavors of UNIX as well as in MS-DOS. For example, to create a directory called mydir, type the following:

```
[root@system /root]# mkdir mydir
```

The only option available is **-p**, which creates a parent directory if none exists. For example, if you need to create /tmp/bigdir/subdir/mydir, and the only directory that exists is /tmp, using **-p** will automatically create bigdir and subdir along with mydir.

> **NOTE** Under Linux, you cannot abbreviate the **mkdir** command as **md** as you can under DOS.

rmdir: Remove Directory

The **rmdir** command offers no surprises if you are familiar with the DOS version of the command. It simply removes an existing directory. For example, to remove a directory called mydir, type the following:

```
[root@system /root]# rmdir mydir
```

One command-line parameter available for this command is **-p**, which removes parent directories as well. For example, if the directory /tmp/bigdir/subdir/mydir exists and you want to get rid of all of the directories from bigdir to mydir, issue the following command:

```
[root@system /tmp]# rmdir -p bigdir/subdir/mydir
```

NOTE   Under Linux, you cannot abbreviate the **rmdir** command as **rd** as you can under DOS.

pwd: Print Working Directory

It is inevitable that eventually you will sit down in front of an already logged-in workstation and not know where you are located in the directory tree. To get this information, you need the **pwd** command. It has no parameters and its only task is to print the current working directory. The DOS equivalent is to type **cd** alone; however, under bash, typing **cd** simply takes you back to your home directory.

For example, to get the current working directory, enter the following command:

```
[root@system src]# pwd
/usr/local/src
```

tar: Tape Archive

If you are familiar with the **pkzip** program, you are used to compression tools not only reducing file size but also combining multiple files into a single large file. Linux separates this process into two tools. The compression tool is **gzip**, which was discussed earlier.

The **tar** program combines multiple files into a single large file. The reason for separating this program from the compression tool is that **tar** allows you to select which compression tool to use or whether you even want compression. In addition, **tar** is able to read and write to devices in much the same way that **dd** can, thus making **tar** a good tool for backing up tape devices.

NOTE   Although the name of the program includes the word *tape*, you do not need to read or write to a tape drive when creating archives. In fact, you will rarely use **tar** with a tape drive in your day-to-day work (aside from your backups).

The format of the **tar** command is as follows:

```
[root@system /root]# tar [commands and options] filenames
```

Some of the options available to **tar** are listed in Table 19-8. Refer to the man page for the complete list.

For example, to create an archive called apache.tar containing all the files from /usr/ src/apache, type the following:

```
[root@system src]# tar -cf apache.tar /usr/src/apache
```

Options	Descriptions
-c	Create a new archive.
-t	View the contents of an archive.
-x	Extract the contents of an archive.
-f	Specify the name of the file (or device) in which the archive is located.
-v	Be verbose during operations.
-z	Assume that the file is already (or will be) compressed with gzip.

Table 19-8. Common tar Command Options

To create an archive called apache.tar containing all the files from /usr/ src/apache and see the list of files as they are added to the archive, type the following:

```
[root@system src]# tar -cvf apache.tar /usr/src/apache
```

To create a gzipped compressed archive called apache.tar.gz containing all the files from /usr/src/apache and list the files as they are being added to the archive, type the following:

```
[root@system src]# tar -cvzf apache.tar.gz /usr/src/apache
```

To extract the contents of a gzipped tar archive called apache.tar.gz and list the files as they are being extracted, type the following:

```
[root@system /root]# tar -xvzf apache.tar.gz
```

cat: Concatenate Files

The **cat** program serves a simple purpose: to display the contents of files. While you can do more creative things with it, you will almost always use the program simply to display the contents of text files, much like you would use the **type** command under DOS. Because you can specify multiple filenames on the command line, it is possible to concatenate files into a single large continuous file. Thus, **cat** differs from **tar** in that the resulting file has no control information to show the boundaries of different files.

For example, to display the /etc/passwd file, type the following:

```
[root@system /root]# cat /etc/passwd
```

To display the /etc/passwd file and the /etc/group file, type the following:

```
[root@system /root]# cat /etc/passwd /etc/group
```

To concatenate the /etc/passwd file with the /etc/group file into the /tmp/ complete file, type the following:

```
[root@system /root]# cat /etc/passwd /etc/group > /tmp/complete
```

To concatenate the /etc/passwd file to an existing file called /tmp/orb, type the following:

```
[root@system /root]# cat /etc/passwd >> /tmp/orb
```

more: Display a File One Screen at a Time

The **more** command works in much the same way as the DOS version of the program. It displays an input file one screen at a time. The input file can come from either **more's** standard input or a command-line parameter. Additional command-line parameters exist for this command; however, they are rarely used. See the man page for additional information.

For example, to view the /etc/passwd file one screenful at a time, type the following:

```
[root@system /root]# more /etc/passwd
```

To view the directory listing generated by the **ls** command one screenful at a time, type the following:

```
[root@system /root]# ls | more
```

du: Disk Utilization

You will often need to determine where and by whom disk space is being consumed, especially when you're running low on it! The **du** command allows you to determine the disk utilization on a directory-by-directory basis. Table 19-9 lists some of the options for **du.**

Options	Description
-c	Produce a grand total at the end of the run.
-h	Print sizes in human-readable format.
-k	Print sizes in kilobytes rather than block sizes. (Note that under Linux, one block is equal to 1KB. However, this is not true for all flavors of UNIX.)
-s	Summarize; print only one output for each argument.

Table 19-9.   Common du Command Options

For example, to display in a human-readable format the amount of space each directory in the /home directory is taking up, type the following:

```
[root@system /root]# du -sh /home/*
```

which: Show the Directory in Which a File Is Located

The **which** command searches your entire path to find the name of the file specified on the command line. If it finds the filename, the tool displays the actual path of the requested file. The purpose of this command is to help you find fully qualified paths.

For example, to find out which directory the **ls** command is in, type the following:

```
[root@system /root]# which ls
```

whereis: Locate the Binary, Source, and Manual Page for a Command

The **whereis** program not only searches your path and displays the name of the program and its absolute directory, but also finds the source file (if available) and the man page for the command (again, if available).

For example, to find the location of the binary, source, and manual page for the command **grep**, type the following:

```
[root@system /root]# whereis grep
```

df: Determine the Amount of Free Space on a Disk

The **df** program displays the amount of free space on a partition-by-partition basis. The drives/partitions must be mounted for **df** to retrieve this information. You can also gather Network File System (NFS) information using this command.

Two options are commonly used with **df**: -h and -l. The -h option specifies to use a human-readable measurement other than simply the number of free blocks to indicate the amount of free space. The -l option lists only the mounted file systems that are local; it does not display any information about network-mounted file systems. Additional command-line options are available; however, they are rarely used. You can read about them in the **df** man page.

For example, to show the free space for all locally mounted drivers, type the following:

```
[root@system /root]# df -l
```

To show the free space in a human-readable format for the file system on which your current working directory is located, type the following (the trailing period is shorthand that means "current directory," just as it does under DOS):

```
[root@system /root]# df -h .
```

To show the free space in a human-readable format for the file system on which /tmp is located, type the following:

```
[root@system /root]# df -h /tmp
```

sync: Synchronize Disks

Like most other modern operating systems, Linux attempts to improve efficiency by maintaining a disk cache. This means, however, that at any given moment not everything you want written to disk has been written to disk.

To schedule the disk cache to be written out to the disk, use the **sync** command. If **sync** detects that writing the cache out to disk has already been scheduled, the tool causes the kernel to flush the cache immediately. For example, to ensure that the disk cache has been flushed, type the following:

```
[root@system /root]# sync ; sync
```

The **sync** command does not have any command-line parameters.

Process Manipulation

Under Linux (and UNIX in general), each running program is composed of at least one process. From the operating system's standpoint, each process is independent of one another, and unless you specifically ask the processes to share resources with each other, they are confined to the memory and CPU allocation assigned to them. Processes that overstep their memory allocation (which could potentially corrupt another running program and make the system unstable) are immediately killed. This method of handling processes has been one of the key reasons that UNIX has been able to sustain its claims to system stability for so long—user applications cannot corrupt other user programs or the operating system.

This section discusses the tools used to list and manipulate processes. This information is very useful to systems administrators, since it's always important to keep an eye on what's going on.

ps: List Processes

The **ps** command lists all of the processes in a system, as well as their state, size, name, owner, CPU time, wall clock time, and much more. The command has many command-line parameters. Table 19-10 lists the ones that are most commonly used.

The most common parameter used with the **ps** command is **-auxww**, which shows all of the processes (regardless of whether or not they have a controlling terminal), each process's owners, and all of the process's command-line parameters. Here is an example of the output of an invocation of **ps -auxww**:

```
USER    PID   %CPU %MEM  VSZ    RSS    TTY   STAT   START TIME   COMMAND
root    1     0.0  0.3   1096   476    ?     S      Jun10 0:04   init
root    2     0.0  0.0   0      0      ?     SW     Jun10 0:00   [kflushd]
root    3     0.0  0.0   0      0      ?     SW     Jun10 0:00   [kpiod]
root    4     0.0  0.0   0      0      ?     SW     Jun10 0:00   [kswapd]
root    5     0.0  0.0   0      0      ?     SW<    Jun10 0:00   [mdrecoveryd]
root    102   0.0  0.2   1068   380    ?     S      Jun10 0:00   /usr/sbin/apmd -p 10
-w 5
bin     253   0.0  0.2   1088   288    ?     S      Jun10 0:00   portmap
root    300   0.0  0.4   1272   548    ?     S      Jun10 0:00   syslogd -m 0
```

```
root    311   0.0  0.5   1376  668   ?     S    Jun10 0:00  klogd
daemon  325   0.0  0.2   1112  284   ?     S    Jun10 0:00  /usr/sbin/atd
root    339   0.0  0.4   1284  532   ?     S    Jun10 0:00  crond
root    357   0.0  0.3   1232  508   ?     S    Jun10 0:00  inetd
root    371   0.0  1.1   2528  1424  ?     S    Jun10 0:00  named
root    385   0.0  0.4   1284  516   ?     S    Jun10 0:00  lpd
root    399   0.0  0.8   2384  1116  ?     S    Jun10 0:00  httpd
xfs     429   0.0  0.7   1988  908   ?     S    Jun10 0:00  xfs
root    467   0.0  0.2   1060  384   tty2  S    Jun10 0:00  /sbin/mingetty tty2
root    468   0.0  0.2   1060  384   tty3  S    Jun10 0:00  /sbin/mingetty tty3
root    469   0.0  0.2   1060  384   tty4  S    Jun10 0:00  /sbin/mingetty tty4
root    470   0.0  0.2   1060  384   tty5  S    Jun10 0:00  /sbin/mingetty tty5
root    471   0.0  0.2   1060  384   tty6  S    Jun10 0:00  /sbin/mingetty tty6
root    473   0.0  0.0   1052  116   ?     S    Jun10 0:01  update (bdflush)
root    853   0.0  0.7   1708  940   pts/1 S    Jun10 0:00  bash
root    1199  0.0  0.7   1940  1012  pts/2 S    Jun10 0:00  su
root    1203  0.0  0.7   1700  920   rpts/2     S    Jun10 0:00  bash
root    1726  0.0  1.3   2824  1760  ?     S    Jun10 0:00  xterm
root    1728  0.0  0.7   1716  940   pts/8 S    Jun10 0:00  bash
root    1953  0.0  1.3   2832  1780  ?     S    Jun11 0:05  xterm
root    1955  0.0  0.7   1724  972   pts/10     S    Jun11 0:00  bash
nobody  6436  0.0  0.7   2572  988   ?     S    Jun13 0:00  httpd
nobody  6437  0.0  0.7   2560  972   ?     S    Jun13 0:00  httpd
nobody  6438  0.0  0.7   2560  976   ?     S    Jun13 0:00  httpd
nobody  6439  0.0  0.7   2560  976   ?     S    Jun13 0:00  httpd
nobody  6440  0.0  0.7   2560  976   ?     S    Jun13 0:00  httpd
nobody  6441  0.0  0.7   2560  976   ?     S    Jun13 0:00  httpd
root    16673 0.0  0.6   1936  840   pts/10     S    Jun14 0:00  su -sshah
sshah   16675 0.0  0.8   1960  1112  pts/10     S    Jun14 0:00  -tcsh
root    18243 0.0  0.9   2144  1216  tty1  S    Jun14 0:00  login -- sshah
sshah   18244 0.0  0.8   1940  1080  tty1  S    Jun14 0:00  -tcsh
```

Option	Description
-a	Show all processes with a controlling terminal, not just the current user's.
-r	Show only running processes.
-x	Show processes that do not have a controlling terminal.
-u	Show the process owners.
-f	Show which processes are the parents to which other processes.
-l	Produce long format.
-w	Show the process's command-line parameters (up to half a line).
-ww	Show all of a process's command-line parameters, despite length.

Table 19-10.   Common ps Command Options

Heading	Description
USER	The user name of the owner for each process.
PID	The process identification number.
%CPU	The percentage of the CPU taken up by a process. Remember that for a system with multiple processors, this column will add up to greater than 100 percent!
%MEM	The percentage of memory taken up by a process.
VSZ	The amount of virtual memory that a process is taking.
RSS	The amount of actual (resident) memory that a process is taking.
TTY	The controlling terminal for a process. A question mark (?) means that the process is no longer connected to a controlling terminal.
STAT	The process's state. S is sleeping. (Remember that all processes that are ready to run—that is, those that are being multitasked while the CPU is momentarily focused on another process—will be asleep). R means that the process is actually on the CPU. D is an uninterruptible sleep (usually I/O-related). T means that a process is being traced by a debugger or has been stopped. Z means that the process has gone zombie. Each process state can have a modifier suffixed to it: W, $<$, N, or L. W means that the process has no resident pages in memory (it has been completely swapped out). $<$ indicates a high-priority process. N indicates a low-priority task. L indicates that some pages are locked into memory (which usually signifies the need for real-time functionality).
START	The date that the process was started.
TIME	The amount of time the process has spent on the CPU.
COMMAND	The name of the process and its command-line parameters.

Table 19-11.   ps Command Output

The very first line of the output is the header indicating the meaning of each column, as listed in Table 19-11.

DEFINE-IT! Going Zombie

Going zombie means one of two things: either the parent process has not acknowledged the death of its child process using the wait system call or the parent was improperly killed and thus the init process cannot reap the child until the parent is completely killed. A zombied process usually indicates poorly written software.

top: Show an Interactive List of Processes

The **top** command is an interactive version of **ps**. Instead of giving a static view of what is going on, this tool refreshes the screen with a list of processes every two or three seconds (the user can adjust the interval). From this list, you can reprioritize or kill processes.

The key problem with the **top** program is that it is a CPU hog. On a congested system, this program tends to make memory problems worse as users start running **top** to see what is going on, only to find several other people are running it as well. Collectively, they have made the system even slower than before!

By default, **top** installs with permissions granted to all users. You might find it prudent, depending on your environment, to allow only root to be able to run it. To do this, change the permissions for the **top** program with the following command:

```
[root@system /root]# chmod 0700 /usr/bin/top
```

kill: Send a Signal to a Process

For some reason, the **kill** program was horribly named. The program doesn't really kill processes! What it does is send *signals* to running processes. By default, the operating system supplies each process a standard set of *signal handlers* to deal with incoming signals. From a systems administrator's standpoint, the most important handler is for signal numbers 9 and 15: kill process and terminate process. (Okay, maybe using *kill* as a name wasn't so inappropriate after all.)

When **kill** is invoked, it requires at least one parameter: the process identification number (PID) as derived from the **ps** command. When passed only the PID number, by default, **kill** will send signal 15, terminate process. Sending the terminate process signal is a lot like politely asking a process to stop what it's doing and shut down. Some programs intercept this signal and perform a number of actions so that they can cleanly shut down; others just stop in their tracks. Either way, sending the signal isn't a guaranteed method for making a process stop.

The optional parameter is a number prefixed by a dash (-), where the number represents a signal number. The two signals that systems administrators are most interested in are 9 and 1: kill and hang up. The kill signal is the impolite way of making a process stop. Instead of asking a process to stop, the operating system takes it upon itself to kill the process. The only time this signal will fail is when the process is in the middle of a system call (such as a request to open a file), in which case the process will die once it returns from the system call.

The hangup signal is a bit of a throwback to when most users of UNIX connected to the system via VT100-style terminals. When a user's connection would drop in the middle of a session, all of that user's running processes would receive a hangup signal (often called a SIGHUP, or HUP for short). This signal gave the processes an opportunity to perform a clean shutdown or, in the case of some programs designed to keep running in the background, to safely ignore the signal. These days, the hangup (HUP) signal is used to tell certain server applications to reread their configuration files. Most applications otherwise ignore the signal.

For example, to terminate process number 2059, type the following:

```
[root@system /root]# kill 2059
```

To kill process number 593 in an almost guaranteed way, type the following:

```
[root@system /root]# kill -9 593
```

To send the init program (which is always process ID 1) the HUP signal, type the following:

```
[root@system /root]# kill -1 1
```

CAUTION   The capability to terminate a process is obviously a very powerful one. The developers of the **kill** command realized this and made sure that security precautions existed so that users can kill only those processes they have permission to kill. For example, nonroot users can send signals only to their own processes. If a nonroot user attempts to send signals to processes that she does not own, the system returns error messages. On the other hand, the root user may send signals to all processes in the system. This means that when using the **kill** command, the root user needs to exercise great care to avoid accidentally killing the wrong process!

Miscellaneous Tools

If this book were devoted to the commands available in your Linux system, the tools discussed in this section would each fit into specific categories. But since this overview is focused on only the most important tools for day-to-day administrative chores, the following tools are lumped together under "miscellaneous." However, even though this section declines to classify them under their own specific categories, that doesn't mean the tools are not important!

uname: Show the System Name

The **uname** program allows you to learn some details about a system. This tool is often helpful when you've managed to log in remotely to a dozen different computers and have lost track of where you are. This tool is also helpful for script writers since it allows them to change the path of a script based on the system information. The command-line parameters for **uname** are listed in Table 19-12.

For example, to get the operating system's name and release type, enter the following:

```
[root@system /root]# uname -s -r
```

It might appear odd that **uname** prints such things as the operating system name when the user obviously will know that the name is Linux. However, such information is actually quite useful because you can find **uname** across almost all UNIX-like operating systems. Thus, if you are at an SGI workstation and enter **uname -s**, the tool will return IRIX; if you enter the command at a Sun workstation, it would return

Option	Description
-m	Print the machine hardware type (for example, i686 for Pentium Pro and better architectures).
-n	Print the machine's hostname.
-r	Print the operating system's release name.
-s	Print the operating system's name.
-v	Print the operating system's version.
-a	Print all of the preceding information.

Table 19-12.   Common uname Command Options

SunOS; and so on. People who work in heterogeneous environments often find it useful to write their scripts such that they behave differently depending on the operating system type, and **uname** provides a wonderfully consistent way to determine that information.

who: Find Out Who Is Logged In

When administering systems that allow people to log in to other people's machines or set up servers, you will want to know who is logged in. To generate a report listing the users currently logged in, use the **who** command, as follows:

```
[root@system]# who
```

This command will generate a report similar to the following:

```
Sshah      tty1      Jun 14 18:22
root       pts/9     Jun 14 18:29     (:0)
root       pts/11    Jun 14 21:12     (:0)
root       pts/12    Jun 14 23:38     (:0)
```

su: Switch Users

Once you have logged in to the system as one user, you do not need to log back out and then log in again to assume another identity (for example, if you logged in as yourself and want to become the root user). Simply use the **su** command to switch to another user. This command has only two command-line parameters, both of which are optional.

By default, running **su** without any parameters results in an attempt to become the root user. For example, if you are logged in as yourself and want to switch to the root user, type the following:

```
[sshah@system ~]$ su
```

Linux will prompt you for the root password; if you enter the password correctly, Linux then drops down to a root shell.

If you are the root user and want to take the identity of another user, you do not need to enter that user's password. For example, if you are logged in as root and want to switch over to user sshah, type the following:

```
[root@system /root]# su sshah
```

You can use the dash (-) as an optional parameter. This character tells **su** not only to switch identities, but to run the login scripts for that user as well. For example, if you are logged in as root and want to switch to user sshah with all of his login and shell configurations, type the following:

```
[root@system /root]# su - sshah
```

Chapter Summary

In this chapter, you first learned about setting some of the key server settings using the built-in graphical tools in Linux. Then you learned about the Linux command line and how to control the system using it.

Of course, this chapter didn't cover everything you need to know about Linux systems administration. But given what you learned here, you should be able to perform basic administrative duties and find your way through the operating system.

The easiest way to gain more information is to spend time playing with both the command-line tools and the various system tools programs. The graphical tools are capable of so much more than was shown here. In fact, for simple servers, it is possible to perform system maintenance using the graphical tools alone! The command line, on the other hand, is the core of Linux's flexibility.

If you want to learn more about systems administration for Linux, be sure to check out *Linux Administration: A Beginner's Guide, Sixth Edition,* by Steven Graham (McGraw-Hill Education, 2012).

Now that you've learned about installing Linux and about administering a Linux system, in the next chapter, you learn about installing one of the most common network services that are run under Linux: an Apache web server.

CHAPTER 20 | Setting Up a Linux Web Server with Apache

One of the most popular web server applications is the Apache web server, a free program that runs under a variety of operating systems, including Linux, Windows, Mac OS X, and Solaris. The Apache web server is a robust, proven platform on which to host a web site. The fact that it is open source and available for free, running on the UNIX-like operating system Linux, which is also often available for free, is a huge plus, and no doubt helps drive its continuing popularity.

This chapter introduces the Apache web server. You learn the basics that you need to install it, find web-based resources to support it, and set up a basic web site on a Fedora Linux system.

Overview of Apache Web Server

The Apache web server started out as a small development at the National Center for Supercomputing Applications (NCSA) in the early 1990s. Beginning as a very simple UNIX *daemon* (pronounced the same as "demon"), it was initially programmed by Rob McCool. McCool left NCSA in 1994, and the project began to be extended by a number of different programmers, some of whom added packages (modules) to the core program to enable it to support new web technologies. In those days, the web server was referred to as "patchy," because it kept getting new patches to correct problems or extend functionality. Eventually, it came to be called the Apache web server.

Version 1.0 of the Apache web server was released to the public at the end of 1995, and by 1996 was the most popular web server on the Internet. The latest statistics at the time this chapter was written (available from http://news.netcraft.com/archives/web_server_survey.html) reveal that Apache is being used to host approximately 53 percent (more than 359 million web sites) of the active web sites on the Internet. Microsoft's Internet Information Server (IIS) is in second place, with around 17 percent (about 112 million web sites). The Apache HTTP Server project is presently coordinated through the Apache Software Foundation (www.apache.org), a nonprofit corporation formed in 1999.

Apache is unlike most other server applications in that it is not a graphical program (despite the fact that its main purpose is to serve up graphical web pages) and has no graphical installation routine. Instead, Apache runs as a background process, or daemon, on the operating system. The background process is typically called **httpd** (Hypertext Transfer Protocol daemon). The management of an Apache web server is handled by editing its text-based configuration files, and by stopping and starting the daemon to cause any changes to those configuration files to take effect.

The fact that Apache is text-based and is administered through a command-line interface should not daunt you. It is straightforward to install and administer an Apache web server, and you should have no trouble doing so. In fact, if you followed the Oracle Linux installation instructions in Chapter 18, you already have Apache installed on that computer, and you just need to activate it (it is not turned on by default in an Oracle Linux installation), as described in the next section.

Activating Apache Web Server Under Oracle Linux

The simplest way to install Apache web server under Oracle Linux is to perform a default installation using the Oracle Linux installation routine, as described in Chapter 18. After Oracle Linux is installed, you can start and test Apache with the following steps:

1. Open a terminal emulation window.
2. Change to the superuser (root):

    ```
    su
    ```

3. Provide the root password when prompted.
4. Type the following command to start Apache:

    ```
    apachectl start
    ```

To test your Apache installation, you can use the **ps** command to verify that the daemons are running:

```
ps -e |more
```

The **ps** command will display all running processes. Because the preceding command pipes the output of **ps -e** through the **more** command, you might need to press the SPACEBAR a number of times to see all of the running processes. In the output, you should see one or more copies of a process called httpd, which is the Apache daemon. You might see many of these processes, because Apache usually starts a number of them, depending on the computer on which you have installed it, but this is perfectly normal.

After you've verified that Apache has started, you can also test it using a web browser. Enter either of the following web addresses, both of which should display the web page shown in Figure 20-1:

```
http://127.0.0.1
http://localhost
```

Both of these commands access any running web server on the computer on which they are used. (Remember that the address 127.0.0.1 is always shorthand for the local computer, as is the name *localhost*.)

You should also be able to access the page from another computer. Assuming that the computer on which you installed Apache has an IP address of 209.200.155.49, the following web address should bring up the page:

```
http://209.200.155.49
```

If you cannot access the page from a remote computer but can on the local computer, you should check basic IP connectivity using the **ping** command and typical network troubleshooting techniques. It's also possible that you have a firewall running on the machine with Apache on it, and the firewall is preventing access.

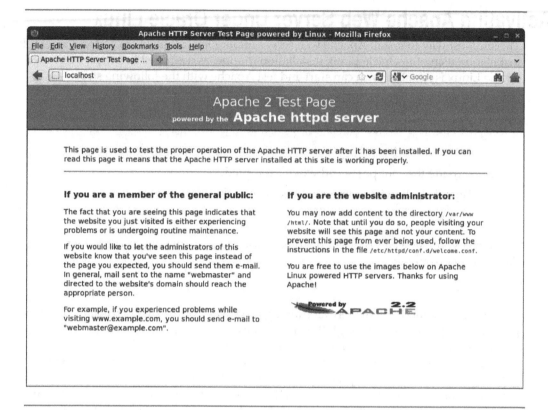

Figure 20-1.   The Apache test page viewed in a web browser

Administering Apache Web Server

You will need to perform a number of basic administrative tasks on an Apache server, not the least of which is publishing a web site onto your newly installed Apache web server. This section briefly describes basic administrative tasks.

Stopping and Starting Apache

You use a script file called apachectl to start and stop the server. For a default Oracle Linux installation, the apachectl file is located in the /usr/sbin directory and takes three main parameters: start, stop, and restart. For example, the following command will restart the server:

```
/usr/sbin/apachectl restart
```

Changing the Apache Configuration

As mentioned earlier in this chapter, Apache is essentially controlled through text-based configuration files, the main one of which is called httpd.conf. The httpd.conf file is located in the /etc/httpd/conf/ directory.

The httpd.conf file works through the use of plain-text directives contained in the file, along with the associated settings. For example, the following directive defines where Apache is installed:

```
ServerRoot "/etc/httpd"
```

If you wanted to move the Apache installation to a different directory on your Linux computer, you could certainly do so, but you would want to be careful to change the ServerRoot setting before attempting to restart Apache in its new location.

NOTE   For any changes to the httpd.conf file to take effect, you must restart Apache using the **apachectl restart** command.

The httpd.conf file is divided into three main sections:

- Global environment
- Main server configuration
- Virtual hosts

Each of these sections contains a large number of directives that control how Apache works.

When learning about Apache, you should spend some time studying the contents of the httpd.conf file and reading the extensive comments included in it. You should also look up the various directives in the online Apache documentation (http://httpd .apache.org/docs/) to get more information than that provided by the comments in the httpd.conf file.

Publishing Web Pages

By default (for Apache version 2), the main web site published by Apache is located in the /var/www/html directory, and this directory is blank.

Once you are ready to publish a complete web site, you can place the files into /var/www/html, with the home page stored as index.html. The easiest way to do this is to connect to the computer running Apache by using the FTP program and then upload the web site's files, either directly to the /var/www/html directory or to a temporary directory on the server's hard disk. Once in the temporary directory, you can move them to the correct location on the server itself using the **mv** or **cp** command (these, among a number of other useful Linux/UNIX commands, are covered in Chapter 19).

Chapter Summary

Most networking professionals will need to set up and maintain a web server in the course of their work. All server platforms have web servers available for them. An excellent web server that is available for just about all platforms is the Apache web server. As you saw in this chapter, Apache is easy to install, administer, and get up and running. If you have followed the instructions in the previous chapters and have set up Oracle Linux on a test system, I recommend that you also follow the steps in this chapter and set up and run Apache. Then add some files for a simple web site to it and browse the web server, first from the computer on which it's running, and then from another computer on the network.

This chapter was intended to get you started with the Apache web server. If this is an area in which you wish to gain greater expertise, you will find more details in resources devoted to Apache server.

CHAPTER 21 | Introduction to Virtualization

One of the most exciting areas to develop in networking over the past several years is *virtualization,* which is a method of creating multiple *virtual machines* on a single computer. These virtual machines operate as if they were running on their own computer, and the computer's actual resources—its processor, hard disk space, network connection, and other hardware—are virtualized so that they can be shared among the various virtual machines.

This chapter introduces virtualization. It discusses some of the main benefits of virtualization, and then provides of an overview of Microsoft's and VMware's virtualization offerings. To get you started, the chapter walks you through an installation of Oracle VirtualBox, a free—for personal use—virtualization offering, along with the setup of an Oracle Linux virtual machine.

Benefits of Virtualization

The ability to virtualize computers can pay rich dividends. The following are some of the chief benefits of virtualization:

- **More efficient use of server resources**   As noted in previous chapters, dedicating one server application per computer is the most reliable way to provide the services, and it's more maintainable as well. However, you often will have server applications that don't use that many server resources. For instance, you may have a web server that is used by 30 to 40 people within your organization on an occasional basis. With virtualization, however, you can run multiple virtual machines—all completely independent from one another—on a single server and more efficiently utilize the server's resources.

- **Ability to run multiple operating systems on a single computer**   With virtualization, there is a *host operating system,* which is the operating system installed on the computer itself, and *guest operating systems,* which are the operating systems installed within each virtual machine. So you can, for instance, have a Windows Server 2012 host operating system installed on a computer, and then run operating systems like Windows (both desktop and server versions), Linux, or Solaris within the virtual machines themselves. Or you can have Linux installed on a computer, and then have a variety of Linux and Windows operating systems running within virtual machines. You can even have no host operating system and instead install what is called a *hypervisor,* which is a bare-bones operating system that only supports virtual machines.

- **Ease of moving virtual machines**   You can easily move virtual machines from one server to another in order to better manage and balance resources like disk space, RAM, and processor utilization.

- **Reduced power requirements** You can reduce the energy required to run your IT infrastructure. By consolidating servers, your power requirements are reduced.

- **Simplified maintenance** When you put a lot of applications on a single server operating system, it becomes difficult to maintain each individual application without affecting the others. For example, if you upgrade an application and need to restart the server, you must restart the *whole* server, affecting all of the other jobs it may be doing. With a virtual machine setup, you can easily restart individual virtual machines without affecting how the other machines operate, and without interrupting their services.

Introducing Windows Server 2012 Hyper-V

Microsoft now offers Hyper-V technology within Windows Server 2012. Hyper-V is a full-featured hypervisor that runs within the Windows Server 2012 environment and allows you to create and manage virtual machines within Windows Server 2012. This provides an easy way for a Windows 2012 Server–based organization to easily start using virtualization.

 NOTE Windows Server 2012 Standard Edition includes the license rights for up to two virtual machines per Windows Server 2012 license. You can purchase additional Windows Server 2012 Standard Edition licenses to increase that license limit, with license rights for two additional virtual machines per license. Windows Server Datacenter Edition includes license rights for an unlimited number of virtual machines.

Microsoft's Hyper-V supports a single host operating system, of course: Windows Server 2012. (Windows Server 2008 also included an earlier version of Hyper-V). It supports the following guest operating systems:

- Windows Server 2012
- Windows Server 2008 (64- and 32-bit)
- Windows Server 2003 (64- and 32-bit)
- Windows Server 2000 SP4
- CentOS
- Red Hat Enterprise Linux (64- and 32-bit)
- SUSE Linux Enterprise Server (64- and 32-bit)
- Windows 7 (64- and 32-bit)
- Windows Vista (64- and 32-bit)
- Windows XP Professional (64- and 32-bit)

These are the *supported* guest operating systems. Note that variants, such as other distributions of Linux, may—and often do—work perfectly fine.

Microsoft has dramatically improved Hyper-V since it was first released as part of Windows Server 2008, and it is now considered a capable competitor to VMware's offerings.

Introducing VMware Virtualization Products

Currently, VMware has the most mature virtualization infrastructure available. VMware has a wide variety of products designed to help companies of any size manage virtual machines. Two powerful virtualization products are offered for free:

- VMware Server, which is a full virtualization product designed to install onto a wide variety of host operating systems

- VMware vSphere Hypervisor (built on VMware ESXi), which is a small (144MB) hypervisor that is installed directly onto a bare-metal computer, and can efficiently host guest operating systems

One of the nice features of VMware Server is that it is supported on a wide variety of host operating systems, including many that are designed as client operating systems. This means that you can install VMware Server onto, say, Windows 7, and then install the full range of guest operating systems within virtual machines. This allows IT professionals to run a wide variety of operating systems, or to test various operating system and application combinations, without even starting with a server operating system.

VMware Server and vSphere Hypervisor require that they be installed on a computer that has a processor capable of supporting virtualization. Fortunately, virtually every Intel or AMD processor available these days supports virtualization. VMware Server can also be installed onto either 32-bit or 64-bit processors. However, keep in mind that if you want to install a 64-bit guest operating system in a virtual machine, the host operating system must also be 64 bits.

VMware Server supports the following host operating systems:

- Windows Server 2008 (64- and 32-bit)

- Windows Server 2003 (64- and 32-bit, including Small Business Server)

- Windows 2000 Server

- Various 64- and 32-bit versions of Red Hat, SUSE, Ubuntu, Mandrake, and Mandriva Linux operating systems (the detailed list of supported versions changes, so consult VMware documentation for the version you wish to install)

VMware Server supports the following guest operating systems:

- Windows Server 2008 (64- and 32-bit)

- Windows Server 2003 (64- and 32-bit, including Small Business Server)

- Windows 2000 Server
- Windows Vista (64- and 32-bit)
- Windows XP Professional (64- and 32-bit)
- Mandrake, Mandriva, Red Hat, SUSE, openSUSE, Open Enterprise Server, and Ubuntu Linux
- Sun Solaris
- Novell NetWare

As with the Hyper-V list, these are the *supported* operating systems. Variants, such as other distributions of Linux, may work.

Introducing Oracle VM VirtualBox

Originally developed by a company called Innotek GmbH, VirtualBox was acquired by Sun Microsystems in 2008, and then in turn by Oracle in its acquisition of Sun in 2010.

The main part of Oracle VM VirtualBox (which I'll refer to as simply VirtualBox from now on) is provided under the GNU General Public License, with some proprietary components offered under a Personal Use and Evaluation License. The net of this is that VirtualBox is free for personal, educational, or evaluation uses.

VirtualBox is a very capable virtualization solution, and it is similar in functionality to VMware Server. It supports Windows, OS X, Linux, and Solaris host operating systems. It also supports a wide variety of guest operating systems, including numerous versions of Windows Server and desktop versions, Linux, Solaris, FreeBSD, OpenBSD, and reportedly even some versions of OS/2 Warp. Of special note, with some limitations, it supports 64-bit guest operating systems, even when VirtualBox is running within a 32-bit host operating system. You can download VirtualBox and obtain its user manual at www.virtualbox.org.

How Is "Personal Use" Defined for VirtualBox Licensing?

The VirtualBox licensing FAQ has a generous interpretation of "personal use," which permits use in a commercial setting, as follows:

"Personal use is when you install the product on one or more PCs yourself and you make use of it (or even your friend, sister, and grandmother). It doesn't matter whether you just use it for fun or run your multimillion-euro business with it. Also, if you install it on your work PC at some large company, this is still personal use. However, if you are an administrator and want to deploy it to the 500 desktops in your company, this would no longer qualify as *personal use.*"

The installation of VirtualBox is very straightforward. You're prompted for where you wish to install it, and also whether to install some additional components that can support USB devices for virtual machines, extra networking drivers for bridged networking, and Python support. For all of these components, you can accept the default choices provided.

Once the installation of VirtualBox completes, you will need to restart the system.

Creating a Virtual Machine for Oracle Linux

In this example, you will see how easy it is to create a virtual machine running Oracle Linux as a guest operating system. You will install Oracle from a CD image file (an ISO file). You can download the current version of Oracle Linux, as an ISO file, from http://edelivery.oracle.com/linux.

Virtual machines are created using a wizard-like process that walks you through making all the appropriate choices. Here are the steps:

1. From within VirtualBox, click the New icon, or access the New command in the Machine menu, or press CTRL-N. You see the Create Virtual Machine screen, as shown in Figure 21-1.

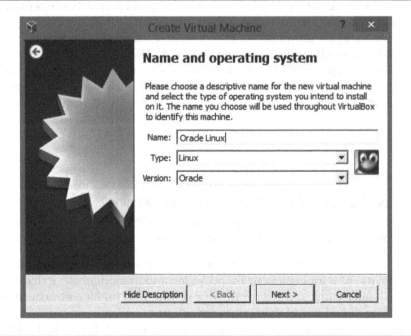

Figure 21-1. Starting to create a virtual machine

2. Type in the name of the virtual machine, which in this example is Oracle
    Linux. Also ensure that the Type field is set to Linux and the Version field says
    Oracle. (While in this first screen, you might want to look through the available
    options for Type and Version to get a better idea of what guest operating
    systems VirtualBox supports.) Click Next to continue.

3. Next, you're prompted to choose how much of the host computer's RAM
    you wish to devote to the virtual machine while it is running, as shown in
    Figure 21-2. In this case, the recommended memory size is 512MB. If your
    machine has plenty of available RAM and you'd like the virtual machine to
    perform better, you can choose higher values. Just keep in mind that when the
    virtual machine is running, that memory will not be available at all to the host
    operating system. And if you run multiple virtual machines simultaneously,
    the total of the memory allocated to all of the running VMs will not be available
    to your host computer. In this example, the host computer has 8GB of RAM,
    so I chose 1GB to devote to the virtual machine.

4. Next, you're prompted to create a virtual hard drive for the virtual machine,
    as shown in Figure 21-3. This will be a file, stored within your host operating
    system, that will mimic a dedicated hard disk for the virtual machine and will
    store all of the virtual machine's hard disk contents. Click Create to continue.

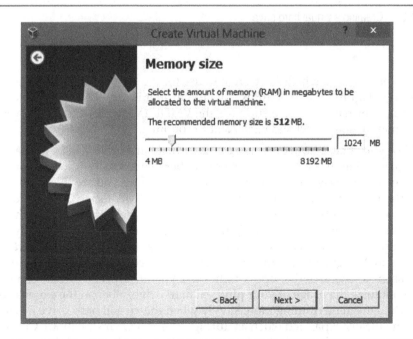

Figure 21-2.   Choosing how much RAM your virtual machine will have

Figure 21-3.   Creating a virtual hard drive

5. You now choose which file format to use for the virtual hard drive file, as
    seen in Figure 21-4. VirtualBox's default format is the VDI (VirtualBox Disk
    Image) format, but it also supports the VMDK (VMware) and VHD (Microsoft)
    formats. Choose VDI and click Next to continue.

6. Next you choose how the space of the virtual hard drive will be allocated,
    shown in Figure 21-5. You can choose either Dynamically Allocated or Fixed
    Size. Both choices can be expanded later if you find you are filling up the
    virtual hard drive. When you choose Dynamically Allocated, the system
    creates a VDI file that is very small initially (despite "appearing" as the full size
    to the virtual machine) but is then expanded as it is used, dynamically. When
    you choose Fixed Size, the file will be created at the full size of the virtual
    hard drive right away, whether anything is stored on it or not. There are good
    reasons to choose either option: Choose Dynamically Sized when you want
    to optimize the usage of your physical hard drive, albeit at the expense of the
    virtual machine running more slowly when the virtual hard drive has to be
    dynamically expanded (such as during the guest OS installation). Choose Fixed
    Size when you have plenty of extra capacity on the host hard drive and want
    the virtual machine to always run at the full speed of which it is capable.

Figure 21-4.   Choosing a virtual hard drive format

7. Your next step is to choose the location and size of the virtual hard drive file, as shown in Figure 21-6. Unless you have a special reason to locate the virtual hard drive file in a different location or to change the size of the virtual hard drive, you can accept the defaults and click Create to create the virtual hard drive.

TIP   Virtual hard drives, whether allocated using the dynamic or fixed methods, can be expanded later if necessary using the VirtualBox command:

```
VBoxManage modifyhd -resize <new size in megabytes>
```

8. You're now returned to the main VirtualBox screen, which you can see in Figure 21-7. The virtual machine is selected, and its details are visible in the main display area. While the virtual machine is ready to run, you're not quite ready to start it up yet. You first need to set the virtual machine to use the Oracle Linux installation ISO file as a virtual DVD-ROM. To do this, select the virtual machine in the left pane, and click the Settings icon in VirtualBox.

Figure 21-5. Choosing a virtual hard drive allocation method

9. You will see the Settings dialog box. Along the left are various categories of settings for the virtual machine. Choose Storage, and then click the CD icon labeled Empty. Then, click the CD icon on the right side of the window, immediately next to the CD/DVD Drive field, and choose the Choose A Virtual CD/DVD Disk File option. You will then see a standard file selection dialog box and can choose the Oracle Linux ISO file that you downloaded, as shown in Figure 21-8.

Running Oracle Linux in the Virtual Machine

Now that you've created the Oracle virtual machine, from the main VirtualBox display, click the virtual machine in the left pane, which will then display the details of the virtual machine.

If you made any mistakes, you can change the virtual machine parameters by using the Settings dialog box. Otherwise, all you need to do is virtually "power on" the virtual machine by clicking the Start icon in VirtualBox.

Figure 21-6.   Finalizing the settings and creating the virtual hard drive

Since the virtual machine's virtual hard disk is blank, and since you've connected the Oracle Linux ISO image file to the virtual machine, the virtual machine will boot from that image file, just as any computer would under those circumstances (bootable CD or DVD inserted and blank hard disk). The Oracle image file is then used for the boot and displays the installation program, as shown in Figure 21-9. You can now proceed with the installation of Oracle Linux, as discussed in Chapter 18.

 NOTE   When you install a guest operating system into a virtual machine, it's just like installing it onto a bare-metal computer. You will need to partition and format the hard disk for the virtual machine during its installation because the virtual hard disk starts out completely blank. The first time you install a guest operating system into a virtual machine, you might be concerned that all of the typical warnings about deleting the hard disk's contents might possibly affect the host computer. However, as long as you're running in the virtual machine, only the virtual hard disk can be partitioned and formatted by the guest operating system; your host system is completely insulated from the virtual machine.

Figure 21-7.   Virtual machine created

At this point, there are some particulars you should know about interacting with the VirtualBox virtual machine console. When you click in the console, the console "owns" the host computer's mouse and keyboard. To release the mouse and keyboard so that you can interact with the host system, press the right CTRL key. When you want to return to the console, just click in it again. Also, rather than press CTRL-ALT-DELETE for a virtual machine, you press the right-hand CTRL key on your keyboard and the DELETE key. CTRL-ALT-DELETE is always interpreted by VirtualBox as being intended for the host operating system.

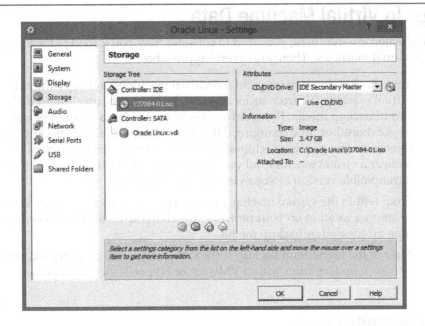

Figure 21-8.   Setting the virtual machine to boot from the Oracle Linux ISO

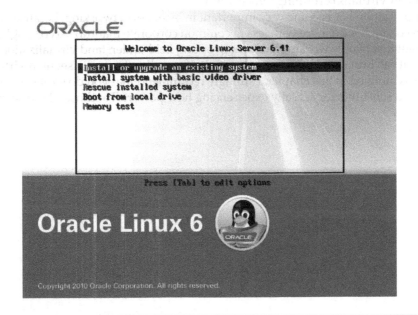

Figure 21-9.   The Oracle Linux installation in the virtual machine

Backing Up Virtual Machine Data

In a production environment, you need to consider how you intend to back up the data on your virtual machines. There are several approaches:

■ You can shut down or suspend the virtual machines and copy the entire virtual machine file from its location on the host computer's hard disk to some sort of backup media. If the virtual machine contains a number of installed applications but little changing data, then this can be a good backup strategy. (Note also that virtual machines can be moved between computers, so to recover a virtual machine, all you need to do is move it to a computer running a compatible version of your virtualization software.)

■ From within the virtual machine, you can set up a process to copy its data files to another location on your network, which in turn might be backed up onto a tape drive or other backup media.

■ Most of the higher-end backup software solutions sell add-on products that let you back up files from within VMware or Hyper-V virtual machines.

Chapter Summary

In this chapter, you learned the essentials of virtualization and the benefits it can bring to networks. You learned about enterprise virtualization solutions from Microsoft and VMware, as well as Oracle VM VirtualBox, and you learned how to set up a virtual machine in VirtualBox running Oracle Linux.

Virtualization has become very important in business networking, because ultimately it helps companies do more with less (a common corporate mantra). Accordingly, it is important that people working in the networking field understand virtualization, the benefits it can bring, and how to work with it. If you didn't actually set up a VirtualBox system as outlined in this chapter, I strongly recommend that you do so at some point. There's no substitute for actually experiencing how powerful and useful virtual machines can be.

Glossary

10Base-2 Specification for 10 Mbps (baseband) carried over coaxial cable. Also called Thin Ethernet or Thinnet.

10Base-5 Specification for 10 Mbps (baseband) carried over thick coaxial cable. Also called Thick Ethernet or Thicknet.

10Base-Fx Specification for 10 Mbps (baseband) carried over fiber-optic cable.

10Base-T Specification for 10 Mbps (baseband) carried over twisted-pair cable.

100Base-Tx Specification for 100 Mbps (baseband) carried over twisted-pair cable.

1000Base-T Specification for 1,000 Mbps (one gigabit) carried over twisted-pair cable.

802.x Specification for various types of Ethernet networks.

AAUI Apple Attachment Unit Interface. Used to connect older Macs to an Ethernet network.

access In the telecommunications context, this refers to the method and cost components for a connection between a customer location and the provider's wider network. It applies to both voice and wide area data networks.

Access Control List (ACL) A list of security permissions for a Windows server's files, directories, and other resources. Access Control Lists are also used on other devices, and are essentially lists of who can access what.

access rights The rights that control what a user can and cannot do with a particular network resource.

account On a server, the definition for a user of the server's services. A user cannot access a server or a network without a valid account.

Address Resolution Protocol (ARP) A protocol that resolves a destination's media access control (MAC) address from its Internet Protocol (IP) address.

administrator The chief administrator of a network. The administrator generally has permission to perform any task on a network and access any resource, and can assign rights to network users. Sometimes called *supervisor* and *super user.*

AFP Apple Filing Protocol. A file access protocol for working with files through a network.

analog An electrical signal that is multistate and usually has an infinite number of values. For example, a volume knob on a radio is usually an analog adjustment.

ANSI American National Standards Institute. A private, nonprofit organization that coordinates standards in the United States.

AppleTalk A set of networking protocols for Macintosh computers.

application layer The seventh and highest layer in the OSI networking model. It handles communication between applications across a network. The application layer often performs user authentication on networks.

archive bit A bit flag that indicates which files need to be archived (backed up). When a full backup is done, the archive bit is cleared. Any subsequent changes to the file cause the archive bit to be set to on, indicating the need for an archive.

ARCnet A token-passing network protocol rarely used these days.

ATM Asynchronous Transfer Mode. A high-speed switched and multiplexed network specification.

attributes (file) Characteristics given to files. For example, in DOS files, attributes include read-only, system, hidden, and archive. Network systems generally add such attributes as shareable and delete inhibit.

AUI Attachment Unit Interface. A box that connects a network cable to a transceiver.

backbone A common cable shared by segments of a network. Usually, the backbone portion of a network operates at a higher speed than the individual segments, since it has to carry most of the traffic of all of the connected segments.

bandwidth The amount of data that can be carried over a network, usually expressed in mega (million) bits per second, or Mbps. Sometimes bandwidth is also specified in Hertz, as in 10 megahertz (MHz).

baseband A network cable that can carry only one signal at a time. See *Broadband.*

Basic Rate Interface (BRI) A package of ISDN services that includes two bearer channels at 56 or 64 Kbps each (64 Kbps is common in the United States), plus a single data channel that carries 16 Kbps. BRI is sometimes also called 2B + D.

baud rate The speed at which an analog signal is carried. Baud rate is analogous to bits per second (bps). Thus 2,400 baud is roughly equivalent to 2,400 bps.

B-channel A channel in an ISDN connection that carries (normally) 64 Kbps of data.

bindery A database that contains account and security information for Novell networks, versions 4 and earlier.

bit Short for *binary digit,* a single digit having a value of either 0 or 1.

BNC connector A bayonet-style connector used in 10Base-2 (Thin) Ethernet networks.

bottleneck In a complex system, the part of the system that limits the rate of work for the entire system.

bridge A networking device that connects two networks to each other using Layers 1 and 2 of the OSI network model.

broadband A network cable that can carry multiple signals at once. See *Baseband*.

broadcast A network transmission sent to all nodes of a network or subnetwork.

browser An application that interprets and displays data formatted using Hypertext Markup Language (HTML) on the World Wide Web.

buffer Memory set aside to cache data between two devices, providing faster access to frequently used data. Operating systems often use buffers to hold frequently used data stored on disks.

bus (1) A network topology in which a cable runs from node to node, terminating on each end. (2) A connection backbone used in a computer. Most peripherals connect to this backbone.

byte A collection of eight bits that can represent up to 256 distinct values.

cache Memory set aside expressly for holding data frequently accessed from a disk.

capture A mechanism that enables a network printer to act like a local printer for a specific computer. Output sent to the computer's printer port is "captured" and redirected to a network printer.

central office (CO) A local switching facility, run by the Regional Bell Operating Company (RBOC), that provides an access point to the RBOC's network.

Challenge Handshake Authentication Protocol (CHAP) An Internet communication standard for validating encrypted passwords.

client A computer on a network that uses data provided by a server.

client/server A network design model in which data processing work is divided between a client's processor and a server's processor, letting each perform the jobs to which they are best suited.

CNE A Certified NetWare Engineer.

coaxial cable Cable with a center conductor surrounded by a shield. Common coaxial cable types are RG-58 and RG-8.

Common Gateway Interface (CGI) A programming standard that connects databases and web browsers.

concentrator A network device that connects multiple user devices to a network. Sometimes called a *hub*.

console A NetWare server's administrative interface. Also, as a generic term, used to refer to a command prompt or terminal window interface to an operating system.

crossover cable A cable that allows the connection of two types of communications equipment that normally do not communicate directly with one another. For instance, data communications equipment is classified as data terminal equipment (DTE) or data communications equipment (DCE). Normally, DTE equipment can only communicate with DCE equipment. A crossover cable allows two DTE or two DCE devices to communicate.

CSMA/CD Carrier Sense Multiple Access with Collision Detection. A method used with Ethernet networks to manage packets on a segment.

CSU/DSU Channel service unit/data service unit. A hardware device that interfaces between a network's signals and the signals carried over a public network connection, such as a T-1 line.

customer premises equipment (CPE) Telephone company lingo for interconnection equipment located on a company's premises.

cyclical redundancy check (CRC) A method to detect errors in transmitted or stored data.

DAT Digital audio tape. A digital tape often used in network backup devices.

data communications equipment (DCE) One end of an RS-232C or other serial connection. DCE and DTE are analogous to "male" and "female" cable connectors, in that both types are needed for a connection. See *Data terminal equipment.*

Data terminal equipment (DTE) One end of an RS-232C or other serial connection. A DTE device communicates only with a DCE device, and vice versa. See *Data communications equipment.*

datagram On an IP network, a collection of network data along with associated address and header information. Also called a *packet.*

data-link layer The second layer of the OSI network model, the data-link layer handles error-free connections between two devices over a common physical connection.

DBMS Database management system. Usually a relational database.

D-channel One of the channels used in all ISDN interfaces; it carries 16 Kbps of data and is used for call setup and other signal control duties. Called the *data channel*, the channel actually carries no user data.

deadlock A situation in which two computers or two processes attempt to access a resource simultaneously, and both wait indefinitely for the other one to finish using the resource.

delayed write A method used in writing new or changed data to a network server's disks to improve overall performance. Data to be written is temporarily held in memory until the system is not busy (or for a set maximum amount of time), at which time the data is committed to the disk.

dial-up networking (DUN) A Microsoft term for a dial-up network connection over a modem.

differential backup A backup that copies all files with their archive bit set and does not clear the archive bit when done.

digital A signaling method in which all signals are binary (1s and 0s only).

digital signature An authentication code embedded in a network message.

direct cable connection A serial (RS-232C) connection between two computers. You can also accomplish a direct cable connection between two Ethernet-equipped computers using a crossover RJ-45 cable.

directory In the tree-shaped structure of a disk's file system, a logical container for files.

disk mirroring A method, also known as RAID 1, that writes data redundantly to two separate disks.

domain (1) On the Internet, a network identified by a name, such as yahoo.com. (2) On Microsoft Windows NT networks, the smallest administrative unit in a network.

Domain Name System (DNS) An Internet system that resolves domain names to IP addresses.

drive map A method that uses a network directory to simulate a local drive letter (such as F: or G:) for a client computer.

DS0 A basic telephone line.

DS1 A digital telephone line used for both voice and data applications. A DS1 carries up to 1.544 Mbps of data, split across 28 separate channels, or carries up to 28 voice channels. Often called a *T-1 line*.

DS3 A digital telephone line that carries up to 44.736 Mbps of data. Often called a *T-3 line*.

Ethernet A network standard that uses CSMA/CD methods to carry network data over many different types of media at many different speeds.

EtherTalk An Apple protocol for connecting Macintosh computers to an Ethernet network.

Fast Ethernet An Ethernet network that runs at 100 Mbps.

FAT File allocation table. A table used by several operating systems to allocate space for files on physical disks.

Fiber Distributed Data Interface (FDDI) A fiber-optic LAN that operates at 100 Mbps.

File Transfer Protocol (FTP) (1) An Internet protocol for copying files between two computers. (2) A program that uses the FTP protocol to do its job.

fileserver A network server that primarily is responsible for storing, sharing, and retrieving files for network clients.

firewall A network device that protects a network from outside intruders.

Fractional T1/T3 A T1 or T3 (also known as DS1 and DS3 telecommunications connection) in which only some of the channels are leased for use.

frame A data-link layer unit of transmission in the OSI network model. Frames can be of variable length.

frame relay A telecommunications server that carries asynchronous data between two points on a WAN. For efficiency, frame relay does not perform error detection and correction, leaving this task up to software on the two connected points.

full backup A process where all files on a network drive are copied to tape or other archival media. Each file's archive bit is cleared as part of a full backup.

full-duplex A connection in which both ends can transmit and receive simultaneously.

gateway A device that connects two networks together at all layers of the OSI network model. An example is an e-mail gateway that transmits e-mail from one network to another.

Gb Short for *gigabit*, or one billion bits.

GB Short for *gigabyte*, or one billion bytes.

generational backup A tape-swapping methodology that gives good restoration granularity without consuming too many tapes. Also called the grandfather/father/son method.

GHz Short for *gigahertz*, or one billion cycles per second.

half-duplex (simplex) A connection in which only one end can transmit at a time.

handshaking Negotiating a connection and data transmission between two devices.

header Control information carried along with a file or a unit of network data, such as a packet.

HTML Hypertext Markup Language. A formatting language used to format web pages.

HTTP Hypertext Transfer Protocol. A network protocol used to retrieve web pages from a web server.

hub A network device that connects multiple nodes to a network segment.

IEEE Institute of Electrical and Electronics Engineers. A body that defines standards for electrical devices.

incremental backup A backup method that backs up files that have their archive attribute set and then clears the archive attribute.

Internet A worldwide public network of services for businesses and consumers.

intranet A company-specific network modeled after the Internet.

IPv6 Internet Protocol version 6, which increases the number of IP addresses available dramatically and includes other enhancements to the IP protocol.

IPX A network protocol used with NetWare networks.

IRQ Interrupt request line. A hardware switch in a computer that allows a device to signal the processor.

ISA bus Industry Standard Architecture bus. A computer bus originally developed for the IBM PC-AT.

ISDN Integrated Services Digital Network. A telecommunications standard for providing digital telephone services to consumers and businesses.

ISO International Standards Organization. A body that defines many computer standards, including networking standards.

ISP Internet service provider. A company that provides Internet services directly to businesses and/or consumers.

Java A programming language, derived from C, that allows the development of programs that can be run on many different computer platforms, and that is also used for automation on Internet web pages.

Kb Short for *kilobit,* or 1,024 bits.

KB Short for *kilobyte,* or 1,024 bytes. KB represents 1,024 bytes instead of 1,000 bytes because 1,024 is the closest binary-driven (powers of 2) number.

key A digital password used to sign electronic documents to guarantee their authenticity.

LAN Local area network. A building-specific network.

LAN Manager An older Microsoft network operating system.

leased line A dedicated, always-on, telephone connection.

Linear Tape Open (LTO) A tape backup standard created originally by an industry consortium made up of Hewlett-Packard, IBM, and Seagate. Different levels of LTO tape specifications exist, numbered LTO-1, LTO-2, LTO-3, and so forth.

LocalTalk An Apple networking system for connecting Macintoshes and Apple laser printers together on a low-speed (230 Kbps) network over twisted-pair wire.

login The process of providing account and authentication information (such as a password) to a computer or network to gain access to its resources.

login script A set of commands that runs automatically when a user logs in to a computer or network.

MAC Media access control. A sublayer (Layer 2) of the OSI networking model. IEEE 802.*x* networks divide up Layer 2 into a MAC layer and a logical link control (LLC) layer. The software at the MAC sublayer is unique to every different network media type. In other words, the MAC sublayer software for Thin Ethernet is different from the software used for twisted-pair Token Ring.

Mb Short for *megabit*, or approximately one million bits. Usually used for speed ratings, such as 100 Mbps, or 100 million bits per second.

MB Short for *megabyte*, or 1,048,576 bytes.

MCA bus Microchannel Architecture bus. A computer bus standard introduced by IBM that was not widely accepted.

MCSA Microsoft Certified Systems Administrator. This is a subset of the requirements for the MCSE certification and is oriented toward network administrators.

MCSE Microsoft Certified Systems Engineer. A person who has completed a set of tests given by Microsoft to certify him or her as a networking engineer.

MHz Short for *megahertz*, or one million Hertz (signals per second). Roughly equivalent to Mbps (million bits per second).

MIME Multipurpose Internet Mail Extension. A standard for the attachment of binary data (attachments) to Internet e-mail messages. Also available as S/MIME, which is a secure form of MIME.

modem Modulator/demodulator. A device that allows digital signals to travel over an analog telephone line. Each end of the connection requires a modem.

MSAU Multistation access unit. A hub used to connect Token Ring nodes together.

multiplexing A technique that allows multiple signals to be aggregated onto a single channel.

multiprocessor A computer, operating system, or application that uses more than one processor to accomplish its work.

multitasking Running multiple programs simultaneously on a single computer.

NetBEUI NetBIOS Extended User Interface. An enhancement to the NetBIOS protocol.

NetBIOS Network Basic Input/Output System. An older and slower networking protocol originally developed by IBM.

NetWare A network operating system developed by Novell Corporation.

NetWare Core Protocol (NCP) An underlying protocol that manages server and workstation communications on a NetWare network.

NetWare Directory Service (NDS) A directory service for NetWare networks. NDS is also available from Novell as a tool to manage other types of servers, such as Solaris, Windows, and UNIX.

network layer Layer 3 of the OSI networking model. The network layer defines different packet protocols, such as IPX or IP.

nibble Four bits.

NIC Network interface card. A peripheral card attached to a computer that lets it interface to a network.

NLM NetWare Loadable Module. A special program that runs only on NetWare servers.

node A computer or device that is a distinct network entity, such as a computer or printer.

NOS Network operating system. An operating system that runs on network servers.

OSI Open System Interconnection. A reference model that conceptually describes how networks work.

packet A collection of data sent as a single entity from one node on a network to another node.

packet filtering Examining packets coming into and going out of a network in order to prevent unauthorized traffic and to identify bottlenecks, failing hardware, and other network problems.

partition A logical division of a hard disk.

patch cable A cable that connects between a patch panel and a network hub, or from a wall jack to a computer.

PCI Peripheral Component Interconnect. A very fast bus introduced by Intel Corporation to allow high-speed communications between peripherals and the computer in which they are installed.

PCI Express A newer version of PCI that runs at much higher data rates. PCI Express used to be called PCI-X.

peer-to-peer network A network that spreads shareable resources among all of the client computers on the network. A peer-to-peer network has no central network servers.

physical layer Layer 1 of the OSI networking model. The physical layer defines the specifications for the physical wiring of a network.

Point-to-Point Protocol (PPP) An IP-specific protocol that enables remote nodes to connect to a network over telephone connections.

Post Office Protocol (POP) A communications protocol for the exchange of e-mail over the Internet.

presentation layer Layer 6 of the OSI networking model. The presentation layer "presents" network data to the system and may include compression/decompression or encryption/decryption functions.

Primary Rate Interface (PRI) An aggregation of ISDN B-channels plus one D-channel that provides 1.544 Mbps of network bandwidth through the telephone network.

print job A unit of printing from a client computer to a network printer.

print queue A place on a network server that accepts and accumulates user print jobs and then sends them to the network printer in sequence.

print server A computer or dedicated device on a network that accepts jobs from print queues and sends them to the individual printers.

protocol A syntax for communication over a network.

PSTN An abbreviation that stands for Public Switched Telephone Network. It refers to traditional voice service, when calls are routed over switched connections.

RAID Redundant array of inexpensive disks. A variety of methods that allow high-speed, fail-safe arrays of disks to be used in concert.

ReFS Short for Resilient File System, which was introduced with Windows Server 2012. It is not a replacement for NTFS, but rather is a file system intended for highly critical data and includes features to reduce the chance of stored data corruption.

registry A database used on Microsoft Windows operating systems that stores computer and user settings.

remote access (node and control) The process of accessing a network from a remote computer, usually over a data connection, usually the Internet. Remote node access makes the remote computer a node on the network. Remote control access lets the remote computer "take control" of a computer that is already a local node on a network.

Remote Access Service (RAS) A Windows NT service that provides remote node access to remote computers. The newer variant is called Routing and Remote Access Service (RRAS).

Remote Authentication Dial In User Service (RADIUS) A networking protocol that provides centralized authentication, authorization, and accounting (AAA) management for computers that connect to and use a network service.

repeater A device that extends the distance that a network segment can be run.

requestor Special networking software that runs on a client computer that interfaces between the computer's operating system and the network operating system. Requestors are specific to each different type of NOS.

ring topology An electrical arrangement of nodes on a network in a ring configuration.

RJ-45 A snap-in connector used with some kinds of network media, similar to modular telephone connectors (called RJ-11) used in homes, but larger.

router A device that routes network traffic from one network to another.

Routing Information Protocol (RIP) A protocol that allows routers to communicate with each other to discover the best route between networks.

SCSI Small Computer Systems Interface. A high-speed interface used primarily to interface hard disks to network servers.

segment An individual part of a network that connects two or more computers together.

server A computer on a network that provides some kind of network service to client computers.

session layer Layer 5 of the OSI networking model. The session layer controls a persistent connection between two network devices or programs.

share A Windows NT or UNIX shared directory, available for use over a network, provided the user has permission.

SMTP Simple Mail Transfer Protocol. An Internet standard for the exchange of e-mail between systems on the Internet.

SNMP Simple Network Management Protocol. A protocol that enables special management software to manage network devices.

SONET Short for Synchronous Optical Networking, a protocol that defines digital transmissions over fiber-optic cable. Usually used for very high-speed telecom data networking connections.

SPX Sequenced Packet Exchange. A NetWare protocol used in concert with IPX.

SSL VPN A virtual private networking technology that works through a web browser's Secure Sockets Layer capabilities.

star topology A network arrangement in which individual cables connect a central hub to the nodes that it services.

switch An Ethernet device that switches traffic between two or more network segments.

TB Short for *terabyte*, or one trillion bytes.

TDM Short for Time Division Multiplexing. Usually used when referring to telecom access connections that use DS1/DS3 (T1/T3) or E1/E3 circuits.

token An electrical signal circulated around Token Ring networks. Only the computer that "has the token" can transmit on the Token Ring network.

Token Ring A network designed by IBM that uses a ring topology and circulates a token to manage traffic on the network.

transceiver A device that connects a computer to a network cable. Often, transceivers are built into NIC cards.

Transmission Control Protocol/Internet Protocol (TCP/IP) A standard network protocol used on the Internet and on many private networks.

transport layer Layer 4 of the OSI networking model. The transport layer coordinates the packet exchange between network nodes. Examples of transport layer protocols are TCP and SPX.

twisted pair Cable that uses small-gauge wires twisted together within a common sheath to carry network or telephone signals. Twisted-pair cable comes in unshielded (UTP) and shielded (STP) varieties.

UPS Uninterruptible power supply. A battery-driven power supply that allows a server to continue operating when a building's power supply is cut off.

URL Uniform resource locator. An address that allows a resource on the Internet to be located and accessed.

Virtual Private Network (VPN) A secure, virtual network connection formed over a public network, such as the Internet.

wiring closet A closet or room that brings together all of the cables needed for a building's network. Some buildings have separate wiring closets on each floor of the building, or for each 100 meters of horizontal distance.

workstation A generic computer client on a network. Sometimes also a high-powered computer used for engineering purposes.

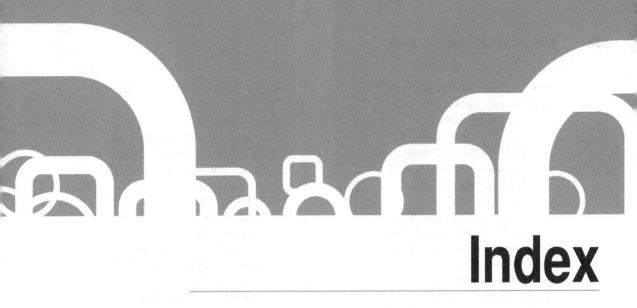

Index